WHY
S.O.B.'S
SUCCEED
AND NICE GUYS
FAIL IN
A SMALL BUSINESS

DISTRIBUTED BY
BUSINESS FINANCIAL CONSULTANTS, INC
P.O. BOX 15567
PHOENIX, ARIZONA 85060

Fifty Second Printing

Library of Congress Cataloging in Publication Data Main Entry Under Title:

WHY S.O.B.'S SUCCEED AND NICE GUYS FAIL IN A SMALL BUSINESS.

DISTRIBUTED BY
BUSINESS FINANCIAL CONSULTANTS, INC
P.O. BOX 15567
PHOENIX, ARIZONA 85060

ISBN-0-930566-01-7   76-40771

TABLE OF CONTENTS

Preface

You will run into some salty language in this book. It is there because it expresses a sense of outrage at the conditions under which the small businessman operates in this country. The game is business and the rules are written by big government, big business and big labor. Even though there are ten million small businesses who account for 50% of the goods and services produced and 58% of the jobs, they have little or no say in how the rules are made.

To survive, the small businessman has to bend or break these rules from time to time. We are told that this is a government of laws, not of men. *"bullshit!"*. The laws are made by men, interpreted by men and enforced by men. Those who have the power use laws to subject or destroy those who do not. There is an old Roman saying, *"multitudes of laws are a sign of tyranny in the emperor"*. In 1975, we had over a thousand new laws passed and over 7,000 new rules laid down by bureaucrats in this country.

So, survival for the small businessman is keyed to how well he can operate inside or outside these rules until he is large enough to benefit from them. The key rule is, *"don't get caught!"*

If this sounds cynical or immoral to you, you are on the right wave length. To win, you must play to win. There is another saying, *"show me a good loser, and I'll show you a loser."* After you win, and are on top of the heap, you can do what the IBM's, Standard Oil's, General Motors and the rest of the big boys do. You can write codes of ethics, make speeches about morality, and at the same time kick rocks down on all the scratching, scrambling little bastards below trying to climb to the top.

The small businessman has two traits that cause him difficulty. First, is the lack of the herd or flock instinct. You can't be a cut throat and an ass-kicker to get ahead in a corporate or bureaucratic structure. Secondly, this trait prevents him from having a powerful organization to represent him against the bigs. He can't organize any more than eagles can become a flock of chickens. But, being an eagle instead of a chicken, he can fend for himself if given enough operating room. By letting his natural instincts operate, he can become a successful S.O.B.

This book cannot change chickens into eagles, but it can show an eagle how to gain some elbow room to fly to the highest spot on the mountain he wishes to reach. Stick it to 'em.

Prologue

This book is about the game of business. The successful players in business buy low — sell high — and expand on the difference. The key to success and fortune in business is the ability to first discover one winner. Any winner will do, as it is the elevator on which you can ride to the top. It can be a hamburger stand called MacDonald's; a fried chicken take-out started by an old Colonel whose operating capital was his social security check; a funny machine that took twenty-five years of salesmanship to sell to a company to produce it called Xerox; an idea for renting people to businesses on a part-time basis called Manpower; an idea for a status symbol credit card to be used in better class restaurants called Diner's Club; a method of syndicating a real estate sales program to establish businesses called Red Carpet; a book full of skin pictures and bawdy cartoons called Playboy; an idea for building and franchising high-rise motels called Holiday Inns; a method of selling cosmetics door-to-door called Avon; or inventing a game in the middle of a depression that allowed people to become vicarious millionaires called Monopoly.

The successful small businessman then expands his success in geometric steps (1-2-4-8-16-32-etc.) At some point he comes to a fork in the road and either sells out to a large corporation for personal reasons and profit, or he has managerial genius to employ aggressive people to build his business into a giant of its own.

BOOKS BY CHICKENS FOR EAGLES

There are many books published on starting small businesses, and oddly enough almost all of them are published by professors, C.P.A.'s, consultants or corporation employees. The feeling of almost all of these books in the beginning, is that small businessmen have little chance of success. They use various tables, statistics and other material available to show the high mortality rate in small business start-ups. The recurring theme in these books is that the small businessman is essentially an undiscovered moron who steps out into the jungle full of big business tigers and is immediately gobbled up. A current book titled "Where Have all the Woolly Mammoths Gone?" by a C.P.A., makes this statement quite early in his book: "How can you, a small firm, possibly compete with big businesses outside sources of capital, political clout, prestige, computerized efficiency, departmentalized specialization, vertical and horizontal monopolies?"

"The awful truth is — you can't! Let's face it. Small businesses' biggest enemy these days is big business. Big business domination extends further and further into every nook and cranny of the economy. Small business is being continually forced onto higher ground — where the soil is barren and the vegetation sparse."

THE BIGS MAKE COMPETITORS

Nothing could be further from the truth. Big business, as it grows bigger, creates more and more opportunities for small entrepreneurs to move in and compete against muscle-bound giants on a very successful basis. A point of fact, IBM, one of the biggest, has created more competition for itself than probably any other major company in the world. Former employees joined together people with capital to start peripheral computer companies in direct competition with IBM and some have been fantastically successful. Max Pavlezsky's Scientific Data Systems and Ken Norris Control Data Corporation were two very successful break-aways from IBM. Also, Kenneth H. Olson's Digital Equipment Company was spawned from an IBM break-away. Interestingly enough, Tom Watson, Sr., the architect of IBM's fantastic success, left National Cash Register and moved to IBM, a direct competitor of National Cash.

The best known story of an IBM break-away is that of H. Ross Perot. He was their star computer salesman in Texas, and sold so much equipment that he made more commissions for himself than the Chairman of the Board of IBM was earning. This, naturally, forced the bureaucrats into putting ceilings onto IBM's commission salesmen, so that this couldn't happen again. The ceiling was $250,000, and Perot made his maximum in the first couple of weeks in the year, and then quit. He invested some of his commissions in a company called Electronic Data Services, which would provide operating services for people who had purchased IBM computers. The company was so successful, that at one point its stock market multiple had reach a place where it was worth $645,000,000 in 1972.

Another story is that of Mary Kay Cosmetics, which was started by a young woman who left a party-plan cosmetics sales organization because she didn't like the treatment she was getting, and started her own. She started by using supplies made by a small proprietary product manufacturer in Texas, who supplied her with private label cosmetics she could use in her program. Not long after she got started in her program, she bought out the manufacturer of her private brand, and continued to grow, until 1966. In 1976, Mary Kay Cosmetics applied for a listing on the New York Stock Exchange.

BETTER OPPORTUNITIES NOW!

In point of fact, there are more opportunities for smart, aggressive, tunnel-visioned, persevering small businessmen today than ever before in history.

The Small Business Administration published a research report some years back titled "The First Two Years: Firm Growth and Survival Problems". In this book they analyze the reasons for success and failure of some 81 business start-ups over a period of two years. The actual research was done by a team of investigators from Brown University in Providence, Rhode Island over a two year period, in which they did intensive interviewing and surveys of 81 small businesses to determine why some succeeded and why some failed. Of the 81 businesses they studied, 40 had failed within the first 2 years. Thirty-two had failed financially and eight closed their doors for other reasons. The study goes into considerable analysis of the personalities of the individuals involved, how much capital that they invested, their working reserves of capital, their ability to manage, what personal deficiencies they displayed, etc.

THE SUCCESS NEED

The interesting point of the study is in the analysis of those who survived and the reasons for survival. The key conclusion in survival was persistence. The ability to hang in there no matter how rough the going got. But, beyond that there was the ability to realistically view the situation as it progressed. They come to their conclusions in a story illustrating their survival and success as they start up small business enterprise. To quote from the book :

"The survival and success of any particular enterprise is usually the result of an interplay of several factors. The fact that the same cases can be used to illustrate different factors attest to the validity of this conclusion. On the whole, analysis of reasons for survival and success suggests that survivors were characterized by a higher degree of rationality and more suitable personality characteristics than failures. To be sure, as discussion of the conditions under which the businesses were opened as shown, very few cases qualified as highly rational undertakings. Rationality cannot be statistically measured, but if it is judged in terms of capitalization, realistic expectations, and managerial competence, then the data of this study indicates that the greater the rationality, the higher the chances for survival, and among those who survive, the greater the chances for success. To the extent that rational practices are supplemented by favorable personality traits, the chances for survival and success are correspondingly enhanced. In this study, the ideal combination of rationality and personality traits is best illustrated by the case of Royal, the operator of a door-to-door vacuum cleaning sales operation.

Royal was a 24-year old, married, college graduate. During the last two years of his college career he had worked as a part-time salesman selling vacuum cleaners door-to-door in his college town. He liked his work and found it lucrative. Having established a good record as a salesman, he regarded the experience as valuable training for self-employment. Upon graduation, he accepted a franchise from the vacuum cleaner company in another part of his state. After 14 months, he was offered the choice of a larger territory by the company, since his performance as a franchised operator had impressed them favorably.......... Royal himself was supremely confident that his sales would increase from 30 units per month, which he achieved during the first two months of operation, to 75 per month by the end of six months, and to 100 units by the end of the first year.

After his first two months, Royal moved to a more spacious location. By September — seven months after opening — business had expanded so much that he rented an adjoining store, knocked out the wall and added it as a show room to his facilities. His whole staff had expanded to 12 persons.

The second year exceeded all expectations. Every interview reported expansion of staff and improvement at headquarters.

When the two-year observation period had ended, business had developed far beyond Royal's fondest dreams. Sales volume had risen to 500 units per month and Royal was confident that sales would fluctuate between 500-700 units a month from then on.

Royal had built up a very lucrative enterprise. His success is particularly impressive in view of the fact, previous to his taking over the franchise, three or four distributors of this vacuum cleaner in Rhode Island had given up the franchise either because of failure or because they saw better opportunities elsewhere. None of their operations had approached Royal's volume. The secret of his success lies in the combination of shrewd managerial practices, boundless enthusiasm, and enormous drive."

THE S.O.B.

Now this is a story of a successful operation, started from scratch, and the point to the reader of this book is the comment that Royal made to the interviewer at their final interview. When asked what satisfied him the most about starting and operating a successful business, and beating the game, he replied thusly: "I like to have two secretaries and a nice office. I like to be a businessman and hire and fire people. These are things that make a business interesting."

In other words, you have the definite characteristics of the dedicated S.O.B. who is going to succeed, who likes the struggle, doesn't mind doing what is necessary to achieve his personal goals, and he did not regret that the monetary return is the most satisfying aspect of the business. To him, winning was the most important, and money was the way he kept score.

There is a formula for success, and it is a simple one. While it is simple to understand, it is extremely difficult to operate.

SELF MOTIVATION IS THE KEY

Self-motivation is everyone's key to success. The ability to do what one dreams of doing comes from *mood to do it.*

SUCCESS MUST BE NEEDED

You must need success Not desire it or only want it, but need it above all else. Needs are what people must have to survive. Humans need food, air to breath, clothing, shelter, sleep etc. What you need to survive, you get at any cost. When you can convince yourself you need success, just as you need to eat when you are hungry, it comes without your even having to think about it.

Most people want to be successful or desire to be successful, but very few need to be successful. This is why the success story is news. It's uncommon. Success doesn't have to be a fortune. It can be inventing a product, learning a skill, climbing a mountain or succeeding in business. We've all different mental pictures of success, but few of us ever really totally achieve it.

There is one major reason for this. Our mental image of ourselves is poor. "We are what we think we are." That is pure truth. We may show the world an image of self-confidence and even arrogance, but inside we may know its a sham. We lack self-confidence because we believe we can't do the thing we most want to do. Therefore, we convince ourselves we don't really need to do it.

How can this be changed? By the simple process of making the want or desire into a need. To create a need, you must first set up a goal. The goal is placed before you,and by using self-motivational techniques, *you make that goal a need.* It becomes a driving force, you convince yourself that the goal must be reached in order for you to survive. Once that state of mind is achieved, you will succeed.

As an example, you are lost in a desert without water. You are weak, and you despair. But, suddenly a water hole appears. It is some distance away, a hard, painful effort is needed to reach it. You know this, but you also know something else. If you don't reach it, you will die. The choice is automatic...... No degree of difficulty, or level of pain will stay you. The need to live will see you through any amount of difficulty to reach that water hole.

So, the need must be established in order to motivate you to pass the difficulties you can see ahead. If you had plenty of water, and you saw the water hole, you might think it would be nice to get some more water, take a cool dip etc. But, the degree of difficulty might well put you off. Here you are only dealing with a desire, and they are easy to put aside. But, once it is a need, *nothing will stay you.*

SET A GOAL

Goal setting is not difficult. You know what you dream of having. You just write it down in a note book. You know it says I want my business to gross a million dollars. You plant that in your mind. I want my business to gross one million dollars. Say that over ten times. Everyday when you wake up, put a note or a device to jog your memory beside your bed that will remind you of your goal. Say it to yourself, I want my business to gross one million dollars. Arrange for at least five other reminders you come in contact with each day to force you to remember to say I want my business to gross one million dollars.

CREATE A SUCCESS HABIT

What are you doing this for? You are engaging in a simple system of self-hypnosis. *You are creating a habit.* You are convincing yourself you need something. the mind is a powerful stimulator. Once it becomes convinced you are serious, and you do need that to survive, it will supply the energy, adrenal and pressure you need to move ahead. *Your mind is both your master and your servant.* It will do what you convince it needs doing. It will make you a drunk, a dope addict or a thief if you want it to. It will take you to the peaks of the highest mountain, drive you across parched deserts, help you solve difficult and intricate problems, if you tell it to often enough and seriously enough. It will make whatever you want made into a habit, including achievement.

SET A TIME LIMIT

The next step *is to provide a time limit* for your goal. A goal without limits is like a gun without ammunition. It has potential, but no fire power. You say, "I want my business to gross one million dollars in five years." This puts the game on the field, you know where you are now, you know where the goal line is, and you know how long the game will last. This adds the necessary pressure to your program.

CHANGE YOUR ATTITUDES

Now, you are ready to start to reach for your unreachable star. But first, *you must change your mind.* Your mind has been conditioned up to now to be a partial achiever: To provide the motivation to keep you alive, and at whatever level of success you may have reached. It is not now conditioned to do more. *It must be!*

You must first change your attitudes about the things around you. Whatever you feel might hold you back must be removed. You must face these fears openly, and tell your mind they are no longer a problem. To forget being afraid, and move on. How is this done? By repetition, *by believing in yourself*, by facing fear you conquer it. Once your mind understands that fear is no longer a problem, it will recategorize it, and it will no longer bother you. You will reprogrammed your mental computer. It is as simple as that.

ADD A PLAN

Now to achieve your goal, you must add a plan. The plan becomes the motor that makes the goal reachable. The plan should be broken down into simple steps that can be reached in appropriate time segments. A trip of a thousand miles starts with the first step, and that is the way you make your plan, one step at a time.

THREE STEPS TO SUCCESS

To achieve success and reach your goal, your plan will be operating in three steps. They are the learning step, the self-confidence step and finally the persevering step.

STEP ONE — LEARNING

The first stage is learning. Information gathering, analyzing and understanding. Before you start the journey towards your goal, you want to know what you are doing. The history of what had happened before, the current state of the art, and the educated estimate of what can happen in the future. You must, in short, become an expert in what you are about to do.

Too many people launch into ventures, or start expanding businesses without enough information. They start out with blind enthusiasm, and wind up sooner or later in total despair. *They fail to understand the game,* or in some cases even know the rules of the game.

For example, only an idiot would sit in a poker game where he couldn't see his cards, had no control over how much he had to bet, didn't know in advance which hands would win or lose while all other players did. Yet, business ventures and plans are started everyday by people playing exactly that kind of game. The results are obvious, sooner or later they lose everything.

So, before you take that plunge, know what you are doing. Be fully informed, know what can go wrong, anticipate trouble and problems, know their solutions, and be ready to face adversity that you realize will come up. When you know what you are doing, and where you are going, then you automatically acquire and move into the second stage of your drive to success. *Self-confidence!*

STEP TWO — SELF-CONFIDENCE

It is axiomatic that when you know what you are doing, and how to do it, you are confident of success.......... To illustrate this, I want you to think about the first time you got behind the wheel of a car and were responsible for driving it by yourself. You were at least nervous, possibly frightened and maybe terrified. Here you are with a couple of tons of metal that you have to precisely control in a narrow area and be able to manuever it properly without hitting anything or doing damage to the vehicle. Those attempts were at best clumsy, and at worst disastrous. But, after some practice, you gained confidence and control. Now, you drive where you wish to go almost without thinking. You have total confidence you can handle a car in any situation that comes up in traffic. *Self-confidence takes you where you want to go.*

So it is with your venture. Once you learn all there is to know about it, you have confidence you can overcome the difficulties and finish what you have started successfully. This confidence puts you on the final plateau to reaching your ultimate goal.

STEP THREE — PERSEVERANCE

Perseverance! This is the real key to all success. The willingness to hang in there, take the lumps that come, and get up off the floor more than once, is the attribute that you must have.

Not long ago Mc Donald's Hamburger Chain published an ad that sums up the value of perseverance, it reads like this:

> Press on. Nothing in the world can take the place of persistence. Talent will not; nothing is more common than unsuccessful men with talent. Genius will not; unrewarded genius is almost a proverb. Education alone will not; the world if full of educated derelicts. Persistence and determination alone are omnipotent.
>
> It is a fact that more people have given up the game on the goal line simply because they didn't know they were there, than at any other point on the field. Just one more try, one more bit of stubborn determination could have carried them on to success.
>
> Why didn't they know? First, because they didn't fully understand what they were doing, and second, they lacked

the confidence that knowledge would have given them. It takes all three to make a dream into reality.

The person who perseveres is destined to succeed. Talent, genius, education and even money are worthless without it. Only personal dedication to a goal by a self- assured person will do it. When the going gets tough, the tough get going sums it all up.

If this sounds like a lot of simplified hogwash or a Sunday school sermon, you are missing the point. The most difficult things to accomplish are most often the most simple to comprehend. Becoming successful in the field you have chosen is simple to understand, but not simple to do. And only by really meaning to do it, will you do it.

This then is the beginning. The place to take the first step on your journey to a goal. Let's recap the procedure.

1. Set a goal

2. Set a time limit for that goal 3. Develop a basic plan for reaching that goal.

To make this system work, you have to become a dedicated, single-minded S.O.B. You have to change your thinking, your attitude towards reality, and develop what could be described as a Machiavellian outlook on the world.

First, you cannot be overconcerned with morality in the conventional sense.

You must become convinced there is nothing essentially wrong with exploiting people and situations. The game of business is like the game of football. If the quarterback on the offensive team discovers that a defensive halfback simply cannot cover one of his pass receivers, he will use that weakness to his maximum advantage. The defender may wind up losing his job, but this is of no concern to the quarterback. The name of the game is winning, and exploiting situations and people is part of that game.

2. You have to learn to become cool and detached in dealing with other people. You never get emotionally involved with people or situations. Essentially you view everything in terms of objects and situations. You do not suffer with intellectual analysis of the results of your actions.

3. You actually enjoy the game. You enjoy the exploitation, you derive the satisfaction from using people, things and situations to achieve your goal. You do not do this for amusement, or self-aggrandizement, but simply to get that which you are after.

4. Above all you have a rational view of society as it exists. You are neither impressed nor bothered by philosophical viewpoints that stress that the greatest goals in life are serving your fellow man.

5. In short you are not a nice guy, you are an S.O.B., dedicated to success, and having convinced yourself you need that success, it will be achieved.

As for money, that's the way you keep score.

If this attitude puts some strain on your psyche, and you feel it is over cynical or outright debasing, I would like to engage in a brief, philosophical dissertation concerning the reality of such things as truth and morals.

In point of fact, *there is no such thing as real truth in human affairs.* Let's examine the most often quoted rule of behavior, the so called golden rule. "Do unto others as you would have others do unto you". This sounds as though it is the perfect philosophical solution to human action. However, all humans are not the same, and there are aberrations in the human psyche. If, for example, a masochist was to apply the golden rule to everybody he came in contact with, there would be many unhappy people in the vicinity.

So even the most likely sounding philosophy has holes in it. The plain truth is, that truth is a point of view.

For example, let's take a common happening that effects everybody in the vicinity. Rain! Rain falls universally on everybody in an area. The farmer says the rain is good because it makes his crops grow, and this is the truth. The road-builder, the owner of the baseball team and the people going on a picnic, say the rain is bad because it stops them from doing what they need to do. And, that is the truth. So we have two people with exactly opposing opinions about an event, and both are telling the truth. So in fact, the truth is little more than a point of view, and it depends on whose moccasins you are standing in as to whether good or bad.

The problems we have, with things of this nature, are that people tend to take extreme view points. Thus, the farmer who demands that it always rains, is advocating flood. The road-builder who advocates that it never rains, is advocating drought. The truth has to be a reasonable compromise between these points of view. And so it is with all affairs of mankind, there had to be a compromise from the extremes in order to arrive at a livable situation. But, those moralists, who set down rules carved in stone, and hand them down as the great truth from above, are little more than con men attempting to force people to live in a society that advocates a single truth or a single point of view. It very seldom works.

Morals are nothing more than social customs. They change with time, generations and societies... For example, a cannibal is moral in a cannibalistic society. He is obviously immoral in a non-cannibalistic society.

In this country we have had great changes in moral attitudes over the years, and they change everyday. In the old West, horse stealing was a hanging offense. Today it is a misdemeanor. In the early days of this country, political corruption, business corruption, prostitution, slavery and other moral outrages were common coin. Yet, we had a higher percentage of people going to church in those days than we do today. Some of the most thoroughly debased, and worst offenders who always considered the moral code, in those days, today have their names engraved on the front of great institutions.

A perfect example of this situation is the recent Watergate mess. We have the President, Richard Nixon, commonly considered, at the time of this writing, the biggest crook that ever occupied the White House.

But, as a matter of fact, the Franklin D. Roosevelt administration made Watergate look like a penny-ante poker game. Roosevelt's political allies were some of the most dedicated rogues in American history. Pendergast of Kansas City, Hague of Jersey City, Curley of Boston, Tammany Hall in New York,

Crump of Memphis and many other political bosses who stole votes, stole money, received payoffs from every crook and rascal in their community on a regular basis, were the people who kept Mr. Roosevelt in office. In the South, his allies were members of the Ku Klux Klan who engaged in lynchings and some of the most terrible racial degradations in our history. Yet, today, his name is invoked as though he were the patron saint of American politics.

Such is the continuous holds of morality on a society. Therefore, the small businessman who is stepping out into the business world, can be little concerned with the changing fads of human morals, or philosophical opinions about what is or is not truth.

The reality of the situation is to reach the top. Each entrepreneur before him has traveled the same road, recognized the same realities, and once at the top, does pretty much the same thing.

When you have made it up the mountain, reached the pinnacle, you can then do what the rest of those successful entrepreneurs have done before you. You can write a code of ethics, make speeches about morality to business and civic groups, and look down with a cold smile on all the scrambling, scratching, little bastards below, trying to find their path to the top. You can even do what some of the rest of them have done — roll rocks down on them just for the hell of it, and make the road a little tougher.

I like to think of the small businessman as an eagle. A high-flying loner, whose only morality is to get that which he deems is his right. He flies alone, finds what he needs himself, and lives where and as he chooses.

I think of corporations, government bureaucracies and others as vultures. Vultures operate in groups, picking the bones of the dead and defenseless, and are simply put here to demonstrate Machiavelli's rule that only the fittest survive.

START NOW!

CHAPTER 1
HOW TO GET AND USE POWER

How To Get And Use Power

One of the most overlooked and least used tools to achieve success in small business is the power button. The average small businessman simply does not think in terms of getting access to and using the power centers in our society to achieve financial success. He is a loner who does not have a powerful organization representing him, and therefore, is prey to those who do.

GAINING A POLITICAL POWER BUTTON

The political power structure consists of those who are elected or appointed to office. It is the easiest power center to infiltrate and gain power button sources. Because the political structure is constantly in need of support and of money, it invites the dedicated S.O.B. into its midst and will reward him in direct proportion to what his apparent service is.

The first and easiest power button source is the political candidate. He has to campaign for office therefore he needs money and support. He looks in all directions for this, and since he is a dedicated S.O.B. himself, is always willing to give *quid pro quo* for support.

The best candidate for your power button is a young aggressive attorney, small businessman or professional man who you view as a comer. He is probably running for a local office, but you view him as a potential for higher office. By latching onto this power button candidate early, you put yourself in the driver's seat, and assure yourself of a long-term power button in ever higher political circles. It is best to avoid an incumbent, unless he is in some political difficulty running against an attractive candidate, and is in need of obvious help, with a good chance to win. But, the established incumbent already had his backers, and unless you could come in with a lot of money or a lot of votes, you won't gain much control by acting on his behalf.

Now it is obvious that you must pick and choose with some care, because backing losers gets you nothing. So, I am going to give you a form chart that you can use, to evaluate candidates for political office in your area, and by filling it out correctly you are going to come up with a pretty good indication of who is going to win and who is going to lose. There are twenty points of evaluation on this chart, which you will find in the appendix with an explanation on how to use it. This chart will not only enable you to have a pretty good advance look at who is going to win a campaign, but will also enable you to pick potential candidates at a later time, tailor make them for political office and become a power broker, with many buttons to push.

Now you are probably saying to yourself, I am running a small business and I don't have time for political nonsense. Let me point out a couple of facts of life to you. First, solid political contacts are fortune builders. Successful politicians are money magnets, who not only get rich themselves, but enable those who back and support them to get even richer. Every major fortune built in this country, has done it with the liberal use of political connections. It is somewhat time consuming at first, as you feel your way along, but as you develop a reputation for being the backer of political winners, and make the many contacts that successful political campaigns bring you, you will find many important opportunities not only to advance your business fortunes, but advance your personal fortunes as well in side deals that will come your way.

It's important to note that a political power button, is not necessarily a corrupt politician. It is simply a politician who will do things for you on request, throw influence and prestige into a situation that will help in resolving it in your favor. But, there is something more important than simply the ability of the politician to take some bureaucrat off your back, or get you favorable attention in terms of a government contract, or tip you off in advance to certain opportunities or sure speculative profits. It is the contacts you will make through your affiliation with the politician and his organization that will bring your fortune.

Politicians make strange bed fellows. Politics is the great social leveler in this society. People of very unequal means will hustle together to elect a candidate neither of them knows very well. It's the place where the ward leader and his 500 sure thing votes stands on equal footing with the millionaire and his money machine. It is the one place you don't have to worry about your social connections, your present occupation or your bank balance when looking for opportunities. The sole criteria in the campaign are your political reliability, and what you can bring to the campaign in terms of money and votes. The connections you will make with the other backers of this politician during a campaign, win or lose, will serve you in good stead. You will meet many present incumbents, you will get to know some of the bureaucrats holding down important government positions, you will meet other business and financial leaders, all which can lead to important connections for you later on.

In making your contact with a potential successful political candidate, you have two ways to go. First, you can come to the candidate offering money and software support. Software means you can use your business to mail letters, make phone calls, and do other things that would cost the candidate money which you will absorb as a personal expense in order to help him get elected. This approach while appreciated, is not nearly as important to the candidate as large amounts of money or large blocks of support. So, the second approach and the most effective one, is to offer the candidate your services as his small business chairman. But you will undertake to contact other small businessmen on his behalf to raise money and get votes. If you could deliver as few as ten small businessmen into his campaign, with money and personal support, you are then in the driver's seat, and your power button will be a big one.

It is not difficult to do this, because you simply point out to your fellow small businessman the theory of the political button... We all need help in fighting the bureaucracy, and here we have a candidate that we can call upon to help us fight back when we are attacked by government. As you well know, this strikes a very responsive cord in the small businessmen's mind, and you would have little difficulty in forming a committee for your candidate.

BECOMING A PARTY WHEEL

If your community is one in which one party is consistently elected and consistantly in control and there is no danger of losing that position, then you could become a party wheel. A party wheel is someone who controls votes. If you could walk into the political headquarters, with fifty to a hundred votes in your pocket, you are an automatic wheel. You can do this by forming a small business organization, a neighborhood improvement organization or other type of politically oriented organization devoted to the specific interests of the members. You are the president, and you can deliver the votes.

Putting yourself in this position, you then gain access to many power buttons. You have access to incumbents presently in office, you get to know promising new candidates, bureaucrats and others in the government power structure. Using these connections you have many possible methods of advancing your own business fortunes, and making a lot of money in personal investments you would otherwise not be aware of.

It is a very simple procedure to form such an organization, and once formed, it is your open sesame to the political vault. In essence, here are the steps you have to take:

1. Find three or four interested and motivated people.

2. Hold a meeting to form the association or group.

3. Arrange for informal initial meetings at the homes or offices of your co-founders.

4. Prepare application blanks for membership, give pep talks in direction in enrolling members.

5. Sign up about twenty to twenty-five members.

6. Hold an organization meeting, set up the rules and by-laws of the organization, and make sure you get elected president.

7. Organize further meetings to enroll members til you have approximately one hundred.

8. Then hold an initial banquet, block party or other function to get newspaper coverage and put on an enrollment drive to get out each of your hundred members to get two more members.

9. Start political action, petitions, demands on city hall or county government bodies to achieve some worthy goal.

10. Take your package to the political organization with the votes in your pocket, and you are a party wheel.

RUNNING FOR OFFICE

If you have the time, and like the idea, you can run for political office yourself. You can start at any level you think you are capable of handling, and once elected, you are immediately a member of the political power structure with access to all the buttons in the organization. It is not too difficult to get elected to small boards, such as school boards, planning commissions and other local elective governing bodies, because by controlling just a few primary votes, you are able to get elected. These types of offices are generally not contested by any dedicated political types, and a modicum of organization, and a few dedicated workers, can result in easy election.

In the appendix you will find a step-by-step organization chart for a political election, so you can get an idea of what needs to be done in its exact order in order to conduct a successful political campaign for yourself.

APPOINTIVE OFFICE

If you are a party wheel, or have backed a successful candidate, you can get appointed to boards and commissions by the politician. This again gives you access to the power structure, contact with many potential political buttons, at very little cost of your time or your money.

WHAT ALL THIS CAN BE WORTH TO YOU

Now, we have given you a general idea of how you can infiltrate the political power structures of your community, and you might wonder in reality, what is all this really worth?

I'm going to give you a perfect example of pushing power buttons to achieve a commercial goal. This may or may not be a true story, it is told about Joe Kennedy, father of the late President, but true or not, it is one that gives you a perfect example of how access to power buttons can overcome a business problem.

In the 1930's Joe Kennedy was sent out to Hollywood to take over a bankrupt movie studio. Joe Kennedy was a powerful Democrat, a good friend of President Franklin D. Roosevelt, and had personal contact with political bosses in every major city in the country.

As head of the studio, and a newcomer to Hollywood, he was not aware of all of the ins and outs of the motion picture business. He assumed that you made a picture in a studio, and sent it out for distribution to the theatres, and collected your money. So, he reorganized the studio and made some pictures, and proceeded to offer them in the distribution channels to theatre owners.

However, he discovered that the best motion picture houses, (in those days the first run houses that collected the most money for a picture), were all controlled by one group of owners, who were directly controlled by the owners of the other major motion picture studios.

Therefore, his pictures were simply not accepted for use in the first run theatres, and he lost the major market he needed to make the kind of money necessary from the movies that were made in his studio.

For someone without access to specific power buttons, this would have been a total disaster. The movie studio would have indeed closed its doors, and the other motion picture studios picked its bones clean.

However, Joe Kennedy was used to dealing in this kind of an atmosphere, and simply picked up the telephone and made a few calls. He called the political bosses in the major cities in the United States who he had personal contact with and made this suggestion to them.

"I want you to send the fire inspectors, the health inspectors and the building inspectors around to the motion picture houses whose names I am going to give you, and I want them cited for every violation that is true or can be imagined, and have them shut down until all these violations are taken care of."

Each of the political bosses was happy to accommodate Joe, and dutifully all of the bureaucrats went out and cited all of these motion picture theatres for every imaginable violation of the municipal code they could think of. It would have cost the theatre owners hundreds of thousands of dollars in many cases to correct the violations they were cited for. There was panic in the streets in Hollywood when this situation developed, and when they called the various cities to find out what could be done about this, one word always came back, "see Joe Kennedy."

The movie moguls knew when they were licked, so with hats in hand to Joe Kennedy to see what could be worked. What was worked out, was that the pictures that Joe Kennedy wanted displayed were given top billing in the best moving picture houses in the country, and in turn all the citations were dropped and forgotten.

This is a perfect example of a businessman caught in a squeeze where he has no resources of his own to fight back, but having access to power buttons, he can turn the situation around instantly by retaliating in another area. The small businessman, with access to power buttons, can do the same thing in his own community and area when necessary.

I can give you a local example of this, that I know from personal experience. A local businessman we shall call Henry owned a pizza parlor in a middle-sized American town. One of the major pizza parlor franchises was planning to open up near him, and was going to cost him a great deal of business should they be allowed to open. He pushed his local political buttons, and all of a sudden the franchise operation had road blocks tossed in their way they had not anticipated. There were problems with the health department in the design of their building, they couldn't put up the kind of sign they wanted, they would have to redesign their parking lot, they would have to pay a business license based on the total volume of the chain, rather than on the volume of the individual unit, etc., and the franchiser wisely decided to try some place else. So Henry protected his business without spending a dime of his own money, and having learned the franchiser was convinced there was room for another pizza parlor, opened another one himself in a part of town they were planning on locating in, and doubled his business.

Big businessmen do their utmost to encourage the politicians natural greed and desire to live well. In America, the huge cost of getting elected at almost any level and the impossibility of winning an election without sufficient funding, opens the door to the political power structure for the businessman. That politicians do well, by acting as political power buttons for businessmen had been proven many times over. Hubert Humphrey, admittedly was bankrupt when he lost the West Virginia primary to John F. Kennedy in 1960. In 1964, when asked for a financial statement as a candidate for president, he showed a net worth in excess of $300,000. Both Nixon and Eisenhower were men of moderate circumstances prior to coming on the national political scene, and both left it wealthy men. Lyndon Johnson was an impecunious congressman from Texas, a former school teacher, who entered government service at a salary of $25,000 a year, and after serving in the House, Senate, as Vice President and President, left office with a fortune estimated between nine to fourteen million dollars.

All these funds were obtained by the politicians because they acted as political power buttons for wealthy side kicks. It is no accident that politicians invariably have advisors, and close friends who are wealthy. Those who don't have big money, are fascinated by those who do. And they are willing to perform reasonable services in order to achieve some of that wealth and prestige for themselves.

As it is true on the national scene, so it is true all the way down the line. And the small businessman who will take the time and the trouble to collect some power buttons in the political structure, will not only be able to protect himself and his business when necessary, but will be able to take advantage of many opportunities to make extra money that would not otherwise come his way. It is reality, and the smart S.O.B. will take full advantage of it.

THE FINANCIAL POWER STRUCTURE

Money is the life-blood of business, and every businessman needs access to a money blood bank. As a rule, this takes the form of having contacts at a commercial bank where he can borrow money when he needs it in order to expand his business. In a future chapter we are going to go into detail concerning gaining control of a banker, and thereby getting access to the bank vault.

Suffice it to say here, that every businessman knows the value of good banking connections, and smart S.O.B. is one who takes the time and effort to develop one or more power buttons in a bank that can be pushed when necessary to obtain funds as needed.

CONNECTIONS WITH WEALTHY PEOPLE

A second source of money, and one that should not be overlooked, is making personal contact with people of wealth. Often times, when bank sources are exhausted and additional funds are needed, these are the life savers that can provide the necessary funds to get over the hump. As a rule, connections are made in a political area where you meet them during political campaigns, through politicians or party workers. They are also met when you make contact through the social structure, which we shall get into later in this chapter. But, always keep a weather eye out for somebody who is loaded, and can be contacted and tapped for funds if necessary. Many times such a wealth connection of this kind does not need to put up any money, simply to make a guarantee in order to make the funds available, or give you an introduction or a recommendation to his own bank where funds would be made available. Every smart S.O.B. had a few of these wealth connections in reserve if needed. They are cultivated carefully, favors done so that quid pro quo can be utilized when necessary.

BROKERS AND FINDERS

There are many operating brokers in money fields, ranging from stock and real estate brokers to money brokers, commodity brokers and so called finders who are nothing more than contact brokers.

Often times solid connections with active brokers in any field, can lead to interesting financial opportunities and sources of additional capital when needed. Most brokers operate at low visibility levels, and often the most successful are not even found with their names in the phone book. But by mingling in the financial community, and making as many contacts as possible, you will run across these people from time to time. It is wise to recognize their potential, and to cultivate them as best you can when the opportunity presents itself.

Many times as your business expands and you require additional capital from banks, you will run into the necessity of having compensating balances in order to obtain a loan. Here is where a smart money broker can come in handy, because he can instantly provide the funds (for a fee) that would enable you to get a sizable loan that would otherwise be denied you. Stock brokers often have contact with wealthy investors, who have surplus funds to invest in good propositions that you might have access to. The same is true of real estate brokers. You can gain their confidence and respect by steering a little business their way from time to time, having lunch with them occasionally, and turning them into financial power buttons by doing them a favor. Most of these people are not wealthy themselves, because they simply don't have the drive to accumulate wealth, but are useful to others who have. Shop the field carefully and be sure you are getting in touch with the right people because there are many.

Analyze the local civic organizations such as Kiwanis, Rotary, Lions, Chambers of Commerce and other such groups and determine which are those where the successful people congregate. When you find out which it is, make every effort to join. This allows you weekly meetings with these people on a peer group basis, and enables you to judge the potential value of each, and by cultivating them turn them into financial power buttons you can use when necessary.

LEGAL AND JUDICIAL POWER SOURCES

One of the slickest power moves you can make in your community, is to get in contact with and have access to a judge. Often this is easily done by simply helping a judge with a political campaign to get elected. While the advantages of having access to a judge are not so much financial, and you can't expect them to fix traffic tickets or cases for you, it allows you to mix with the hierarchy of the judicial system in your community, which can be of tremendous advantage to you in many ways.

For example, in finding a good lawyer. The one person who can rate lawyers from the standpoint of ability and responsibility is a judge. When a judge is your confidant and your friend, he will give the names of lawyers for particular situations who can do the job for you. They'll even pick up the phone and call them and make an appointment for you assuring you of red carpet treatment when you arrive at the office.

Many times a judge can give you legal advice that would cost you several hundred dollars to get from a lawyer, just talking to him over cocktails.

If you have good political and financial connections, you can introduce the judge into your circle of contacts, in exchange for being introduced into his.

Since campaigns for judges are not generally hard fought, and are more or less foregone conclusions, you don't have to invest a great deal of time or energy in helping a judge get elected, but supply some money and a little help once in a while, that will pay off handsomely in the future.

So, when the opportunity presents itself, try to find a judge who will become a legal power button for you and you have many advantages in dealing with the power structure of the community.

MEDIA POWER SOURCES

The most powerful shapers of public opinion and reaction in a community are the newspaper, radio and TV stations. In every community there is one dominant newspaper, one dominant radio and TV station. The smart S.O.B. will look for power buttons in the structure of these groups, in order to have access to favorable publicity, and the ability to water down unfavorable publicity.

Most communities are fairly well dominated by newspapers as the most powerful media in the community. Most people think that having good contact with the publisher of a daily newspaper is the way to go in having media influence. This is probably not true in 90% of the cases. The publisher has little day to day knowledge of what is or isn't being printed, and is far more concerned with advertising linage, circulation income, payrolls and expenses than he is with content. Therefore, in developing a power button in a newspaper, you are far better off dealing with an editor than with a publisher in most daily newspapers. While it certainly can't do any harm to know the publisher, and have some social contact with him, in terms of getting news in the paper, or keeping out of the paper, the publisher is not the person to contact.

The man or woman to look for, is a senior editor. For example, if it is a daily newspaper, they probably have a business editor. He is the first step. Getting to know him, doing him some favors, and getting favorable publicity from him from time to time is not difficult.

One of the easiest ways to put him in your pocket, is to get together some fellow businessmen and have an award banquet which he is the star attraction and receives an award as the best newspaperman of the twentieth century, or something similiar. Giving him an occasional PR assignment for fifty or a hundred dollars as a sideline, (in newspaper terms this is putting him on the pad) is also not a bad idea because it solidifies your connections with him or her.

Once you have a solid connection with the business editor, or the reporter who covers the business news and is called the editor, you can use him to move on to the next power button source, which would probably be the city editor or managing editor. By playing essentially the same game with this editor, an awards banquet or some other personal tribute to the individual engineered and sponsored by you, you will have another receptive power button within the media structure.

If you are looking for publicity for an event, or for a business opening or other commercial project, having access to these editorial types is of great importance. Many businessmen feel because they buy a substantial amount of advertising, that they can get publicity in newspapers either favorable to them or unfavorable to somebody else whenever they wish. This is seldom the case. The editorial side of a newspaper is extremely jealous of their prerogatives, and any suggestion from the advertising side that they give free stories to advertisers is taken with great umbrage. But, where you have direct access to them, bypassing the advertising department entirely, you will have little difficulty in getting the stories in the paper you wish to plant.

I learned about this situation very early in life. At one point I was promoting an air show, and thought by buying a great deal of advertising in the newspapers and on the radio at the time, that I would be entitled to free publicity in the newspapers. During the time I was initially buying the advertising, I got nothing.

Then, I contacted a reporter, and offered him $50 to give me some publicity, and wound up with front page stories both in the newspaper he worked for, and in the competing newspaper across town. Subsequently, whenever I had an idea that I needed publicity for, $50 bought me all I could use, and I never had to spend another dime for advertising.

I would think the situation is true or even truer in radio and television stations. In the first place, in small communities particularly, radio and television people are paid something less than janitors. So consequently they are always in need of money, and always looking for something like an awards banquet that they could put in their portfolio that would enable them to get a higher paying job in a larger community. By a judicious inquiry, you can find out who is the power button in the broadcast media in each station, and cultivate them pretty much the same way you cultivate newspaper editors.

I want to say a word here about weekly newspapers, because they differ in structure from dailies. In a weekly newspaper the publisher generally controls the content of the paper to a great extent. To get on the good side of a weekly publisher, all you need to do is help him get some advertising. This is his biggest problem, and the one he is the most appreciative of help with. So by using whatever influence you have in other centers, to be sure that this weekly newspaper publisher gets his share of political advertising, advertising from fellow businessmen etc., you will have a friend for life. And he is a good deal more pliable concerning publicity material, and virtually anything will go if you have him on your side.

Generally in the community there are small magazines, shoppers and other publications which have very little impact on community opinion, but sometimes can be used for such things as political campaigns, advertising promotion etc., to some advantage. It is not really worth your time to cultivate power buttons in this type of media, though as you run across them in your social, political, financial and other contacts, it is well to make note of who they are, and if you can do them a favor without a waste of time or money, it could pay off to some extent later on.

A good media power button used judiciously, can be worth a great deal to a smart S.O.B. in developing a business, and doing favors for other power buttons on occasion to keep them in line.

SOCIAL POWER CENTERS

In a community, there are generally four major social power centers. These would be church groups, civic groups, special interest groups and in some places ethnic groups.

A little investigating, or simply listening to people in the community will alert you to the church group that is the most powerful, the civic group with the largest number of potential power sources in it, and the special interest.

It is worth the time and effort for a smart S.O.B. to become a member of one or more of these groups, giving some of his time and perhaps a little of his money in order to become solidly established. Oftentimes, you can volunteer for the Community Chest, the Boy Scouts, Cancer Drive or other charitable institutional efforts and make some excellent contacts in other areas. It also helps to have an appellation of a good citizen in a community, and some small effort on your part can get you that by working within and for one of these groups.

Many times, you can meet the potential power buttons in the other power centers through membership in these influential groups, and it usually the best place to start your campaign in developing power sources in the community.

Almost all professional people — doctors, lawyers, accountants and others, use memberships in these groups as one of their major forms of advertising. So by joining and working with the proper group, you are meeting the top-level professional people in your community and from those meetings can develop power buttons in other areas of the power structure.

TO SUM UP

As you read all of this material you are probably thinking, who in the hell has time to do everything that is suggested in this chapter? The answer to it is this: By budgeting some of your time to develop contacts with the power centers in your community, you have made the best investment of your time you can possibly make outside operation of your business.

Let me give you a specific example of what power button contact can mean. In a recently released IRS operating manual, they revealed that the "sensitive — case" label is applied to audits of politicians and their close friends, nationally-known businessmen, racketeers clubs with large influencial membership, and colleges and universities. If the Internal Revenue Service is going to treat politicians and their friends, well-known successful people gingerly in making audits in their tax returns, this will give you some idea of what power and contacts with power are worth. You should give very serious consideration to developing these sources in your community, and stretching them as far beyond your community as time and resources will allow. As we have stated previously in the chapter, it not only will result in you being able to defend yourself against bureaucratic attack, against larger business organizations, against assaults of any kind in the business world, but it also gives you many opportunities to make money, expand your business and otherwise become far more wealthy than you would without them. These kind of contacts open doors that you never dreamed existed, and properly developed and maintained virtually assure your success. So, don't sell them short, but give serious consideration to developing as many power buttons as you can in order to survive and prosper.

CHAPTER 2
THE FINE ART OF EMPLOYEE EXPLOITATION

The Fine Art Of Employee Exploitation

SMALL BUSINESSMEN ARE 4 F's IN PERSONNEL COMPETITION

The small businessman is in competition with big business, big government and the welfare rolls in obtaining help. He is a 4F in this battle, and therefore operates under a distinct handicap. His four F's can be termed as: Lack of funds, fringes, facilities and future.

In other words; he can't pay as much as a large firm for help; he can't offer the same type and quality of fringe benefits; he rarely has the same working facilities as a large corporation; and, the future he can offer most employees (particularly young ones) is much more limited than a large company.

For this reason, the smart S.O.B. has to make up for these deficiencies with some careful planning and careful dealing with his employees.

RAPE VERSUS SEDUCTION

Intercourse between owner and the employee in a small business is similiar to that in a bedroom.

The intercourse can take two forms, rape or seduction.........Rape is performed with an unwilling partner, and only one receives any satisfaction from the act. Seduction on the other hand, is willingly participated in by both partners, and both enjoy it. The results are the same, but only in the latter is the enjoyment mutual.

Therefore, the art of employee seduction is something the small businessman should consider very carefully in an effort to make his business more successful and his life a lot easier.

In this chapter we are going to try to explain the art of employee seduction to you, in terms of minimum cost to you and maximum results from those you employ.

TYPES OF EMPLOYEES AVAILABLE

The small businessman generally finds four types of people applying for position in his company. You must remember, small business is the minor leagues, and you primarily have to deal with minor leaguers as employees.

The first type is the transitory worker. This is the individual who is simply putting in time to get a pay check while looking for something better. Often times they are excellent workers, but will jump ship as soon as a better offer comes along. On occasion, these people are open to seduction and can be retained by making them believe there are better days ahead.

The second type is the newcomer, trainee or young person who needs experience and will always move along when something more interesting shows up. Since they are young, seduction does not generally work well with them, and they should always be employed at minimum wages with a realization that six months to two years will be their maximum stay as employees with a small businessman.

The third type are the flakes and failures. These are often people who have failed in the big leagues and are on their way down. They will often come with impressive credentials, often be over qualified for the job they seek, and you can be positive there is a reason why they are back in the minor leagues. This does not mean that they can't be turned into good and useful employees, but they must be hired with great care and watched constantly.

The fourth type, is a desperation case. These are people who need a pay check at any cost, willing to accept almost any terms of employment in order to get it, and often have serious personal problems that can cause a great deal of difficulty to their employer. This individual generally applies for work with a very convincing sob story, and literally begs for the job. The smart S.O.B. never employees this type of individual.

Lastly, is the rare gem. This is the individual who is a competent worker, satisfied with minor league employment, likes you and likes the operation, and will be an extremely valuable employee for your organization.

Often times, these people simply do not feel comfortable in large organizations, where they are simply ants in an ant hill. They enjoy some responsibility in an organization and perhaps for personal reasons either like or must live in the area your business is located in, although they could do much better elsewhere. For whatever reason, these are obviously the first choices for any small businessman, but unfortunately, like valuable gems, are rare and hard to find.

FINDING A GEM IN THE GARBAGE

Locating potential employees who will be valuable to your organization is an art you should develop. Regardless of how much seduction you indulge in, and how well you handle your people, you're still going to have a turn-over of employees for personal reasons, for lures of more money in the big leagues, or who simply go off to engage in their own pursuits. Many times, you are doing no more than training competitors in your particular business.

So, there will be a fairly constant need to find new employees as your business expands, and, at least in the beginning, you will be the personnel manager who must hire them.

We are going to try to reveal the sources of locating employees, the good and bad features of each method, and how to set up a scouting system similiar to that run by professional athletic teams so that good potential employees can be spotted and signed up when available.

The first and best source of locating such an individual is from your own employees. By alerting them to keep their eyes open for people you need for specific positions, they will often tell you about a neighbor, a friend, a relative, someone in a club or organization that they know who may not be as happy in their present situation.

The simplest way to contact these people is to get their home telephone number, call them and ask them to come in for an interview about a potential job with your company.

If the employee works for somebody you know, or could give you some difficulty, then you should arrange to have a third party make the contact. Rather than have your employee go to them directly, you can arrange for somebody you know to pose as an employment agency, head hunter etc., and contact the dissatisfied party and arrange for you to meet with that party at some convenient time and place. Perhaps a Saturday interview at your office, or a lunch or other social contact could be arranged in this manner. Using this technique, you can act innocent when accused of stealing the employee away from their present employment.

Another method of doing this and cutting the cost of having a head hunter working for you, is to contact some counsellor working for an employment agency who runs across the kind of people you are looking for. This can be worked out when the employment agency calls you to ask if you have any openings, and you determine that this counsellor is a commissioned salesman for the employment agency, you offer to have lunch him or her. At lunch you offer them a flat $50 or $100 to find the kind of individual you are looking for and arrange a meeting. It is understood that this will be paid to them directly, and will have nothing to do with the employment agency. This way you will have someone constantly scouting for the kind of individual you are looking for, and whether they are employed or unemployed, can put you in touch with some valuable potential employees.

One of the more imaginative schemes that was told to me by a successful small businessman who has working for him a very competent executive secretary to handle his business because he was away from the office a great deal of the time, was a letter-writing campaign. He called companies who he knew hired exceptionally good people, and got the names of the executive secretaries in that company, and sent each of them a letter outlining the job that he was offering, at a somewhat higher salary than they were probably receiving, with the added benefit that it would be a situation where they would take on a great deal of responsibility for the company, in effect be an assistant to the president rather than an executive secretary, and listed the fringe benefits, and asked them if they know anybody who would be interested in obtaining such a position. They could call him confidentially at home, or at his office.

The obvious intent of the letter was to hire or raid a secretary directly from these letters, and it worked. He got the girl he was looking for away from one of the corporations in the area, and if anybody accused him of raiding, he could point out that he wasn't asking those people to take his position, but was simply asking them if they knew somebody.

Obviously, the same technique could be used with almost any judgement position that you had open. You obtain good people who are simply convinced that their future in the ant hill is not all that good.

USING EMPLOYEES AS SOURCES

For the "grunt" jobs, those semi-skilled and low-level positions in your organization, one of the best sources of potential employees is from your own employees. Almost all of them probably know people who would make better than average employees, and by simply letting them know what you are looking for, you can get a great number of people to interview at no expense to yourself.

You should not, however, use this source too often for judgement jobs. Here you could get into a problem with the perception of your employees as to what a job requires. For judgement or management position jobs, you need to deal at arms length with everyone. You don't want to risk upsetting or irritating your employee by turning down the individual who they consider perfectly suited for the job, and who have gone out and shot their mouth off by telling this individual that they can get him this particular job because they have great influence with you.

But, for the grunt jobs your employees will be excellent sources, and you can get quick action without any great waste of time or money.

USING NEWSPAPER ADS

Most small businessmen who have a job opening instinctively think of the help wanted column of the local newspaper as the best method of contacting potential employees. But, this is more fallacy than fact. Newspaper advertising is the first thing read in the morning by the unemployed, and you get a constant flow of desperation types, flakes and failures, transitory types and potential trainees; *but very few gems*.

The second problem these days with newspaper advertising, is the equal opportunity club that the government holds over the head of employers. If you get applicants from minorities, and don't hire them, you can wind up with a discrimination suit against you sponsored and paid for by the federal government. You can find yourself with a suit by a 110 pound woman who wants a job in a warehouse moving 500 pound packages, on the grounds of sex discrimination and other nonsense of that kind. Because of this sex discrimination ruling you can't write your ad to specify that you are looking for somebody with a size 17 shirt and a size 6 hat for the job, so many problems can evolve from current use of newspaper advertising and employing people in a small business.

If you do use newspaper advertising, ask for resumes and letters of application, sent to a blind box number at the newspaper. By looking them over, you can weed out the obviously unqualified individuals, and then arrange interviews for those you feel have some talent that you might be able to use. But avoid using a telephone number or an address that they can come to.

USING THE FEDERAL UNEMPLOYMENT OFFICE

You have much the same problem in contacting the employment service sponsored by the federal government, at the unemployment office. You will often get a parade of weirdos, desperation cases and mostly unqualified people in answer to your request. The unemployment office makes little attempt to screen anyone. But for jobs that may last a day or two, you can get fast action from the unemployment service for this type of help.

USING EMPLOYMENT AGENCIES

Using employment agencies to find good employees has its good and bad sides. The good side is that you can stipulate the kind of applicant you want (within the federal guidelines of fair employment practices) and let them do the advertising and initial searching for the employee. The bad side is, that many employment agencies pay little attention to the qualifications you have stipulated and will send anybody and everybody who is registered with them out for an interview. This is particularly true of those agency counsellors working on straight commission. In order to eat they must find jobs for people. So, they are inclined to use the shotgun approach and send everybody everywhere in the hope that something will fall into place and they will make a commission.

There are two methods of using employment agencies. One is where the employer pays the fees, called "EPF" in employment agency lingo, and of course this is much preferred by employment agencies because it makes their collection problems a good deal less difficult. However, their fees are extremely high for what you get, for example it can run as high as $4,000 for somebody earning a $20,000 salary, and $900 to $1,000 for somebody in the $10,000 range.

By the same token, when you use the employment agency where the employee pays the fees, these high fees can cause the employee a good deal of financial strain in the initial weeks or months of his employment.

There are also arrangements where employers pay part of the fees, or reimburse the fees if the employee stays on the job for six months, and of course if you are paying the fee you never accept the first offer anyway. You could probably get the same service for about half of their first quotation if you are going to pay the fees.

One smart S.O.B. who wanted to set up a branch manager in a city, and wanted to use employment agencies to find a good prospect, used this scheme. He had his brother-in-law call the employment agencies in that city, and offer them a fee-paid deal to find a branch manager with the proper qualifications. He then arranged to go to the city and take a motel room and interview those that the agencies found for him. He interviewed those the agencies sent, and under instructions from the S.O.B. picked the best one that he felt would handle the job properly, and sent back his name, address and telephone number. The brother- in-law then contacted the employment agency and stated that he was interested in one or two of the people he sent, and would be getting back to them in two or three weeks when the branch office plans were firmed up.

In the mean time the S.O.B. called the individual the brother-in-law had picked out, and arranged to meet with him and subsequently held him for the job, bypassing the employment agency. The brother-in-law then wrote a very sad letter to the employment agency stating that his plans for a branch office had been cancelled, and the S.O.B. was home free with his employee and neither of them had to pay employment agency commissions.

In dealing with employment agencies, the best kind are those that specialize in the specific types of jobs you are trying to fill. General agencies simply don't get the kind of people that are needed in specific areas. By using the specialized agency and agreeing to pay the fees, you get access to people who more nearly fill the specific needs for the job. In fact, in a manual on how to start an employment agency, I quote from one paragraph: "The employer-paid fee offers many advantages to the agency for all or most of its jobs. The employers advertise jobs directly, many good potential applicants prefer to answer these ads rather than pay an agency fee. When you can advertise your agency's job as "fee paid", these applicants will become willing to register with you and you *obtain more and better applicants.*" For this reason you can negotiate the fee with an agency on the basis of strength. Since they are getting specific advantages from the employers fee-paid offering, they get additional applicants they could possibly place in other jobs, as well as your own position. Basically the fee structure is on the jobs in the $9,000 to $10,000 range, 10% of the salary. It generally goes up about 1% for each $2,000 increment above $10,-000 till you get to $20,000 when the fee is supposedly 20%. Obviously a $4,000 fee would be highly negotiable, and should have clauses in it that the employee must remain on the job for a period of one year etc., or proportions of the fee are refundable.

USING TEMPORARY EMPLOYMENT SERVICES

The small businessman just starting out can use temporary employment services for office help, and sometimes other help at a considerable savings to himself of time and paperwork. Temporary agencies pay all social security, withholding, disability etc. fee for the employee, and you pay the temporary agency so much an hour for the employee's services. This way you don't have any registration with the government as an employer, and avoid all of the paperwork, forms, paying half the social security fees, etc.

It is also an excellent way of finding people for eventual hiring. By working through temporary employment agencies, and getting different people each time , you have an opportunity to find somebody who likes you and your operation, and who you can hire away from the temporary agency on a clandestine basis, paying them less than you pay the temporary agency, but more than they receive net from the agency. You can sign them up as independent contractors, and avoid the payment of social security or withholding etc., by establishing them in their own business and having them submit invoices to you for services rendered.

INDEPENDENT CONTRACTORS

There is much to be said for the small businessman employing independent contractors to do as much work as possible. These are people who essentially are set up in their own business, and who collect their income from services performed, submit invoices, pay their own taxes, insurance etc. In the appendix you will find a contract written up that they can sign as independent contractors, which gives you legal standing (but it isn't guaranteed the IRS will accept it if they get nasty about it) in hiring independent contractors to do work for you.

The main thing is to have them establish a business, help pay for a business license at city hall, get some invoices and business cards printed so they can actually be in business. The fact that you are their only client, is in reality their problem and not yours.

THE RESUME EXCHANGE

If you are in a business where you are hiring a good many people for judgement jobs or intend to, you might work out a resume exchange with firms in a similiar business, who are more established and better known than you are. You agree to send along any resumes you receive from people you cannot use in exchange for those received that they cannot use. This way you establish a flow of resumes, at no cost to you, and possibly can spot some gems in the garbage from what you read.

YOUR EMPLOYMENT APPLICATION

Many small businessmen aren't aware of the federal restrictions on what you can ask an applicant in an employment application blank by federal edict. The Equal Employment Opportunity Commission (EEOC) generally stipulates that the following pre-employment inquiries are unlawful.

1. The original name of an applicant whose name has been changed by court order or otherwise.

2. If they have ever worked under another name, requiring them to state that name and the dates when they worked under it.

3. The birth place of the applicant. (unless it is a job that had national security sensitivity)

4. Birth place of applicants' parents, spouse or other close relative.

5. Requirement that applicant submit birth certificate, naturalization or baptismal record.

6. Require that applicant produce proof of age in a form of a birth certificate or baptismal record.

7. Inquiry into applicants' religious denomination, religious affiliations, church, parish, pastor or religious holidays observed.

8. An applicant may not be told that this is a catholic, protestant, or jewish organization.

9. Complexion or color of skin.

10. Coloring.

11. Require that applicant submit a photograph with his application form at any time before hiring.

12. Of what country are they citizen.

13. Whether the applicant is naturalized or native born citizen; the date when the applicant aquired citizenship.

14. Require that the applicant produce his naturalization papers or first papers.

15. Whether an applicants parents or spouse are naturalized or native

born citizens of the United States; citizenship date of parents or spouse.

16. Inquiry into applicant's lineage, ancestry, national origin, descent, parentage or nationality.

17. Nationality of applicants parents or spouse.

18. What is their native language.

19. Inquiry into how applicant acquired ability to read, write or speak a foreign language.

20. Name of any relative of applicant other than applicants father and mother, husband or wife and minor dependent children.

21. Address of any relative of applicant other than address (within the United States) of applicants father and mother, husband or wife and minor dependent children.

22. Inquiry into an applicants general military experience. (But may inquire into their experience in the U.S. armed forces.)

23. Requiring them to list clubs, societies and lodges to which they belong.

The federal law does not expressly forbid pre-employment inquiries about a job applicant's race, color, religion or national origin — it is silent on that point. However, the EEOC has stated that it regards such inquiries *with extreme disfavor* and that any investigation of charges of unlawful employment practices, the fact that such questions were used may, unless otherwise explained, constitute evidence of discrimination.

The Federal Rights Act of 1964, also added discrimination because of sex to other practices already forbidden. The employer may treat the sex of an applicant as a legitimate job factor only if it is "*a bonafide occupational qualification*" (BFOQ) reasonably necessary for the normal operation of a particular business or enterprise.

The courts have indicated that sex will be found to constitute a BFOQ only for a job where an employer can prove he has reasonable cause to believe — that is *factual basis* for believing — that all or substantially all women would be able to perform safely and efficiently the duties of the job involved. In interpreting the BFOQ exemption, the EEOC has found a job for which sex is a BFOQ alone indeed. We may presume that playing defensive right tackle for the Los Angeles Rams is one. But, beyond that, you never know what a bureaucrat will do.

In essence, the only situations in which the commission has indicated it would find sex to be BFOQ involves one or more of the following factors: — the need for authenticity or genuineness (actor, actress, model) — community standards of morality or propriety (restroom attendant, lingerie sales clerk) — jobs in the entertainment industry for which sex appeal is the essential qualification. The burden of establishing that sex is a BFOQ *rests on the employer.*

The best way for the small businessman to stay out of this morass, is to avoid using the more public means of hiring. It is doubtful that if a small business firm with from five to twenty employees could be proven to have discriminated in its hiring practices if there were no public evidences around of advertising or pre-employment qualifications given to employment agencies. As long as your application blank does not contain any of the former no no's, you are probably on pretty safe ground.

HIRING PROCEDURES

Hiring people for small business jobs is a highly personal experience. The owner is the personnel manager, does interviewing and makes his decision based more on a *gut feeling* than on the scientific methods used by large corporations. If the small businessman is a fairly good judge of human nature, he probably does pretty well. If he is not, he probably has difficulty both in hiring good people and keeping them.

Keeping in mind that it is better to be a seducer than a rapist, the seduction process begins with the hiring. Just as people on the make have found that the best working partners aren't always the best in bed, so the small businessman discovers that the seemingly most likely job applicant doesn't make the best job holder. As you interview people for jobs, you have to make an educated guess as to their future behavior.

While behavioral psychology is almost an exact science in predicting mass behavior (shouting fire in a theatre and causing panic), it is far from an exact science in predicting individual behavior. While we are all products of a common culture, we all do not react exactly the same in identical situations. If you put the possibilities of individual reactions to all the possible situations they come face to face with in their jobs, it becomes a mathematical impossibility. Therefore, even the most scientifically controlled estimate is little more than an educated guess, and no one has ever been perfect in this field.

So, the best bet is going to be to exceed the law of averages in picking good employees, and fifty percent batting average in this field is superior.

When you have the resume or the filled out job application in front of you, there are some immediate bits of information you can collate to get a picture of your potential employee.

Their neatness and preciseness in filling out the application (all spaces filled in or dashes put where not applicable) gives you an indication that this is an individual with some pride in themselves, and probably someone who will have some pride in their work. One that is hastily filled out, somewhat illegible, and inprecise about dates and salaries, addresses etc. is an individual who is probably careless, probably arrogant and starts off with a strike or two against them.

In the application blank there is a space indicating position desired and earnings expected. This particular space has a tendency to separate the sheep from the goats. If an earning figure is set down, and it is in line with, or perhaps slightly below the average earnings for that type of job, you have a sheep who needs a job and is willing to start at perhaps a lower salary than they would like. This does not mean that they would not be good employees, but gives you an idea that this is not an overly aggressive person, not a person who will be constantly hassling you for more money, and somebody pliable enough so that you can deal successfully with them. In other words, they are round heels, easily seduceable. These are often times excellent prospects for the grunt jobs in your organization, because they are probably fairly easy to please.

On the other hand, if the salary expected is higher than you had in mind, or negotiable is written in there, you have an aggressive individual who may be an excellent prospect for a judgement job, but would be a hell of a lot of trouble in a grunt job.

In checking their education, you can get a determination of their actual expectations. The higher they went on the educational level, the more they expect. Those with supplemented education with a business or trade school training, are better prospects than those who have not. These people have shown enough initiative to spend their own time and money in furthering their education, and have every evidence, barring personality problems, of being good employees with the skills they have mastered. The obvious point here is, that people with college and graduate school degrees may often be over-qualified for what you have to offer. If you are looking for a salesman to call on gas stations selling refinished spark plugs, there is no point in hiring somebody who is a graduate of Harvard Business School. By matching the level of education with the job opening, you can make a quick determination of who is about qualified for the job, and given the expected earnings, pretty much determine whether they are trying to be hirable or not.

In looking at armed forces records, anyone applying for a grunt job who has had a hitch in one of the services is somebody accustomed to discipline, taking orders; working in a structured organization, and if they achieved some rank during their service, it indicates the ability to operate successfully under tight control. In the face of judgement jobs, military experience (unless it included the rank of Major or higher) is not of a great deal of importance.

In checking their job history, you are looking primarily for two things. Their salary levels at each position, and the continuity of the jobs. At the interview you can discuss their accomplishments on the jobs, but in looking at the cold figures on the paper, concentrating on those two factors will give you a rounded out view of the individual you will be interviewing.

If the salaries were constantly increased in each job situation, (and these are verifiable on checking), you have an upwardly mobile individual who was a successful job holder. Of course, if their last job was of considerably higher salary, and with a much larger organization than yours, you may assume you may be dealing with someone in the flake or failure category who is being banished back to the minor leagues.

The second thing that you want to watch for in the sequence of jobs is gaposis. This is where there is a long period of time between one job and another, which indicates the applicant was unemployed or doing something other than working. This could indicate anything from a term in jail to having won a Rhodes scholarship.

At the interview, the applicant should be questioned closely on this time gap, because commonly it represents a job situation that they left under circumstances unfavorable to them. Where they won't get a good reference and they don't wish to reveal it. Another thing to watch for is an indication of a job over a long period of time with a defunct company. Where there is no way to actually check the references given, as the smart job hopper often uses this ploy to cover up a series of misadventures in job situations, or long periods of unemployment. The simple way to catch them up in this, is during the interview you may off-handedly ask them if they know Charley Hopper, who was the sales manager, personnel manager or somebody that they would have known according to their job description. The common answer for the liar will be I didn't know him but I heard of him. Or he was there after or before I was. If he simply says no, I didn't hear of him the only one I knew was, then you've either got an extremely sharp individual or one that's telling the truth, and in either case he might make a good employee.

BEWARE OF THE PSYCHOLOGICAL MIRROR

One of the failings we all have in being objective is in seeing things or hearing things that relate to our own personalities. Too often when you are interviewing somebody for a job, your tendency is to become very much impressed with somebody who likes the same things you do, talks about things the way you do, perhaps has the same hobbies or avocations and generally reflects your general opinion and outlook on things. You are looking into a psychological mirror, and being impressed by yourself. The only question you have to answer in this case, is would you make a good employee in the job you are hiring for. If you wouldn't, neither will the person you are talking to.

The second problem that the small businessman has is that he falls in love with every new employee, new machine and new procedure that he develops. He spends anywhere from one week to one year being almost emotional about it, and then the light of reason begins to creep in, and he generally turns around 180 degrees and begins to dislike everything about it. Primarily, because it wasn't perfect and he feels duped. Beware of this, as it is very common among small businessmen and the smart S.O.B. is always objective and never subjective about things dealing with his business and the art of making money.

There is a ton of material written on the psychology of interviewing people, and all kinds of tricks and various methods of extracting so called secret signs from them from rapid blinking of the eyes, to clenched fists, to muscles rippling along the jaw line, etc. This is all very good stuff as far as it goes, but since everybody is different, they have different problems and different outlooks to a great degree, much of this stuff is a lot of nonsense. There are things that people do and do unconsciously, that can give you a tip off as to the kind of people they really are. By using a few techniques in an interview, you can quickly discover whether you are talking to a phony or somebody solid enough to make a good employee.

The first thing to probe for is *rationalization* . Rationalization is nothing more than an excuse for failure. We all do it, attributing our failure to other things in our own stupidity, misconduct or inability to master a problem situation. To avoid dealing with ourselves harshly, and to bring about greater peace of mind, we often reconstruct past events so that we turned out to be winners instead of losers. The rationalization comes in where the failure was laid squarely upon anything from bad weather to bad breath.

In discussing employment situations with an interviewee, and you hear a story about the situation that places the interviewee in a favorable light and events or others in an unfavorable light, you are dealing with a rationalization. This is not a fatal flaw, or indicative of somebody who is a congenital liar, but it is simply a human failure we all suffer from. The thing you want to try to discern is whether this individual is full of such rationalizations, or are there only one or two in the conversation.

This trait is very common in salesmen. They will explain that while they were setting the world on fire in their territory, the sales manager, the home office, quality control etc. are letting them down time after time and they were forced to leave because they had too much pride to work for inferior companies or sell inferior products. If he has more than one such story, you smile politely and show him the door. You have to remember once you learn how to do these things, you can trip people off on all kinds of little psychological hang-ups and just plain human frailities, and because you are able to do it, you may not be able to hire anybody because if you set your goal as perfection you are in a lot of trouble. It's been a long time since Jesus Christ went around looking for a job, and everybody else falls so much short of that level of perfection. All you are trying to determine is whether the person is relatively competent or relatively incompetent. Relative competence is all you can expect, and if you find it, hire it.

Now another gimick is called *projection*. This is when somebody attributes their own motives to other people. This can be a very telling thing if you handle it right because you can find out who is going to tap the till and who isn't.

Psychologists tell us projection is one of the most common and most important ways that human beings proceed and think about objects in the external environment. The process is probably unconscious in the sense that the individual does not know that he is coloring or perhaps distorting his perception of external objects and people by imbuing them with his own characteristics.

The way you can use this successfully in an interview is to tell a story about somebody in a light and off-handed manner as though you were just relating a tale in which the protagonist has some undesirable trait, such as a cheater, a drunk, a chaser, etc. If the interviewee comes back with a story of similiar nature, always talking about a third party and seems to enjoy the tale, you've got a case of projection on your hands. This indicates that that individual subconsciously approves of or enjoys that type of conduct. If they have no story for you, but smile dutifully as an interviewee must when the boss is laying the B.S. on them, then you don't have a projection problem and you can go on to the next point.

The next point of the interview you want to determine individual's *self-image*. Everyone has an image of themselves that is created from his aspirations, experiences and ego structure. Decisions are often made to either protect or enhance a self-image, and you want to know whether it is a good one or a bad one in order to determine the individual's reliability in making those decisions.

There is an old saying that *we are what we think we are, and we become what we think we are sooner or later.* Therefore you should try to determine this individual's own self appraisal and self image. The easiest way to do this is to talk informally about his past jobs, his avocations and his general life experience and look for statements of positive achievement in past situations with a general tone of self-approval and enjoyment. The thing to beware of is the masochistic self-image where the interviewee is constantly talking about struggle and adversity, and goes into some lengths about illnesses, accidents and other misfortunes to himself or others. This is an individual with a bad self-image, and one who is probably not going to do you much good in any position.

One of the problems in determining the potentials of any individual is that of role playing. Everybody is playing a role in life, to loosely quote Shakespeare, "The world is a stage and we are all actors upon it." There is a psychological axiom that when two people meet and discuss something, six different people are involved. Each person actually represents three different people or roles. Role one is the person he thinks he is — his self-image; role two is the person he appears to be to others; and role three is the person he actually is. These three fold personalities make it difficult to predict what people will do under stressful circumstances, or in a position where daily decisions have to be made.

If the individual you are talking to, like you, has these three different personalities, you have to attempt to dig around a little bit to find out if your perception of the individual you are interviewing is in actual line with the real person you are talking to.

The problem we all have in this regard is the inability to stand in the other person's shoes and see the world through his or her eyes. In general terms it goes back to our discussion previously about truth and morality, and the fact that truth can be two different things to people in different circumstances.

Part of this problem is dealing with people in terms of what they consider rational behavior. Rationality is the ability to perceive things as they really are. For example, take a room full of people in a gambling casino. Since the odds are rigged heavily in favor of the house, anybody gambling in that casino is essentially irrational in terms of reality. However, the man or woman there who is cheating in order to bring the odds in their favor, is acting rationally. Now it is both immoral and illegal to do so, but we are talking about rationality and not legality. When we are talking to people about accomplishments, you will discover they have set up many self-made barriers to themselves because they believe these barriers are rational results of their experiences.

The old story about the farmer who put up the electric fence to keep the cows in is a perfect example. He erected the fence, and the farmer across the road observed that the cows in the field surrounded by the electric fence never went near the fence. Upon meeting the farmer who owned the electric fence one day, he commented that it was certainly a wonderful way to keep the cows in the field and that he noticed they never went near the fence, but he felt it was far too expensive in paying for the necessary electricity to keep the fence electrified. The other farmer smiled and commented that he had kept the electricity on for the first three days, and once the cows had learned their lesson and never went near the fence, he had never turned the electricity on again. This points out the self-imposed restriction one sets on oneself based on previous experience.

So when you are interviewing a potential employee, and you come across a self-imposed restriction where they feel they cannot do this or they cannot do that, but you observe in them enough drive and ambition to hold down the job, don't let their self-imposed restrictions deter you from employing them. To their great surprise they may find themselves capable, because once they are shown that these restrictions they have placed on themselves are not rational, they will proceed to do them with a great deal of pride and sense of achievement and be very valuable additions to your company.

HOW TO HIRE THEM AT THE BOTTOM OF THE PAY SCALE

During the interview, you find an applicant for a judgement or a sales job who you like, and you want to hire him for the bottom rate of the going pay scale, here is a system that was used by one man we interviewed, with great success.

After he had determined in the first part of the interview that the individual was somebody that would fit into the company picture, he began to discuss company prospects with him. He filled the sky full of pie about the future of the company, how fast it was growing, what great potential it had, and in going back and forth with the interviewee, gradually increased the interviewee's enthusiasm for the ideas and the prospects of the company. He began to elicit from the interviewee ideas and suggestions and other positive reactions to the conversation so the interviewee became enthusiastic about company prospects and wanted to definitely participate in the growth of the company and do what he could to make the company more profitable and so forth. Once this level of conversation had been achieved, Charley reached down on his desk and handed the interviewee a chart. This he said, handing it over, you have three choices of pay scale if we employ you with this company.

Scale number one was the straight salary scale which was generally at the top range of what the job called for that the company could pay. Salary schedule two was about $1500 a year under the top scale but tied to a partial profit sharing program which was projected out to show that the potential income from this pay scale plus profit sharing would equal two or three thousand dollars more than the top pay scale. The third one was the lowest pay scale but, had the most profit sharing potential and projected out into a profitable year would get the applicant considerably higher income than the top pay scale.

The psychology of this was simple, the applicant had already dug his own hole by getting enthusiastic with Charley about the prospects of the company and giving him ways he thought he could be helpful and how interested he was in seeing the company grow etc., so when he had the card in his hand he was virtually obligated to take the lowest pay scale tied in with the highest amount profit sharing. To ask for the top salary with no profit sharing would have been ridiculous at this point, because it would have gone against everything he had just got finished saying. So this little psychological ploy enabled him to get good people hooked into his company at the minimum rate, tied to the most potential profit, and as the profit sharing accumulated, they were tied in to essentially a low paying job, but were smiling everyday.

Let's assume that the average range in the job would be between twelve and fifteen thousand dollars a year. On the chart, a $15,000 a year salary would be offered with no profit sharing participation; the second column would offer say $13,500, with a small profit participation that could ad two to three thousand dollars a year to the applicant's income; and the lowest pay scale, say $12,000, but offered the applicant a chance to earn as much as $10,000 a year in profit sharing. If these were the figures under the circumstances, Charley initially saved $3,000 a year in flat salary payments, and the fortunes of the employees were tied to the company and its profitability.

You can use this scheme for every employee in your organization if you wish, but its much more effective in management and sales jobs than it is in grunt jobs. A grunt employee doesn't have the imagination, nor will they have the authority or power to effect the company's profits that much, and the salary ranges are so low to begin with, that even the top one is probably somewhat under the market. But it's very effective with judgement and sales jobs, and every small businessman should consider using it when hiring in this area.

KITA VERSUS POTB

The Harvard Business School has developed a thesis on motivating employees called KITA (kick in the ass), which they present as a negative or positive KITA. The negative KITA is a literal, physical kick, or a psychological one. It is pointed out that the negative KITA accomplishes little in terms of anything but immediate motivation, and constant repitiion can simply result in the kicker getting a tired leg and the kickee getting his butt out of there.

The positive KITA of course is using a larger carrot to induce employees to motivate themselves to do better jobs, and is considered at the Harvard Business School to be the proper way to motivate employees.

The small businessman, however, should consider the POTB system. This is the pat on the butt. This is both a sign of affection and encouragement, and one that would have much greater positive effects on the employee and their morale when judiciously applied.

The POTB is simply the prelude to employee seduction, and represents the employers approbation of the employees efforts. You will note as you watch a professional football game on TV, how the POTB is applied by players for those they wish to compliment for performing extremely well in a given situation. You use the same system in your business operation for the best results.

One thing you must remember about POTB, and your relationship with the employees is the atmosphere is which you work. It is not very smart to become one of the boys or girls in the organization when you are the boss. Familiarity breeds contempt, and worse, inability to have a disciplined organization. Lack of discipline, leadership and organization causes bad morale and lousy business. You should remember you are the boss, and your name isn't George or Mary, it's Mr. Jones or Mrs. Smith, and you are to be respected and obeyed.

When this condition exists, the POTB is much appreciated and it tends to keep morale at a high level.

In analyzing the art of seducing employees, you want to understand their levels of concern with their job in the order of their importance. A good many studies have been made on this, and it may vary slightly from time to time, but in this order most employees have these concerns about their employment.

1. Security
2. Interest
3. Opportunity for advancement
4. Appreciation
5. Company and management
6. Intrinsic aspects of job assignment
7. Wages
8. Supervision
9. Social aspects of job
10. Working conditions
11. Communications
12. Hours
13. Ease
14. Benefits

You will note with some interest, wages come in number seven on this list. If the employees are relatively satisfied with the wages they are drawing for the work, the importance of job security, having an interesting job, opportunities to advance and an appreciation of management are the four most important things in employee seduction. One smart S.O.B. that we interviewed that was running a happy ship, made a suggestion I thought was excellent. He had observed that all his employees in non-management capacities, would suffer a great frustrations from time to time, and they really needed something or somebody to kick once in a while. Since he couldn't hire any donkeys for them to have authority over, he did the next best thing. Starting with the janitor, and working through every employee in his staff, he set them up with a purchasing budget. He allowed them to choose their own suppliers, and purchase their own supplies for their particular job. This simple move gave them power and authority over something in their working situation. They could go home at night and tell the spouse how they told that stupid salesman from so and so's company off, or got the best of him on a deal, and had something to brag about and take their frustrations out on. In short, he used vendors as the donkeys, and gave the employee something to vent a little steam off on and at the same time have some pride in having specific authority over something in their job.

That struck me as an excellent method of employee seduction and one that all small businessmen could consider. It has another advantage in that it enables you to talk to your employees on a man to man basis about business problems in connection with their purchasing. It shows them that you are interested in them, you trust them, and when they come to you and tell you about a particularly good deal they got, it is well to congratulate them heartily and give them a good POTB as a reward.

This is one benefit that costs you little or nothing as long as you maintain the budget and see they stay within it. It gives you a situation where people are working with you instead of for you and makes them enthusiastic members of the firm.

Another deal that we heard about from another small businessman was kind of unique, and one that seemed to pay off handsomely for him. He discovered that there was an insurance policy he could buy on his employees, that gave them life insurance, where he paid the premiums as long as they were employed by the company. If they should leave the company employ, the insurance was cancelled, and the company paid him back every thin dime of premiums he had paid on that policy. This was a substantial fringe benefit, that all employees appreciated, and was another method of seduction to hold them to their jobs. (Financial Assurance, Inc., 900 Grant Street, Denver, Colorado 80201.

Another small businessman made a move that was intelligent in terms of supplying his employees with a fringe benefit that again cost him nothing. He got together with fifteen or twenty other small businessmen in the community and arranged to start a credit union for their employees. The employees held a meeting and appointed and handled all the operations of the credit union themselves, and each employee and each small business was a member, and another fringe benefit that cost the employers nothing. Again, something extra for the employees was nothing out of pocket for you as a method of seduction and holding them on jobs.

Still another one we heard about which was even simpler to put together, was a small businessman who went around to others in the retail business (as he was in) and arranged to issue cards to employees of all stores so they could enjoy 10% discount in the member stores. This gave the employees something similar to those working for a large retail establishment; the employee discount helped all the stores get more business from each others employees, and again was a fringe benefit that was appreciated by the employees and cost the employer nothing.

One benefit that all employees seek is a medical plan that will pay for the great portion of their medical expenses. As a rule, these are too expensive for the employer to bear alone, but you can start one out where the employee pays the major portion of the expense, but as they continue on their jobs, the employer picks up more and more of the cost for years of service. This, again, gives you a seduction lever on the employee, because their medical plan costs them less each year.

Here's a slick deal that a small businessman we'll call Jim worked out. When he was on a trip to Hawaii, he spotted a condominium over there that he could buy for $10,000 down and relatively modest monthly payments. He got the idea of having his employees purchase the condominium for him by setting up a unique vacation plan. He went to a travel agency and made a deal on travel bookings, so that he got a good discount whereby they could sell twenty round trip tickets to Hawaii each year, and offer his employees an inexpensive vacation benefit. They could fly to Hawaii, spend two weeks in the condominium, have a $200 bonus check to spend by deducting small weekly amounts from their pay check. The deductions took care of all the travel costs, which were pre-paid to the travel agency to get the discounts, and the monthly payments on the condominium. The employees used the condominium forty weeks a year, leaving him twelve weeks of free rent in the condominium as no extra cost to him, and when the payments were made the equity in the condominium went to him personally.

This is another form of employee seduction that could be worked out, and there is an extra link to this that would make it even more attractive. There is now an organization called Resort Condominiums International, which will arrange exchanges of condominiums all over the world. In other words, the employee can arrange to exchange their two weeks in Hawaii for two weeks in the Carribean with another condominium owner during the period their con- dominium is available to them. So in effect, with a small up-front investment, you could offer your employees literally world-wide vacations rent free and travel cost free with small deductions from their pay checks which would cover all costs, and be a tremendous seductive method of holding them on their job.

Another plan, simple in its psychology, was given to us by another small businessman who gave all of his employees titles like banks do. The file clerk was the Records Manager, the typist was the Word Processing Manager, the janitor was the Maintenance Engineer etc. The names and titles of these employees were placed in a chart in the outer office of the company, so that everybody calling there could see their names and their titles. Another method of POTB that costs nothing, and makes employees happy.

An offshoot of this was an organizational chart we saw on a wall in an office, that was inverted. The lower paid employees names appeared in boxes at the top of the chart, and the president's name was in a box at the bottom of the chart. Across the top of the chart read: "Our front line troops are our most im- portant employees". Another little psychological POTB that makes employees happy.

There are other methods of POTB and employee seduction you will run across, and the more you apply them the better off you are going to be. The people work for less money, they work more effectively and are happier doing it, and thus you put more money in your pocket by using psychology instead of a stick.

TO SUM UP

We realize that this is all time consuming, it all takes effort and energy, and good management is the difference between success and failure. It's that simple, and whatever time it takes, or effort it takes, pays off more handsomely on the bottom line than anything else you can do.

CHAPTER 3
HOW TO OWN A BANKER AND FINANCE ANYTHING

How To Own A Banker
And
Finance Anything

THE SOB & OPM

One thing we learned about successful S.O.B.'s and business, is that they have learned the secret of operating on other peoples money. Whenever they need money to expand, get into a deal or simply for personal use, they have managed to develop sources for it that are eager to fill their pockets full whenever they ask.

The average nice guy small businessman usually starts his business with his own capital (with help from friends and relatives), and establishes relationships with a bank or other money source to obtain additional funds from time to time as required. By contrast, the S.O.B. rarely uses his own money, even for starting up, and not only used banks as capital sources, but many others as well. They were all developed because others perceived him as a successful operator.

Once you adopt this attitude and obtain this image, finding OPM (other people's money) is not difficult, and often times you have to beat people away with a stick once they discover you are a successful operator, and they can make a few bucks by shoving some dollars in your pocket.

GETTING MONEY FROM BANKS

Someone once asked Willy the Actor Sutton, a famous bank robber, why he robbed banks. He replied, *"because there's where the money is."* Which is as good a description of a bank as you can find.

The small businessman looking for capital probably thinks of banks first. They are stuffed with money, and are into the business of lending it out. That is the appearance, but not the reality. Banks are not in the business of lending money, they are in the *business of making money*. There is a very big difference there, and one seeking money should never lose sight of this in dealing with banks and bankers.

To be perfectly frank about it, most bankers consider small businessmen to be a pain in the ass. They don't want their business, they consider it risky and troublesome, and they can lend the money in large hunks to large businesses more profitably than to fifty or a hundred small businesses in small lots.

Granted, this is not the image their advertising promotes, but this is reality. The only opportunity you have to borrow money from banks as a small businessman, is if you have enough collateral to prove that you really don't need the money, otherwise you will find a great reluctance to extend you much of anything in the way of a reasonable line of credit or a loan.

If you are a new businessman *forget it!* In fact, if you are a new businessman, you're better off not telling the banker about it. Just tell him you have a job with your company, in case he relates to a pay check, and not to free enterprise.

HOW THE S.O.B. BEATS THAT SYSTEM

Given the handicaps the small businessman has in dealing with a bank, it is obvious something other than simply presenting yourself to the banker with a pocket full of financial statements and a request for a loan, is going to be necessary if you are going to have access to the vault.

Fortunately, the S.O.B. learns early on that banks are vulnerable if he makes the right moves. The way to get past the wall of no's and get your hand in the vault is to work on a banker, not a bank.

To do this you have to analyze the position the bank executive is in. First, all bankers are underpaid. This guarantees the bank of employing the proper kind of sheep who will follow the book, and are frankly too lazy to work hard, and too nervous to steal.

The bank executive simply wants to hang in there long enough to get a somewhat more prestigious desk and title, a few more bucks an hour and the right to mingle socially with the community power structure.

Unfortunately for banks, some of their sheep develop personal appetites beyond what their income will provide. Dealing with large sums of money everyday, and getting a pay check that would send ditch diggers out on strike, they are susceptible to being corrupted.

One successful corrupter of bankers explained how he went from near bankruptcy to control of over a million dollars worth of assets in eighteen months, by the simple art of corrupting one banker and getting access to the bank vault.

We shall call him Mike, and here is his story:

"I came into town as a total stranger, and I was nearly $50,000 in debt, with only a small income from a business venture I was operating, and I needed both money to live on and capital to expand my venture which looked promising.

I knew a lawyer in the town who was constantly involved in small business deals, and I went to him and had him introduce me to a banker he knew who was something of a swinger and I discussed five or six potential business ventures with him, giving him the impression I was involved in all of them and all of them were making money at the time. At the time of the conversation I had approximately $300 to my name, and I had a sailor's bank roll with two one hundred dollar bills on the outside and about 35 one dollar bills on the inside. I paid for the lunch by peeling off one of the one hundred dollar bills and tossing it carelessly on the tray the waitress had left, and watched his eyes examine my bankroll as I shoved it back in my pocket. I sensed then, that I had the man I was looking for and I arranged to have a meeting with him in the bank.

At the bank I discussed putting one of my business accounts in his bank (the only one going that was bringing in any income), and told him that it was the smallest of the six I had operating, and inferred that as I got more settled in the community I would be transferring the other larger accounts to the bank as well.

He opened the business account for the other one hundred dollar bill I had in my pocket, telling him I wanted to get it opened now and I would transfer my other funds as soon as I could arrange to have the account closed at the former bank. So, for a lunch and a hundred dollars I had a banker who was impressed with my business potential.

I waited about a week, and took him to lunch again and discussed the closing of the other account and putting some more money in the account in his bank, which amounted to about $1500. I explained to him that the $1500 was just a token deposit just to get things started, and we would soon be discussing larger accounts. Offhandedly, I mentioned a deal I had in mind to him and stated that I needed somebody to handle the financial details, and I would give them a percentage of the deal, which amounted to a couple of thousand dollars. I wondered if he knew anybody that would be interested in handling something like that. As I expected, he indicated immediately that he would, and I told him, fine, I would make the arrangements and get back to him.

I also told him that I was interested in picking up any good deals that he might run across, that if he saw any to be sure and give me a call.

The next morning he called me, and stated that he knew of a small food market that was for sale, and that I could probably swing the deal for $5,000, and get a net cash income of $600 a month with an absentee manager.

I went down to the bank and looked over the papers, and he told me that he was holding the mortgage on the market, and the present owner wanted out. So, I suggested that he act as the broker in the case, and pick a $2,000 commission for arranging the sale, and give me a $5,000 loan to take over the market. That way we would be able to close the deal right away and he could pick up his $2,000 immediately , rather than waiting til I closed something else out to get the $5,000.

He went for the deal, and wrote up the loan papers and OK'd them himself and the market deal was closed. I had now gained a net income of around $600 a month, and after installing a new manager and doing some advertising doubled that income within a couple of months.

I made sure to have lunch with the banker at least once a week, and a couple of times a month would take him and his wife out for dinner at one of the best places in town, and always discussing larger and larger deals with him. He made some other buy-sell transactions with the bank's money, he got a nice commission and I picked up free and clear profits of several thousand dollars without putting a dime of my own money, or even much of my own time as he handled all the details.

Without going into a step by step history of how this thing proceeded, within a year's time I had aquired control of over a million dollars worth of assets, all with cash flows, had at one time borrowed $20,000 thousand dollars on my signature at the bank to invest in my operating business, which quadrupled the income for me, and had that banker introduce me to other bankers in other branches and at other banks, so that I widened my banking contacts and at the end of my first year in that town I had filed an income tax return with a personal income of over $300,000.

As I stated, when I walked into that town I had about $300 cash to my name.

That is an exceptional story, and obviously it doesn't always work that way. It does indicate something that the smart S.O.B. knows. That you can get access to the vault by getting a banker by the balls, catering to his greed.

The one unwritten rule in this case, is to always protect your banker. If something goes sour, and problems arise, you take all the heat on your shoulders. You protect him every step of the way, because this way you really and truly own him.

For the small businessman, looking for access to a bank on the same basis that a large corporation has, you look for a corruptible banker, and give him some participation in deals so that he becomes an eager convert to the idea of loaning the bank's money without requiring you to do any more than sign the papers.

HOW TO FIND THESE BANKERS

Obviously the best way is to find a kinky lawyer. A lawyer who is on the make, and one who will obviously know a banker who feels the same way. Simply have the lawyer give you an introduction, as Mike did, and you are on your way.

Barring that, you simply shop the banks yourself. You sit down and talk to these people, take those out to lunch who look like likely prospects, and keep working through the banks until you find the individual you are looking for.

The psychology is all in your favor, and by not pushing too hard too fast, and making sure you give the banker a participation before you hit him up for a big loan, you have the key to the vault in your hand.

It doesn't hurt to take the banker around and introduce him to other businessmen, urge the businessmen to open accounts at his bank, making sure he gets credit for it, and do anything else in a POTB way that you can to build him up in the community.

Corrupting a banker can be your best investment of time and money you will ever make, and every small businessman should consider the opportunity worth the time and money.

BUILDING CREDIT ON THE BANKS' MONEY

If you are a very small businessman, or just starting out, you will have to establish credit at a bank in order to have the bankers even talk to you. This will have to be done on a personal basis, rather than on a business basis, and it is relatively simple with a little planning to do it on their money. The best asset you can have in borrowing money from a bank is a record of *having borrowed money and paid it back on time* to a bank, any bank. It can be a personal loan, a car loan, home improvement, mortgage, etc. If you have such a record, then use it to *get a personal loan* from your present banker for all the traffic will bear. You may not need the money right away, *but borrow it anyway.* You are establishing credit, and you can take the money and put it in a savings account at another bank to earn some interest while you get ready to use it.

At this point you may be interested in creating a loan source at another bank. If so, take the money you borrowed from Bank A, put it in a savings account at Bank B to draw interest. When the time comes to repay Bank A, to to Bank B and *borrow the money* from them using the savings account as collateral, and repay Bank A. What have you accomplished? You now have a loan record at two banks. Because your loan at Bank B is 100% backed by liquid assets (the savings account), they won't even *make a credit check,* but your loan record will show they made a loan, and were repaid as agreed. You now have a potential source of capital from two banks instead of one.

Actually, if your area is large enough, you can use this loan pyramid technique in several banks to build a potential capital source many times larger than one bank would allow. When it comes time to use these banks for capital, you make simultaneous loan applications at each of the banks. In this way you *don't have to list any of the other banks as creditors,* as they are not at the time you are applying for the loan.

Now, let's see how this can work out in practice. If you have used the savings account-loan program at two other banks besides your regular bank, you have this potential. Bank A will lend you $2500 on your statement and repayment record. You apply the same day to banks B & C for the same loan, $2500. This gives you a potential *capital source of $7500 for a venture.* Now, you can't tell the bankers you want the money for seed capital, you've got to apply for a home improvement (or other personal use loan), but once the money is in your hands, it's yours to do anything you please with. There are no strings on it.

Simultaneous application is important because you can list your obligations without including the loans at the other banks, as they haven't been granted yet, this prevents your applications from being fraudulent. Note of caution, if you have to pledge collateral for the loans, *don't pledge the same collateral to the same banks. Try for signature loans which are granted only on your good credit. This is perfectly legal.*

With this method you can use banks as a source of seed capital without letting them know the purpose. Of course you must have the capability of paying off the loans, or you are in deep trouble.

HOW TO TURN LACK OF FUNDS INTO STRONGER CREDIT

Let's say that you borrow the $7500 for your venture and discover that while still owing $5000 you can't come up with enough money for the payments. Here's the way to turn that disaster into an asset.

Say the payments on your loans are $300 a month total. Your venture will only produce $150 at that time. Go to a friend or relative and make arrangements with them to borrow $5000 to repay the loans that are outstanding....and they get terms of $150 a month. You take over the payments for a couple of months, then with your bank credit shining pure and clean, go back and borrow enough to repay the outstanding loan your relative made, taking him or her off the hook, and you repay the banks at $150 a month. Let's assume that the relative can only borrow a couple thousand dollars. Then give them the entire $2000 and have them pay on the outstanding loans each month from the $2000. You take over the payments on a $2000 loan. Say the $2000 lasts for a year, then you can have the $2000 loan paid down to a $200 balance, and take over payments on the outstanding balance on the other loans. You buy time, keep your credit and at this point can easily go back to renegotiate a loan for even more money because of your prompt payment record. So, disaster can be turned into an asset.

HOW THE BANKER JUDGES YOU AS A LOAN PROSPECT

Banks have a pretty standard system for looking at personal loan applications. Most of them are standardized by a point system so lower echelon officers can make loans on the spot with just an elementary credit check.

The methods of coming up with the numbers will vary, as will the numbers themselves. On the next page you will find a standard point rating system used by the banks (some banks) to evaluate personal loan applicants. Points are awarded by the age, marital status, residence, income, stability, as shown in years at job and at residence, occupation and other factors including loans at banks. In passing you will note on the chart if you got no points for the personal history section, if you had a loan record at their bank, and at another bank in good standing, and a telephone in your name, you would have enough points (8) *to qualify for a minimum loan.* This is the value of establishing a loan and repayment record at a bank.

Study the chart and see where you are weak, the more points, the *more money.* By changing a few items you can upgrade your application to increase your borrowing potential.

Good credit is obviously necessary for a signature loan at a bank, but you can get a loan without it if you have collateral. If you borrow against collateral, and pay it back promptly, then you have the potential of a signature loan the next time around. So, study the chart and see how you shape up, it's the key to your ability to walk in a bank, sign on the dotted line and walk out with $500 to $5000 in your pocket. Remember, the banker wants to make the loan, all he wants to know is, "Can you pay back?"

	Points
AGE	
21 to 25	0
26 to 64	1
65 & over	0
MARITAL STATUS	
Married	1
Not Married	0
DEPENDENTS	
One to Three	1
Over three	0
No dependents	0
RESIDENCE	
Rent Unfurnished	1
Own with mortgage	3
Own without mortgage	4
Any other	0
YEARS AT PREVIOUS RESIDENCE	
0 to 5 years	0
6 years up	1

MONTHLY INCOME
Up to $600	1
$600 to $800	2
$800 to $1000	4
Over $1000	6

YEARS ON THE JOB
Less than one year	0
One to three years	1
Four to six years	2
Seven to ten years	3
Over ten years	4

MONTHLY OBLIGATIONS
Zero to $200	1
Over $200	0

OCCUPATION
Unskilled	1
Skilled worker	2
Executive or Professional	3

IN ADDITION:
Phone in your name	2
Loan at this bank	4
Loan at other bank	2
Savings acct.	2

When you first apply for a personal loan at a bank, you have to fill out an application form. The banker looks it over and decides from the contents whether to give you the loan asked for.

In a general way he applies a formula to the information similar to that on the chart on this page. He rates each ten items on the form, plus four supplemental items to get a reading on your repayment potential. You can give yourself this check in advance and see how he will rate you.

Allow yourself the proper number of points for each section, and see if you can get 8 points. This is the minimum to pass on your loan application. Everything you get over 8 adds to the potential of your loan, ie. more money.

If you come up short, and need more points, then analyze some of the section. For example, if your residence section is 0, then you can state you rent unfirnished and add a point. Or, you can pick up a point on income by adding some expected outside source. Just work up 8 points or better.

By building up your credit in this way at a bank, you will qualify for small signature loans. As you use these loans, and pay them off as indicated, you can keep increasing the size of them slowly but surely until you can get them up in the four figure range.

You can also do this with Master Charge or Bankamericard issued by banks. As a rule their starting credit limit is $500, but if you exceed that limit several times, and pay off immediately, you can get them to raise your limit simply by asking. So the key here, is to use the bank's money to increase your line of credit until it is something you can use in emergencies, or for business start-ups or expansion.

BANKS AS WORKING CAPITAL SOURCES

You might think the banker is solely interested in the rate of interest, or the security of the loan when he is deciding whether or not to lend money. While these are prime considerations, the banker wants more. He can lend money at one rate or another as fast as it comes in. He can put his entire loan portfolio into consumer loans at relatively high rates of interest with little trouble. But this fails to get one thing he is vitally interested in.

MORE DEPOSITS

He is very interested in anyone or any company who will deposit sizeable amounts of cash in his bank. These are the sources for his loan fund. Without them he cannot loan money. So the banker, when looking at a business loan application, is not only considering the amount, rate of interest, security, etc., of the loan, he is trying to determine how much money that business will be depositing in his bank.

The banker will often insist the borrower keep a minimum balance in his checking account at all times as part of the agreement to grant a loan or line of credit. This guaranteed minimum deposit assures him of lendable balances in accounts, and also in effect raises the rate of interest since the business cannot use part of the money.

EVALUATING THE FLOAT

Another factor the banker investigates in a business account is the 'float.' This is money that has officially been paid out by the depositor by check, but which has not reached the bank for payment as yet. This float is best understood by sending a check to the Hawaiian Islands for example, to pay for merchandise. It is written on day number one, and at that point is withdrawn from the bank on your books. But it takes the check three days to reach Hawaii, one more day to process the order and deposit the check, and it takes three more days for the check to clear. This is a seven day lapse from the time the check was drawn until the bank had to honor it. This seven day float allows the bank to earn interest on that money for seven days before they had to transfer it. This float is important to a bank who deals in millions. If they are earning 4% interest in Treasury bills and they have $1,000,000 floating for four days, they pick up nearly $500 extra interest for those five days while the money is in transit, or floating.

YOU MAY BE WORTH MORE THAN YOU THINK YOU ARE

A second factor in the banker's thinking is your average balance in your checking account. If you accumulate funds in it till bill paying time on the first or 10th of the month, you could build up a $20,000 balance before you write checks. Then if you write $18,000 worth of checks, and it takes them an average of four days to clear, while you're putting in an average of $700 more everyday, by the time your checks clear, you will still never have an average balance of less than $4000, and possibly more if you collect most of your income between the first and the tenth.

If he feels that yours will become a sizeable account and you have the other necessary qualifications, he'll be happy to accommodate.

HE WILL REALLY CHECK YOUR FINANCIAL STATEMENT NOW

When you've had experience with the rather informal manner in which personal loans are granted, you will be taken aback by the seemingly vigorous demands of facts and information the bank makes in granting business loans. They not only want your personal history and statistics, but a detailed report on your business activities as reflected in your financial statements. They prefer the statements of recognized accountants, though in cases of small loans your own figures by banking records might suffice.

The bankers, and for that matter all lenders, need certain information on which to base a loan decision. Part of it will be furnished by the borrower, and the rest will come from the banker's own credit files, and from outside sources. This information is related to what credit men call the C's of credit: Character, Capacity, Capital, Collateral, Circumstances, and Coverage (insurance).

Character. To the banker, character means two things in particular:

1. The borrower will do everything in his power to

conserve his business assets and so insure repayment of

his loan. He will manage his business to the best of his ability. He will not squander his own or other funds.

2. The borrower is a man of his word. When he says that he will repay his borrowings promptly, he means it. If he does not keep his promise, he at least will have made every possible effort to do so.

Capacity. The management skill shown by the small businessman using his investment and enlarging it is another important business asset. For those just embarking on a business career or entering a new field, past experience may carry little weight. For example, experience as a machinist, salesman, bookkeeper or scientist, no matter how successful in their field, does not necessarily qualify them to run a restaurant.

Capital. The small businessman's investment in his own business is evidence of his faith in its future. He must furnish the management and most of the capital until others have enough confidence in his business to be willing to invest in it. In other words, he is expected to have the seed before asking for money to buy fertilizer.

Collateral. Businessmen who have a high credit standing do much of their borrowing on an unsecured basis. Others are often obliged to back up their credit standing with collateral. This is especially likely to be true of a new small businessman. If he owns a home or other improved real estate, life-insurance policies with a cash surrender value, or marketable securities, he may be able to use such assets as collateral for business loans.

Before borrowing on these terms, however, he should consider the consequences to himself and his family if he should be forced to withdraw from the business before it becomes firmly established. A small businessman who retires from business prematurely usually does so at a loss.

Circumstances. Some factors over which the small businessman has no control may have a bearing on the grading of a bank loan and its repayment. These include:

Seasonal character of the business.

Long-run business changes.

The level of community business activity.

The competitive position of the firm.

The nature of the product.

Coverage. Proper insurance coverage is extremely important. Small businessmen are subject to possible business losses from many causes, such as these:

The death of an owner, partner, or principal stockholder.

Physical damage or interruption of operations such as the result of fire, explosion, flood, tornado, or other violent causes.

Theft, embezzlement, or other acts of dishonesty by owners-officers, employees and others.

Public liability not covered by workmen's compensation insurance.

A new small businessman may not be able to insure his company as fully as the owner of an established business, but he should recognize the need: A going concern has little excuse for neglecting to establish and maintain adequate insurance protection against basic rasks. (See your insurance broker, agent, or company representative!)

When you present your balance sheet, income statement and other pertinent data to the bank, they immediately check your ratios. Here they are:

1. *Current Ratio...* Current assets divided by current liabilities, which give them an estimate of your working capital, thus your ability to pay your bills. This should be $2.00 in assets for each $1.00 of liabilities—two to one ratio.

2. *Net worth to debt net worth divided by total debt. Ratio of owners investment in the business in relation to the creditors investment. This must always show the owners have more invested than the creditors.*

3. *Sales to receivables...* Net annual sales divided by outstanding accounts not yet paid...This indicates the liquidity (what they are really worth) of the accounts receivable on the balance sheet. Watch out for high ratio of bad debts, write off old one to improve ratio.

4. *Cost of sales in inventories ratio...* They take the cost of goods sold, divide it by the inventory, gives the rate of turnover of inventory (how fast you are selling your goods), and also indicates the liquidation value of the inventory. Turnover rate should match industry average.

5. *Net profit to sales ratio...* Annual net profit is divided by annual net sales...this shows how much money you are making on what you sell after all overhead and expenses and allowances. It indicates your business efficiency.

6. *Operating ratio...* The percentage figure between net income and net sales, to allow them to trust you against the averages in your business to see if you are

doing a good job of management.

7. *Capital employed ratio...*This gives the banker an idea of how you are doing on your investment. He divides your capital investment into your net profits. This lets him know whether you are really making any money in this business, because this figure is taken after you have withdrawn your salary for services.

8. *Fixed property ratio...*He divides your net sales figure by your fixed assets (machinery, furniture, fixtures, etc.) to give him a ratio of how much you are doing with your equipment.

WARNING SIGNS HE LOOKS FOR

1. If you have heavy inventories in relation to sales, he wonders if you are a good buyer, and how long you can carry overloaded inventories.

2. He checks very carefully to see how much is being taken out of the business for personal use, in salaries, advances, withdrawals of capital, etc. If it is excessive, no loan.

3. If there is any hanky panky, such as the business lending sums of money to officers, owners or directors for non business purposes, look out.

4. If your unpaid bills have piled up and you don't have the money to cover them, you are probably too late for a bank loan.

5. If you are carrying heavy long term debts on equipment, land, etc., and it makes your working capital margins too small, he'll probably say no.

6. *Too much invested in fixed assets...*If you have machinery, etc., coming out your ears, and can't show the sales to justify it, he may suggest you sell some off to get capital.

7. *Permanently overextended...*If your financial statements show a lack of budget control and you are constantly robbing Peter to pay Paul, he will back away unless you show positive control of overhead.

8. *Lack of reserves...*This is not critical, and is something that most small businesses suffer from. But you should have personal reserves to show in case of sudden business requirements that might jeopardize the loan.

The reason you should study these problem areas is that your banker is not in business to help you run a failing business. You can't get him to lend money on a sinking ship, anymore than you would yourself. The time to ask for a loan and a line of credit is when you don't need it except to do more business...*more business*...that is what he is interested in lending money for, not to salvage your mistakes. The old gag, *The banker will lend you money if you don't need it,* is right. The word 'need' being equated with desperation. But if the word need is equated with *making more,* then he is very interested. Banks are not charities, and they are not worthy of asking for people to place money in them if they are.

So, remember the point about working capital...it is a tool to use in order to increase your business, not a lifejacket for you when you're drowning.

GETTING A LINE OF CREDIT

In lieu of getting a specific loan each time you might need some working capital, you can arrange with the bank for a line of credit. Again, *the time to apply for this is when you don't need it!* The same criteria is used as would be in judging your specific loan application. But, there is a different relationship between a line of credit and a loan.

First, when the amount of the loan is agreed on, it is put on standby for you. Thus, it is taken from the banks reserves, and there is a small fee for this service. Thus, once granted, you should use it. To use it, you simply sign a note at the bank and the money is transferred to your account.

A line of credit agreement will contain these usual stipulations:

1. There will be a time period, usually one year.

2. The amount to the line (amount you can borrow).

3. Type of note signed and rate of interest charged.

4. The commitment fee (the amount you pay, 1% or less) to have the funds set aside for you.

5. A no-penalty pre-payment clause should be inserted.

6. A due and payable clause in event of failure to meet payment obligations. (If you don't pay part, you owe all of it.)

7. A statement that you will furnish the bank with financial statements (usually quarterly).

A good line of credit at a conservative bank is the best recommendation you can have as to your ability as a businessman.

IN SUMMATION

In getting a working capital loan, prepare carefully before you present your case. Have your figures prepared by an accountant if possible.

With a good presentation you can shop for interest rates (always do this) because there may be cheaper money around.

When you borrow against your line of credit it is good business to rest it (pay all you owe on it) from time to time (at least once a year).

When you see trouble ahead, tell your banker first. They detest surprises, and may help you avoid it.

Use all forms of leverage possible to make your business grow. Borrowing is not a sign of weakness or poor business planning, it's a sign of a smart operator using other people's money to line his own pockets.

As a businessman, a sound banking connection is the best asset you have in making your business grow fast. They have the funds, the know-how, and the connections to help; use all you can of everything they offer.

THERE'S MORE THAN ONE LOAN TO SKIN YOUR CAT

Remember, banks offer many types of loan services, here are a few of them. These services available to commercial accounts are used extensively by businesses of all sizes, and by utilizing them, are able to use the other capital for producing more business and more profits.

Some Types of Short and Intermediate Term Credit: Loans may also be described on the basis of factors other than the time allowed for repayment. For example, type of security required, method of repayment, source, and so on. Some of the most common kinds are described here.

Simple commercial loans. Most of these loans are made for periods ranging from 30 to 90 days. They are usually based on financial statements. Often, they are unsecured, and signed by the maker without other endorsement. In most cases, it is expected that they will be paid from the funds produced by normal business activity. This type of loan is used particularly for seasonal financing and for building up inventories.

Character loans. Character loans are usually made as individual rather than business credit. They are sometimes used for business purposes however.

Installment loans. Loans of this type are made for many business purposes, usually by larger banks. They may be extended for almost any period the banks see fit to offer, with payments generally on a monthly basis.

As the loan is reduced, it is often possible to obtain refinancing at better rates. Also, these loans may be tailored to the seasonal requirements of the business, with heavier payments in peak months and smaller payments during off-season periods.

Lines of credit. A line of credit is an informal understanding between a businessman and his bank. The bank agrees to grant loans as the businessman requests them so long as they do not exceed at any one time, a maximum established in the agreement. The loans are usually unsecured, and are often granted almost automatically during the period of the agreement (usually a year) and up to the total specified. Credit lines are used most commonly by businessmen with a seasonal need for short-term funds.

Account-receivable loans. Accounts and notes receivable can be used as a basis for short or intermediate term loans from your bank, a finance company or a factor. (A factor specializes in lending money on accounts receivable and or purchasing them outright.) If your working capital is limited or your sales volume fluctuates, you will find this type of financing particularly useful.

When you obtain an accounts-receivable loan, you pledge or assign all or part of your accounts receivable as security for the loan. The agreement for the loan specifies what percentage of the volume of receivables you assign will be loaned to you. In the case of a bank loan, this will usually be from 75 to 80 percent of sound receivables; for factor loans, it may be somewhat higher. The agreement also sets forth your rights and liabilities, those of the lender, the conditions under which each assignment is to operate, and the charges, which may include both interest and service charges.

You assign accounts receivable to the lender as you need funds. Each time, you prepare a schedule of assigned accounts and, if a loan is made, you sign a note for the amount. Usually, the lender stamps the assigned accounts in your accounts receivable ledger.

Factoring accounts receivable. In more and more lines of business, factoring companies are being used to convert accounts receivable into cash. This procedure, called 'factoring', is not the same as assigning accounts receivable as security for a loan, though most factoring companies handle both types of financing. In factoring, you enter into an agreement under which the factor buys all your accounts receivable as they arise. The accounts sold are no longer among your assets, nor does the amount received increase your liabilities, since it will not have to be paid. If you borrow on your accounts receivable, on the other hand, they remain as an asset, and the amount of the loan becomes a liability.

With a loan on receivable, you are still responsible for collection, but when you sell the accounts, the factor takes over that function. He assumes all the risk and has no recourse if an account proves uncollectible. Because of this, the factor will pass on the credit standing of your customers. If he does not approve an account, you may still make the sale, but at your own risk. The factor will not buy that account.

The factor typically makes a service charge of 1 or 2 percent on the face amount of the accounts purchased. In addition, he charges interest at the rate of about 6 percent per year for the period between the time you receive funds from him and the average maturity date of the receivables he purchases from you.

Factoring is an expensive method of raising funds, but it does away with the need for a credit and collection department. Also, it is often the quickest way for a small business to obtain cash.

Warehouse receipt loans. Often, a small businessman needs extra cash when he is accumulating inventories for seasonal or other peak demands. When this happens, he may be able to obtain a warehouse receipt loan. Under such an arrangement, the inventory is delivered to a professional warehouseman and stored in a special 'field warehouse' established on the premises of the borrower. The receipts issued to him by the warehouseman are then turned over to the bank as collateral for a loan.

When orders are received, the borrower will 'buy back' from the bank enough warehouse receipts to fill the orders. As more sales are made he will be able to buy back all his warehouse receipts and so complete the repayment of this loan.

Costs of warehouse receipt loans vary widely. The field warehouseman's bill is based on the value of the inventory, the work involved in checking the inventory in and out, and the duration of the agreement. Bank charges run 6 percent or more; combined charges, 6 to 12 percent.

Since the initial costs are high, this type of financing should not be undertaken unless the arrangement is expected to continue for some time. Even so, it is rather expensive financing. It may, however, be the only source open to a borrower who has exhausted his unsecured credit, and it does have several advantages for the small businessman.

He can build up his inventories when he finds it most profitable to do so.

He can maintain a more stable production schedule.

He can take advantage of cash or quantity discounts.

He can get additional working capital at times when operating costs are high and working capital is low.

Floor planning. Floor planning is used mostly to finance the inventories of automobile and appliance dealers and have considerable unit value. In floor planning, the dealer has possession of the merchandise (in exchange for a note), but title to it remains with a bank or other lender who has paid the manufacturer. When the dealer sells a unit, he must pay the lender the amount due on that unit. The agreement contains various provisions for the protection of the lender.

Trade credit. Trade credit is the credit extended by a supplier to a buyer for goods purchased. It is the most commonly used form of short term credit, expecially among small businesses.

If the goods purchased are paid for in time to take advantage of the cash discounts, trade credit costs the buyer nothing. If not, it can be one of the most expensive types of financing.

Suppose you have an invoice for $1,000 with terms of 2/10, net/30. If you pay the invoice within the 10 days, you will pay $980. But suppose you do not have enough cash to pay the invoice within 10 days, although you will be able to pay it within the 30-day period. You will then have to pay the $1,000. In other words, the extra 20 days' credit will cost 2 percent of $1,000 or $20.

On the other hand, if you borrowed $1,000 from the bank on a 30-day note and paid the invoice within the 10 days, you would pay the bank only $5 interest, a saving of $15.

It pays to use the full cash-discount period or, if no cash discount is offered, the full credit period. Delaying payment beyond the credit period, however, injures your credit rating and may be costly in the long run.

HOW THE BIG LOAN IS NEGOTIATED

When you get into the big time money game a bank loan can become a good deal more complicated than just your line of credit or ability to repay. To get big money, you are going to have to offer something quid pro quo to the banker. Here is a typical example of a loan floated in tight money times when the bank if picking and choosing its borrowers with care, and an eye to making an extra buck out of their loan funds.

You go to the bank for a $5 million loan for one year. The bank starts out (remember we are in a tight money period) with 9.75% interest for the year

($475,000). The businessman can pay that, but the banker turns over his next card. He wants a compensating balance of $1,000,000 left in the bank for a year. The businessman has two choices at this point. He can leave a million of the loan in the bank, or go out and hustle up some source who will agree to deposit a million in the bank in a savings account for a fee above the interest the bank will pay on the million...usually two or three points.. Now, the banker moves on the next step...he wants what is termed 'link financing'. This means the businessman will have to find a source who will put $5 million in the bank for a year on a certificate of deposit, paying some $150,000 extra to the CD source. Finally, the banker wants 10% participation in the profits from the venture the $5 million will finance. Thus, his loan will cost him around 20% interest for the year, so he must raise prices that much to come out with his original profit figure.

We point this out to show you that a banker has many ways to arrange financing for you, and you should know about them all, and take advantage of them when you can.

Banks are really your best capital source, and by understanding what they want, you can get what you want.

GETTING YOUR OWN FACTOR

We mentioned previously the system of factoring accounts receivable. Factoring is a very expensive proposition, and most factors are very selective about what they will and won't take on.

The smart S.O.B., can get around this by setting up somebody as a factor who simply wants to earn more interest on their savings.

What you do is find some eager beaver who is interested in making say 20% a year on savings, and set him up as a factor. He purchases your accounts receivable, collects them at his own address, charges you about 2% a month for the money, and won't hassle you nearly as much as a commercial factor about what you are doing with the money, how much you are keeping in reserve to pay off non-payables etc. In other words you can set up a greedy amatuer in the factoring business, and pretty much control the money any way you want to.

To find a factor you simply run an ad under investments and business opportunities in your local newspaper column, which states something like this: *successful businessman offers twenty per cent interest on small loans repayable monthly. No risk, $25,000 required.*

That ad will pull inquiries from people who have the money, and are interested in making more of a return than they are getting in the bank or savings and loan.

When they contact you, you simply explain the fact that you will sell them your accounts receivable on the first of every month, and they will collect them during the month, getting their money back, and you will pay the 2% monthly fee for whatever is advanced. You will also guarantee any accounts that go beyond 90 days, so that they are taking no risks and making considerably more on their money than they would on a savings account.

This will appeal to some of them, and you can have your own factor that you own and control, and free your capital to expand your business. Often times the simple process of factoring will enable a small businessman to expand his business considerably, because he has no problem in financing his sales.

Here is a sample letter of agreement you could send to an individual who agrees to factor your accounts.

Dear Mr. Jones:

This confirms our agreement to sell you our accounts receivable on the first day of each month for a 2% discount, up to a maximum of $7,000 per month.

We agree to accept full risk on the credit of each account, and to pay 2% for each 30-day period the account is open. At the end of 60 days, we will repurchase the account, plus earned interest from you, or pay the interest due and assign another account to replace it.

We agree to be responsible for all disputes with customers arising from sales of our products and services and to reimburse you for any returns made on the accounts prior to payment.

You are assigned full ownership in each assigned account, and have sole collection rights to it while assigned to you. We agree to promptly remit any and all money paid directly to us by accounts assigned to you.

We guarantee each assigned account is a lawful obligation of
the debtor, and that we have fully complied with all obligations
due before assigned each account.

All billing for these accounts will be done by you, all checks
received by you at your preferred address, and you will remit
a statement of payment to us on each account you have received.

This agreement may be terminated by either party on 90 days
prior notice.

If you understand and agree to these terms, please sign and
return this letter.

Respectfully,

_____   _____

This letter of agreement, will be sufficient contract between you and the factor. In the appendix you will find samples of three forms, to use in setting up this factoring plan. Form One is your receipt of monies paid to you by the factor for assigned accounts; Form Two is a form listing the accounts to be assigned and the third is a sample of the remittance form the factor will send you when he receives payment from these accounts.

This is a simple plan to operate, and one that could give you alot more operating capital on the first of each month to more carefully plan and promote your business, and give you some extra capital for expansion.

RAISING INVESTMENT CAPITAL

Most small businessmen don't realize there is alot of risk capital available almost every place when properly contacted and promoted. There are many other small businessmen and professional men, particularly those in the service businesses, who constantly have endless income that will go into investment or into taxes. Since the individual is primarily investing tax money, they are willing to accept higher risks than so called prudent investors might accept, and if the potential return is substantial enough, little difficulty would be experienced in raising the capital.

WHERE IS THE RISK CAPITAL INVESTOR?

He is, of course, everywhere except in jail or in a monastery. He is a doctor, lawyer, stockbroker, merchant, manufacturer, heir or even an uncaught thief. The question of locating him is as varied as your own contacts and place of residence. However, there is one important fact that weighs heavily in your favor. He is looking as hard for you as you are for him, perhaps harder, because time works against him in capital gains situations. Therefore, there is now common meeting ground that has two advantages. It is the advertising pages of financial and local newspapers. Its first advantage is that it reaches a great many interested risk capital investors at once, and the second is that you can retain your anonymity when advertising. They read the columns in these papers where risk capital ventures are offered eagerly. They respond quickly to ads that interest them. So, for quick action, a well written ad, properly placed with the right publication, will put you in touch with the risk capital investor.

WRITING THE AD TO GAIN ATTENTION AND INTEREST

You don't have to be a professional ad writer to put together an ad that will get the attention and interest of a risk capital investor. There are a few simple rules to follow, and they simply represent the application of common sense to the problem. The first thing to do is write the ad.

There are three important things that you should say in each ad you run. First, tell the prospective investor the kind of business you are in. Some people won't invest in certain things, no matter how lucrative the potential. Second, tell him the amount of money you require. Third, tell him the kind of return he can expect. This serves a dual purpose; first, it assures you that the answers will be from people who have no objection to the type of business you are engaged in; second, it assures you that they have the amount of money needed, and last, it provides the potential investor with what he is interested in . . . what he can get from his investment. This type of ad serves as a qualifier. It eliminates the people who would have no interest in your proposition in advance for any of the major reasons given above.

"WANTED . . . $50M for desirable investment with x'lnt returns. HO 7-8646." This ad is a typical example of a "bag deal" advertiser. He tells the reader nothing other than the amount of money required. He may field many phone calls, but he is interested in getting names of people who are looking for investments, and will wind up trying to sort out sharpshooters and phonies who have an angle. If you were to run an ad like this, you would spend all your time showing your deal to bad news people, and rarely, if ever, would come into contact with a legitimate investor.

"NEW ELECTRONICS CO. being formed for production of exciting new inventions. Maximum risk 20%, potential return 10-20 times investment. Minimum investment $5,000. B or A references and full details to qualified investors. Reply to Box J-103 Times." This ad is the kind you want to run. It tells the whole story in a few words. You will have to waste only a minimum amount of time weeding out the phonies. (Every business opportunity ad attracts some angle shooters.)

YOU NEED ONLY ONE INVESTOR

Remember, in most cases when seeking risk capital for a new venture, you only need to sell one customer. So the number of replies that you get from your ad is unimportant; it's the QUALITY of those replies that counts. So when you write the ad, write it with the principle in mind, and you will get the kind of results you want. Don't make it wordy, long or involved; keep it short and sufficient, as the above example. Above all, avoid quotations like, "you'll get rich . . . fantastic returns . . . world's greatest opportunity, etc." . . . these simply turn the investors away. Remember, you're not dealing with a bunch of chumps . . . they didn't get surplus investment capital being stupid.

WHERE TO PLACE THE AD?

The next consideration is where to place your ad. What papers are best to use? Perhaps the best way to answer the question is to consider the nature of your offer. If you are looking for both capital and participation from your investor, that is, you want the investor to be active in the company, then you should stay with the nearest large newspaper. Sunday papers are best, if they are printed and distributed in a major metropolitan area. They are widely read by risk capital investors. You can try smaller papers if the amount you need is not too large (under $50,000), but for the most immediate action, your big Sunday paper is best. If you want capital from an investor without his personal participation, then you can use either the Sunday paper or a regional edition of the Wall Street Journal. Using the Journal you will reach potential investors in other areas, and will have to travel to see them, or have them travel to see you . . . but you reach a much larger potential investment market. If you have a very large proposition ($1,000,000 or more), then the use of nationwide financial publications should be considered. Again, remember, you are only looking for one person, so judge your area of coverage by that. It is wise to start in your own area, and gradually reach out farther from home base if necessary. For 25 cents you can get a handy rate guide, with all major Sunday papers as well as magazines listed, from the Chicago Advertising Agency, 28 E. Jackson St., Chicago, ILL 60604. This also lists combinations of Sunday papers in each state that can be used.

DISPLAY OR CLASSIFIED?

The question of whether to use display or classified space is moot. As a rule of thumb, if you seek over $50,000, display space on the financial pages of a Sunday will be read by more people with $50,000 or more to invest as a rule, and you also have the opportunity to interest someone not actively seeking an opportunity, but who was attracted by your offer. In general, replies from display will be of a better class than those from classified. The disadvantage is that display space is expensive, and you should use at least five to ten column inches to gain enough attention to make it worthwhile. This can cost ten times as much as a classified ad. Classified should be tried at the start anyway, just to save money. In the Wall Street Journal and other financial publications, use their classified sections, as this is where the risk capital investor is looking. You might also consider using trade journals of the industry you are getting into, but this is much slower; you'll be letting your future competitors know what you are up to.

HOW BIG AND HOW OFTEN?

The question of how big an ad to run in classified is decided by the number of words you need to tell your story. Don't use a lot of unnecessary words, and don't use a lot of abbreviations or chop the copy down in order to save a dollar or two. We mentioned that display should be from four to ten inches, large enough to be seen by most people who look at the page. Run the ad just once on Sunday in newspapers, and just once in other journals. Again, you need only one person, so you will need to work through your initial replies before needing more. Speed in answering inquiries is essential. Interest is fleeting and must be capitalized on while it is high, and before something else comes along to replace it. So reply to your original inquiries at once, and only when you discover there were no good prospects among them should you advertise again. Above all, don't keep an ad running every day; it's bad psychology ... potential investors see it, and shy away because there must be something wrong with a deal that has to be advertised over a long period. You can get an interesting little booklet on writing a business opportunity ad by writing the classified advertising department of the New York Times, Times Square, NY, NY (ask for their booklet on "How To Write a Business Opportunity Ad").

HOW TO HANDLE INQUIRIES

Answers to your ad will come in some surprising forms. One will be a postcard with one word scrawled on it, DETAILS, and an almost illegible signature. Another will be a beautifully typed letter on an engraved letterhead; another will be on a desk memo supplied by some trucking company, etc. Your tendency will be to work the nicely typed letters first and ignore the scrawls ... DON'T ... busy men often use scrawls and one word is really all that's needed anyway. Answer them as they come in; if phone numbers are given, call for an appointment; if mailing addresses, send your letter asking for an appointment. Do it the same day they arrive. Don't try to sell anything over the phone or by letter, other than an appointment . . . Don't be too eager, be very businesslike; if the time they wish to see you is not convenient, then say so and suggest another time; make them know you are not a beggar, but someone with a very good deal who is worth seeing. Never shop your inquiries, never try to analyze the prospect from the method he uses to answer your inquiries, and pay no more attention to a telegram than a postcard. And remember, don't give any information to a phone call or by letter, other than where and when you'll be available for a personal interview. Don't pay any attention to letters that ask for full details by mail; just contact them for an appointment. If they aren't interested enough to see you in person, you're not going to sell them.

MEETING THE POTENTIAL INVESTOR

When you meet the prospective investor, you will want to be completely prepared to present your proposition so he will understand it, and have confidence in you and in it. It might be well to point out here that most people fail to raise capital because they would not take the time to do the necessary preparatory work to fully develop the idea and its potential. Make no mistakes, it takes a lot of time and effort to do this, but until you do, your chances of raising capital are almost nil. The people you will be trying to sell the idea to are, by and large, very sharp individuals, and they will have access to experts in the field you are entering; so unless you can touch all the bases and satisfactorily answer all the questions, you'll fail. So when you sit down face to face with your prospects, be ready. A couple of points about that first meeting. Try and arrange neutral ground where neither of you will be disturbed by phone calls or visitors. Be sure that you have at least an hour and preferably more to develop your ideas, and if it's lunch or dinner, be sure YOU pick up the first check. Very important.

THE PRESENTATION

The purpose of your presentation is threefold. First, to gain investor confidence in your program and your ability to manage it. Second, to make the equity interest attractive to him. Third, to prove the potential is above average. Your initial prospectus will concern itself with these major points. After looking it over, and asking some questions (Part 1), the level of interest of the potential investor will determine whether you will show him part two. It is well to point out that there should be definite enthusiastic interest on his part, or you close it out there. Don't have part two with you; arrange another meeting, and now you ask some questions. Who is he, what is his background, and can he show proof of having the necessary capital prior to going into serious negotiations? Don't be afraid to dig right in, because he will respect you for it, and will understand that you are a responsible business man, the kind he wants to bet his money on. If he gets annoyed or hedges, close him out and go on to the next one. Don't waste time on people who have time to waste.

THE SECOND MEETING

At the next meeting he may want to bring along an attorney, and an accountant or friend who may have some expertise in the field. Agree, but bring some reinforcements yourself, and particularly if he brings his attorney, you bring yours. This adds stature to your program and it also will prevent you from being forced into a legal box. You should bring along part two of your prospectus to this meeting.

NOW THE REAL TEST TAKES PLACE

After your prospect has surveyed your prospectus, and you have convinced him your figures are correct, the bargaining will start in earnest. You will start to test each other for flaws and weaknesses. You might as well know it now: there are no friends in a poker game, and that is just what you will be in. His first move will be to try and get control or change the amount of investment, testing to see if you have any more to put up. He may suggest you form a syndicate and he'll get some of his friends to invest as well, or suggest you bring in some of your friends, etc. . . . in short, he is trying to either steal the deal or to get in with a minimum amount for maximum gain. When this starts, don't feel discouraged; if he didn't like it, would he try to steal it? As we mentioned before, have a point beyond which you will not go before you start, and when the point of no return is reached, make him fish or cut bait. If you prove firm and honest, you'll get what you need.

THE ADVISORS AND HOW TO HANDLE THEM

Once in a while you will find a potential investor who has some advisors. This is particularly true with a first-time investor. It may be his wife, a relative, friend or business associate. They want to put their oar in the water by suggesting a different arrangement, or by advising him not to go ahead with the program for one reason or another. The only way to deal with these people, is NOT TO DEAL WITH THEM. If your prospect can be swayed from the kind of presentation you have made by the off-the-cuff advice of someone not familiar with the deal at all, you'll be much better off being rid of him at the start, or you'll have nothing but trouble with him from then on. When he reacts to this advice by backing away, then fold up your papers, thank him for his time and walk away. If he lets you go, fine . . . if he calls you back, then you will be in the driver's seat from then on.

PROTECTING YOUR INTEREST

The problem of how much interest you should retain in the company is always a bone of contention in raising speculation capital to start a new company, and particularly so if you have no capital of your own to invest. The general rule is 50% without capital, and 50% plus the amount you put in when you do invest capital. You will want some return for your development work perhaps, and again this is a hard point as far as the investor is concerned. He hates to pay for dead horses, which your time and effort represent. The best way to handle this problem is to defer payment for the costs until the company is in the black (this shows your good faith). Now, as for your salary as manager of the company, this again represents a problem for the investor . . . You are entitled to be paid for your work, but it should be kept at a minimum until the company can afford more. If you want to set yourself up with a large salary and expense account right at the start, you'll have trouble getting the money. If you are really broke and in debt because of the expense of developing the program, level with the investor, tell him what the problems are and arrange for a loan against your salary to keep your head above water . . . you can't be fighting off personal creditors while trying to get a business going. ASK WHAT IS FAIR, and you won't have any trouble.

THE ATTORNEY

Hiring a lawyer to represent you is an expensive proposition, but a necessary one. There are attorneys, however, who take flyers now and then in propositions like this. They will gamble their time for a share of the business in the hopes that future profits will more than pay for their time in helping with the organization. You can ask around for one of these speculators, almost every community has one, and you have an extra bonus going for you here . . . he will be quite interested in seeing to it that you get all the breaks because he's personally involved. You'll pay more in the long run, but if your deal is good the long run should provide enough for everyone. And you have one extra carrot to dangle in front of him . . . he will be getting the company's legal business as well as part of the profits.

INVESTOR PROTECTION

When you are preparing your prospectus, talk your problems over with your banker and accountant. One of them is the protection the investors require for their investment. Forming a corporation is a form of protection, but there are many more sophisticated methods of providing the investor with additional capital security. One such form is capital notes. These are obligations of a corporation that must be repaid, but have the advantage of definite terms of repayment (and draw interest that must be paid), unlike common stock which relies on profits, or preferred stock which also relies on profits.

Some investors take part in stock, and part in capital notes. They serve another function: the company cannot borrow from a bank unless the holder of capital notes agrees to subordinate his notes to the bank loan (agrees that the bank will be paid first), thus he will know of any bank loans automatically.

UNITIZED INVESTMENT

Here is a classic method of supplying the promoter with 50% of the stock in a corporation, without having a claim on the investor's money once the corporation is formed. It works this way. Suppose you require $100,000. You form the corporation and issue $90,000 in debenture bonds to the investor, and $5,000 in capital stock; you get the other $5,000 in stock. Thus $100,000 has been invested, but you don't own $50,000 of his money after the corporation is formed as you would if you both took 50,000 shares of stock. You own 5,000 shares of stock in a corporation that owes the investor $90,000. Thus his capital is protected from you.

THE THIN CORPORATION

You will have to take the tax position of your investor into consideration, and a tax shelter is always of interest to him. As we stated in the beginning of this report, he is interested in a proposition where he can let Uncle Sam take the lion's share of the losses, while he gets the lion's share of the gains . . . This is where the thin corporation in the form of notes, which are reflected on the balance sheet as advances from stockholders. The ratio of these notes to stock purchased is four or five to one (a rule of thumb set down by the Internal Revenue Bureau). Thus one fifth of the investment is in stock, four-fifths in notes, which bear little or no interest. Now, the first profits of the company go to pay off the notes, thus the investor can get back 80% of his investment tax-free (it represents repayment of a loan), and has his stock interest remaining to share in additional profits. This is allowing him to have his cake and eat it too, and if offered, makes your proposition even more attractive. In the event of losses by the corporation, there are ways he can handle that as well.

SUB-CHAPTER S

In the event of losses, the investor has a unique tax shelter situation. Under Sub-Chapter S of the Internal Revenue Code, investors can elect on an individual basis to be taxed (rather than the corporation being taxed), and they add the corporation profits or losses to their personal income tax returns. Under the thin corporation set-up, the investors can't declare their losses until the company is out of business entirely, and then only as a short-term capital loss. But by invoking Sub-Chapter S provisions, the investor can take the corporate losses off his personal income tax, and thus a high bracket taxpayer reaps a considerable benefit. When the corporation starts making profits again, the stockholders can cease reporting under Sub-Chapter S, and return to a true corporation tax situation and the investor reaps capital gains.

EQUIPMENT LEASING

There is another gimmick where the high bracket taxpayer can get some extra money from Uncle Sam. If your company will need a considerable amount of equipment, the investor can set up a special trust to lease the equipment to the corporation, take accelerated depreciation on the equipment, as well as the initial 7% tax credit for new equipment, right off the top of his income tax. When the equipment has been fully depreciated and returns an income, he can sell it to the corporation for capital notes, etc.

TAX ADVANTAGES

Here is where your accountant can really shine if he knows his tax law. There are many ways to capitalize on tax situations to create extra income for the corporation. First, choosing the fiscal year for the corporation. If the corporation is profitable right from the start, then end the first fiscal year when the corporation has made $25,000. This prevents paying the sur-tax for that period. If the corporation is losing money, extend the losses to 12 full months from the starting date to gain the biggest possible tax loss carryover. The method of accounting chosen can make or cost money. The cash basis or accrual basis; each have advantages and disadvantages, and depending on your operation, one of them can save money for you, so choose with care. Be sure to include the costs of incorporation in your expenses (they can be amortized out over the first five years); if you fail to do so, you can't deduct them until the corporation is closed out. There are definite tax advantages in Medical plans in small corporations. There is a section in the Internal Revenue Code that allows small corporations to set up a medical plan for corporation members that provided the corporation can reimburse plan members for all their medical expenses and take such payments as deductions from their income taxes, and on the other hand the corporation members who receive such payments are not required to include such amounts in their gross income, thus your investor as a corporation member can obtain free medical care for himself and his dependents. You can set up very lucrative retirement funds and pension plans that can be invested and reinvested without tax payments, and the corporation receives full tax deductions from earned income for all payments into the fund. There are many ways to defer income tax payments (which amount to borrowing interest-free money from the government). The method of inventory control, Last In, First Out, commonly known as LIFO, has built-in tax advantages. The point of all this is simply that a good accountant can show you many opportunities to offer real tax savings to a potential investor, and each one is another reason for him to put up the capital.

To summarize, sell him on your project, offer him a good return and be sure you don't paint yourself in a financial corner.

This method of raising capital is probably best for new ventures requiring $50,000 or less.

WHY SMALL BUSINESS SHOULD INCORPORATE

All small businesses, sooner or later should consider incorporating. There are specific advantages to this, and the main one is you separate your assets from debts and liabilities of your business. But, in order to successfully do this, you must have a strong business operation going, or else you will have to be personally liable for everything the corporation does. But if you demonstrate some business strength, the corporation will protect your personal property from creditors should something happen to your corporation.

In addition the corporation offers you the opportunity of having tax free medical, pension, profit sharing and insurance plans; a safe deposit box that your heirs can open upon your death without having a tax and a state tax official present. (To remove any assets that might be there that could be kept out of the estate tax) All personal safe deposit boxes are sealed on the death of the owner, but corporation boxes are not, because corporations don't die until they are bankrupt; there are ways of postponing profit that would have to be paid out in income in a given year with a corporate structure you don't have as a sole proprietor or partnership; you still are able to offset profits made in other ventures against corporation losses; you have the ability to secure additonal capital without debt; methods of eliminating social security taxes from some income received from a corporation; and ability to take higher risks without personal liability is another important advantage.

For these reasons and others, you should consider incorporation. It is not a very difficult process.

HOW TO INCORPORATE A BUSINESS

In many cases it will be easier to raise capital if the venture is incorporated. This allows you to properly divide the interests in the business, protects both your investor's and your personal assets from liability in case of business failure, and offers some interesting opportunities to sweeten the pot for the investor that no other type of business format offers.

It is not difficult to form a corporation, but there are many little things that can cost you a great deal of money and grief if you don't take precautions when you form the corporation.

The general procedure is to determine the business objective, strike a business bargain between the principals involved, then incorporate.

The steps of incorporation are simple enough. You draft a charter; set up bylaws; decide what state to incorporate in; pay taxes and fees; appoint directors, and hold your first meeting.

The time it takes and the cost vary widely from state to state and corporation to corporation depending on the amount it's incorporated for, how it will operate, etc. As a rule, it's a matter of a few weeks at best for a small corporation with an uncomplicated charter.

THE BUSINESS BARGAIN

The elements in a basic business bargain should properly cover the following points:

1. The purpose of the enterprise.
2. The name of the business.
3. Where the business will be located.
4. Names of participants in the venture.
5. Functions of participants and remuneration, if any.
6. How much each participant will invest and on what terms.
7. How profits will be divided.
8. Who will have control.

Prior to any venture each participant needs a clear and definitive picture of the "Business Bargain". This removes later problems which may lead to divisiveness and bitterness if the method of solution is not laid out in advance. A good attorney is well aware of this, and can define the rights and responsibilities of all parties to the "business bargain" so each understands clearly how it's going to work.

INCORPORATION PROCEDURE

After the business bargain has been struck, it is necessary to create the corporation.

First, the choice of state in which you will incorporate is of more than passing interest. The most convenient state may be the most expensive and restrictive. States like Delaware make a good thing out of incorporating, and it is the legal home of many corporate giants who do little actual business there, but make it their "home state" because of the attractive laws dealing with taxes and restrictions.

Other states that offer new corporations some advantages are: New York, New Jersey, Pennsylvania, Maryland, Nevada, Tennessee and to some extent, Arizona.

The major reasons you might consider another state for your corporate domicile would be a broader charter is possible (allowing the corporation to get into other types of business, etc.); the right to issue no-par stocks which is barred or restricted in some states (no-par stocks can markedly reduce corporate taxes and franchise fees); some states require stockholders to become partially liable for wages of employees or services the corporation contracted for; some corporate debt or the right to mortgage property; some have blue sky laws that are highly restrictive to later selling issues of stock to the public; some make redemption of shares of stock difficult; and some simply take far too long to grant the charter.

All these considerations should be weighed when picking the legal home for your new corporation.

TAXES ON CORPORATIONS

Another look should involve a study of the tax structure of your domicile state. Some states hit corporations hard, others are very easy on their corporate residents.

Here are a list of taxes levied by some of the better corporate domiciles:

Alabama: 5%

Alaska: 18%

Arizona: 2% 1st $1000; 3% 2nd $1000; 4% 3rd $1000; 5% 4th $14,000; 6% balance

California: 7% Min. $100

Colorado: 5%

Connecticut: 8% Min. $25

Delaware: 6%

District of Columbia: 6% Min. $25

Georgia: 6%

Hawaii: 5.85% 1st $25,000; 6.435% balance

Idaho: 6% plus $10 excise

Illinois: 4%

Indiana: 2%

Iowa: 4% 1st $25,000; 6% next $75,000; over $100,000 8%

Kansas: 42% 1st $25,000; 24% balance

Kentucky: 5% 1st $25,000; 7% balance

Louisiana: 4%

Maine: 4%

Maryland: 7%

Massachusetts: Excise $6.15 per $100 on tangible values or net worth plus 8.55% of net income; or $144 Min. Direct 4.56%

Michigan: 5.6%

Minnesota: 11.33% Min. $10

Mississippi: 3% 1st $5000; 4% bal.

Missouri: 2%

Montana: 64% Min. $50

Nebraska: 2.6%

New Hampshire: 6%

New Jersey: 42%

New Mexico: 5%

New York: 7% Min. $100

North Carolina: 6%

North Dakota: 3% 1st $3000; 4% next $5000; 5% next $7000; 6% bal.

Oklahoma: 4%

Oregon: 6% Min. $10

Pennsylvania: 12%

Rhode Island: 8%

South Carolina: 6%

Tennessee: 5%

Utah: 6% Min. $25

Vermont: 6% Min. $25

Virginia: 5%

West Virginia: 6%

Wisconsin: 2% 1st $1000; 22% 2nd $1000; 3% 3rd $1000; 4%
4th $1000; 5% 5th $1000; 6% 6th $1000; 7% bal.

Note, be very careful if you are going to issue no-par value stock.
Many states set the arbitrary value of no-par stock quite high, and you
will pay a large penalty in incorporation costs if you are not aware of the
charge, or will have to prove actual value of your stock which is time
consuming and sometimes difficult.

The problems that come up by having a corporation chartered in
another state relate to laws of foreign corporations doing business in
your state. If you live in California, and incorporate in Delaware, you
will have to meet some costs, and some state regulations in order to do
business in California. Always check out these aspects of cost before you
charter in another state. It may prove to be more costly in the long run.
Many states have prohibitive taxes and laws on foreign corporations,
won't allow them to sue, etc. Be sure and check the costs of doing
business as a foreign corporation in your state. TAX PICTURE
 In addition to corporate franchise and income taxes levied by the states,
there are other taxes that bear looking into. *Property Tax*—What is the
rate that will be levied against the corporation, and how does it vary
between domestic (corporation chartered in that state) and a foreign one
(chartered in another state). There may be some dramatic
difference. *Capital Stock Tax*—Check to see if the domicile state im-
poses a tax on the capital stock (the net worth of the corporation, a very
costly tax). *Income & Franchise Taxes*—Check your domicile state rates
against the examples we've given earlier.

Some additional points to check in the income tax picture are: does
the state tax the entire income of the corporation, or just that portion
which represents business done in the state; does the state allow deductions of federal income taxes paid before taxing income (a big difference
here); does the state allow the loss carry-overs from previous years for
purposes of determining tax liability?

CHECKING THE AVAILABILITY OF A NAME

It is possible the name you have chosen is already taken by an existing corporation, and you will have to change the name before you can be granted a charter. You can determine this by calling (or writing) the Secretary of State's office in the state you choose to incorporate in, and have them check the availability of the name.

You cannot include a name in the corporate title that would tend to mislead the public as to the true nature of corporate business. But one had only to look at a list of new stock issues to discover that many states apparently engage in very loose enforcement of this legal point. But with the rise in consumerism, it can cause trouble.

For a complete check, if cleared by the state, you can check the federal register of trademarks to avoid conflicts with a corporation of another state with the same name. If they have trademarked the name you have chosen, lawsuits will result if you use it.

MEDICAL PLANS

Under Section 105 (e) of the IRS Code, an employee of a corporation and his dependents can have a comprehensive medical plan paid for by the corporation. He need not include the services he receives under this plan in his gross income and all payments for the plan are provided by the corporation, which in turn may deduct them as a business expense. This is an extra corporate goodie that you can use to sweeten the pot in a capital raising program and take full advantage of yourself.

PENSION PLANS

The corporation can provide contributions to pension plans for employees as tax deductable expenses, and there is no tax obligation to the employee till the income from them is actually received. If it is after retirement, its at a much lower tax rate than if received during earning years. Another sweetener for capital.

SECTION 1244 RULE

This section of the IRS Code allows corporate shareholders who purchase stock directly from the corporation ($500,000 or less) to take losses as ordinary income, but still allows capital gains taxation on any stock sold at profit.

Unlike Sub-Chapter S, which must be declared at the start of a fiscal year, 1244 stockholders can declare under 1244 and choose their own tax basis anytime. Losses are limited to $25,000 each year ($50,000 in a joint return) and of course profits are unlimited. Another goodie you can offer an investor.

SUB-CHAPTER S

A corporation set up under Sub Chapter S (with under 10 shareholders) can elect each taxable year to either be taxed as individuals on the income or losses of the venture, or to be taxed as a corporation. If business is bad, losses can be deducted from current income. If business is good, they can be taxed as a corporation and take capital gains on the income.

SECTION 1244 & SUB-CHAPTER S

By declaring both 1244 and Sub-Chapter S, current losses can be deducted from income, and any further losses on the disposition of the stock can be deducted as an ordinary loss under 1244. Thus an investor in high income brackets who is bailing out, can take the Sub-Chapter S loss as a participating stockholder, and then sell his stock at a loss, and invoke 1244 to declare an additional loss against income. Two losses for the price of one.

These are just some of the goodies that a sharp accountant can work up for you in making up an investment package.

RULE 146

In order to assist the small business in his effort raising capital through corporate offerings, the SEC has adopted Rule 146.

Rule 146 allows the offer of stock to be made to an unlimited number of investors. Previous rules required only twenty-five investors could be contacted, and if sufficient funds could not be raised from them, then a public SEC filing was necessary. The rule further states that no other than 35 investors can buy into the venture during any 12-month period, but, the offering can be made in a second 12-month period to gain another 35 and so forth. Thus, many more than 35 investors can eventually be included in the corporation.

The vital ruling is that the promoters of the stock must pay very close attention to who the offerings are made. The guidelines state that the investor must be financially sophisticated, either to handle risks and have the same access to information that would normally be provided in a registration statement. The investor should also understand that the stock is unregistered and therefore cannot be resold publicly, and, thus he would have to be willing to buy it as a long-term investment or until the firm went public with an SEC filing.

Offers for Rule 146 stock may also be made through investment counsellors or brokers, as long as they have no interest, financial or otherwise, in the stock of the company. Also, ventures with investments totaling less than $50,000 collected over a 12-month period are exempt. Over $50,000, the corporation making the offer must file form 146 within 45 days from the sale of the stock.

The difference in 146 from regular offers filed with the SEC, are that the offering must be direct communications. That is the officers of the company, or others who are selling it, must present themselves before the investor and answer any questions asked about the offering. This eliminates advertising, direct mail and other methods of soliciting investment.

The SEC also requires that the person being offered the stock is presented with an annual report (the most recent one) of the company, plus a brief description of the securities being offered, the intended use of the proceeds, and any material changes in its affairs not disclosed in the annual report. This material must be filed with the SEC.

There are other rules, that you should be aware of, you can obtain from the SEC should you be interested in selling stock under this plan.

A SMART ACCOUNTANT CAN SAVE BIG MONEY

When your corporation starts in business, a smart accountant who knows corporate law can be a real goldmine to the stockholders. For example, the fiscal year. A new corporation should pick its fiscal year to maximize tax advantages. If the jackpot is hit right off the bat and the money is rolling in, then it's smart to close the first fiscal year when the $25,000 earnings figure has been reached. This is then taxed only at normal rates, and not at the sur-tax rate. On the other hand, if losses are being incurred, he will stretch out the fiscal year for the full 12 months to give everyone a nice tax deduction.

He can pick the accounting method that will save the most dollars. Cash or accrual basis is the choice. Cash is the most flexible. He can choose your inventory accounting method. Example, in an inflationary economy LIFO (last in, first out) is best because it has the effect of valuing the entire inventory at the level of the lowest cost (the oldest items in inventory) while sales costs are charged on the basis of the latest (highest priced) items. This effectively overstates the charge against profit and loss for tax purposes.

He can invoke Section 179 of the IRS Code to provide a small corporation with a "Bonus Depreciation" of up to $2000 of the first $10,000 of property acquired by the corporation in any particular year. The property must be noted specifically as Section 179 property. After that, he can choose accelerated or straight line depreciation for you.

He can arrange under an accrual accounting basis to set up non-taxable reserves against bad depts. This is the only "estimated item" the IRS allows.

He can be sure to set up a five-year amortization of incorporation expenses over a five-year period. If this is not done in the first accounting year, these expenses cannot be deducted till the corporation is dissolved.

He can show you how to borrow some money from Uncle Sam, interest free. By using options available to defer tax payments and other items to conserve working capital...One option is to appropriate charitable contributions at the year's end and add them to business expenses, but the corporation has 142 months to actually fork over the cash (Section 170 IRS Code). He can also arrange to extend payment time on contributions to pension and profit-sharing funds, while taking deductions for such payments from current income.

He can help build some quick and solid tax deductions for high profit margin operations. He can arrange to donate some of the inventory dogs to charitable organizations, and take full value (including the high margin) as a charitable contribution. Thus a corporation with a 60% gross profit figure in the 48% tax bracket would be able to donate $1000 in cash to charity, for a net cost of $520. But, by donating $1000 in inventory, and using the high profit margin and 48% deduction figure, the $1000 would only cost $288.

These are just some of the options a good accountant can work up for a going corporation.

INTEREST IS DEDUCTIBLE

In raising capital remember that it costs twice as much for a corporation in the 48% tax bracket to use money provided from a 6% preferred stock, as from a 6% debenture.

BUSINESS FORM IMPORTANT

The above table shows the tax bite on a man with a $100,000 net business income...as sole owner he has a $43,000 tax bill...as a family partnership with his wife and two children a $29,000 tax obligation, and slightly less for a corporation form.

At some point, a business needs to be incorporated...For example, if the business produced $200,000 income, a sole proprietor would owe well over $100,000 in taxes, as a partnership around $75,000, and as a corporation $76,000.

While the corporate tax is slightly higher, under tax laws the owner would have over $16,000 more for business expansion than under a partnership form.

In the case of the partnership (where the wife and children are the partners), he takes out more for living to justify the partnership angle, pays $29,000 in taxes, and has $32,000 left.

In the case of the corporation, he draws $27,000, pays $28,000 in taxes, and has $44,500 left. This is the tax advantage of incorporating, but it has other advantages as well.

TAX SALARY

In corporate format the owner has to balance his taxable salary against corporate deductions. If the corporation pays a high salary to the owner, his tax bill will more than offset the corporate expense deduction and vice versa.

SUGGESTED SALARY LEVELS

TO SUM UP

Generally, the first step in the required procedure is preparation by the incorporators of a "certificate of incorporation." Most states require that this certificate be prepared by three or more legally qualified persons in a manner prescribed by State Law. Frequently, the certificate must designate the names and addresses of the persons who are to serve as the directors until the first meeting of the corporation. (The certificate is discussed in more detail in a later section.)

If the designated State official determines that the name of the proposed corporation is satisfactory, that the certificate contains the necessary information and has been properly executed, and there is nothing in the certificate or in the corporation's proposed activities that violates State law or public policy, he will issue the charter.

Thereafter the stockholders must meet to complete the incorporation process. This meeting is extremely important and usually is conducted by an attorney or someone familiar with corporate organizational procedure.

In the meeting, the corporate by-laws are adopted and a Board of Directors is elected. This Board of Directors in turn will elect the officers who actually will have charge of the operations of the corporation for example, the president, secretary, and treasurer. In small corporations, members of the Board of Directors are often the officers.

CORPORATE HOUSEKEEPING

One very important point about a corporation, is that it must be treated as such. Many small businessmen form corporations, and ignore the necessary corporate housekeeping, and when the pressure comes, find out that the courts disallow their corporate formation, making them personally liable for everything. This is because they failed to do the necessary things to show the corporation was in fact operating, active and fulfilling the necessary requirements to keep its corporate identity.

The corporation must hold its annual meeting, keep minutes of those meetings, hold meetings with its Board of Directors, keep minutes of those, make sure all necessary facts, tax and other forms are filed when due and properly filled out, and be able to show corporation affairs are in order.

The best source for all the necessary housekeeping materials, minute books, corporation forms, seals and other material is the Excelsior-Legal Stationary, Inc., 62 White Street, New York, New York 10013. There prices are reasonable, and they have everything on hand that you would need.

FLOATING A SMALL STOCK ISSUE

The trickiest part of capital raising is the selling of stock in a company that has no business history. You must first clear your offering with the Securities and Exchange Commission, then with the states you intend to offer the stock for sale in, and finally comply with any local regulations regarding such sales.

It is not easy nor is it particularly an efficient way to raise capital, since sales and promotion costs are invariably quite high, and results are often disappointing. But it can be, and has been done. Jimmy Ling, who started as an electrical contractor working out of a truck, incorporated in Texas, and cleared a stock offering, and sold shares in a booth at the State Fair. The result of this initial offering was Ling-Tempco-Vought, one of the 50 largest corporations in the United States, so it can be done.

When you decide to float a small stock or security issue to raise capital, your first decision has to be what kind of stock or security are you going to offer.

In general, there are three types: *common stock* (the ownership and basic risk of the business); *preferred stock* (guaranteed return; can participate in profits and has superior rights to assets in case of liquidation); *debenture or indentured bonds*(can be issued in various manners; debentures are without security other than company potential income; indentures are secured by physical assets of the company).

Most people understand common stock. It needs no explaining to the average investor; he's buying a share of ownership in the company, and expects to share in the profits, if any. This is the simplest form of equity to market because it is so common. In floating a small issue, this needs less detailed explanation, particularly if you are going after relatively unsophisticated investors.

Preferred stock is the widows and orphans gamble. It usually carries a set percentage of return, is cumulative (that is, if dividends on preferred are passed over because business is bad, they accumulate and no dividend can be paid on common stock until all accumulations are cleared on the preferred). They can be participating or non-participating, which means they can get an extra dividend along with the common (usually after a maximum dividend has been paid common; i.e., if the common dividend is $2 a share, then everything over $2 would be share and share alike with preferred, anything under $2 would not be shared), and they can be voting or non-voting (usually non-voting unless there is a missed dividend, then voting rights may be granted).

The bonds (debentures or indentures) can also take several forms. They have the advantage of obtaining capital without dilution of earnings by issuing more stock. They give the buyer a fixed return on his investment. Indenture bonds are secured by real estate (called mortgage bonds) or by equipment and fixtures (secured by trust certificates on the equipment), while debentures are only secured by the general credit of the company. In starting a new company, unless you plan to use proceeds to purchase real estate and major items of equipment, the indenture bond is not practical.

The sweetener to a bond offering can be a convertibility option. The holder can collect his fixed interest while he sees how the company is doing, and then at a future time (usually a limit is stated on the bond), he can convert the bond into common or preferred stock. This in effect gives him some security in the initial phases of the operation, and also gives him the chance to participate in eventual success.

Another sweetner for a bond buyer can be warrants attached to each bond. These are simply options to buy common stock at a stated figure, usually within a given time limit (although some warrants are issued in perpetuity). This, in general, gives him the same right as a convertible; but he must pay extra for the stock, and his bond cannot be converted.

The techniques of the various securities, and what the best selling type would be is a matter of serious investigation. You should discuss the problem with your banker, attorney, and accountant, and get some advice from a mortgage banker if possible.

If you are going to market the issue yourself, you'll want the type of security or stock that will less with the least resistance.

The problems of bond issues are ever greater, and suffice it to say that the new business planning to float its own stock issue should stay with straight common stock. It is what people understand, and when selling it, you don't have to explain some tricky esoteric financing scheme that will only confuse your prospects.

When you decide to proceed with floating your own stock issue, you will immediately have to contact the Securities and Exchange Commission in your area (by checking the phonebook of the nearest big city) about notification or filing of your offer. For the new enterprise or small business attempting to float and sell their own stock issues there are four courses open which make sense. They are the intra-state offer, which involves selling up to $500,000 worth of stock in your company to residents of your state only. This offer does not require filing, but only notification of the SEC of intended sale.

The major problem with intra-state offers is that if any buyers of the stock were to sell that stock to someone outside that state within a year of purchase date, the offer no longer qualifies as intra-state, but becomes an inter-state offer which requires filing with the SEC. Therefore, an intra-state offer needs some sort of escrow agreement from stock buyers that they will hold their stock for at least 12 months before they sell it to someone outside their domicile state.

The second method of selling stock yourself is under the so-called Rule 257, which limits an offer to $50,000 that is usually sold locally. This requires only a notification to the SEC and does not require filing a prospectus the seller intends to use in selling his stock. However, Rule 257 is not open to new enterprises. It is only available to established businesses with an earnings record. Obviously, Rule 257 is a rather simple way to raise $50,000 if you have an operating business with an earnings history.

The third method of floating your own stock issue is to go what is termed the Regulation A route. Regulation A issues are limited to $500,000. You fill out a set of forms telling the SEC who you are and what you intend to sell, and then file this as a notification of intended sale. This is to be filed at least 10 days prior to making the offering. If the SEC does not challenge the offer, the usual proceeding is to get a "no action letter" from the regional office of the SEC where your materials were filed. This is simply a letter stating the SEC will not stop sales at the present time, but they reserve the right to do so in the future, and that buyers of the stock will have the right to challenge the validity of the Reg. A offering and demand their money back on the basis the offering required a full filing.

The sticky point in filing a Regulation A notification with the SEC will be with your prospectus. In your prospectus, you will have to tell them the truth, the whole truth, and nothing but the truth or the SEC will refuse to let you go ahead with the stock sale. In general this means in a new enterprise, you must state emphatically that there are no earnings, that you are doing no business, that there is risk involved, etc. There is little harm in saying this, because the average investor is aware of this and the sale of stock in a new enterprise is a "ground floor syndrome proposition". People like to get in on the ground floor and are aware there is risk involved. So, by stating this in the prospectus you are doing little to harm your chances of sale. The main thing to avoid is any promises of great return in a short period of time by purchasing this stock or any unrealistic statements that the prospect can't lose, and so forth.

PREPARING A STOCK SALES CAMPAIGN

Our first step is to be sure you are on firm legal ground. Have your attorney clear your proposed offering with the SEC, or do it yourself. You can contact the nearest regional office, and find out what avenues are open to you. They will tell you what you have to do and what must be filed. Rules for small stock issues are changing all the time, becoming more liberal in some cases, so find out all you can from them, then pick the best way to go and launch your campaign.

Selling stock, like selling any other product, requires careful preparation, market analysis, a sales pitch, publicity, advertising, training, a time schedule, and a sales goal. When you sit down to decide how you are going to sell this stock, you must first analyze your available manpower. Remember this, the only people entitled to sell stock in a corporation are officers of the corporation or licensed security dealers. You can't hire salesmen off the street or have housewives going door-to-door selling stock. If you line up some licensed security salesmen to help, well and good. If not, you will have to divide the sales work up among the officers of the corporation.

In order to set realistic goals for each individual who will be selling stock, it will be necessary to sit down and figure out the approximate size of the prospect list you are going to need in order to realistically reach the goal you have set. As a rule of thumb, experienced security salesmen will tell you that you need approximately twenty suspects to equal one prospect, and four prospects to equal one customer. And this is selling recognized security of well-known companies on major exchanges. To sell stock in a new company with no earnings record and no national reputation, it should require something larger of a prospect list than what the average stock salesman uses. But, you have an advantage starting, in that you and your associates can sit down and make a list of people that you know who would be potential buyers of stock in your company simply through personal contact. This then will be your first step. You and your associates sit down and make out what will be called a F.A.R.

list. This means friends, acquaintances, and relatives. This is the list used by all insurance salesmen, security salesmen, and others who are starting out in the field and it is used as their initial prospect list. The length and potential of the F.A.R. list will tell you approximately how much larger a prospect list you are going to need in order to complete your projected sales goal.

If your stock issue is $500,000, and this is your sales goal, then you figure your F.A.R. list will absorb half of that amount, this leaves $250,000 to sell to a general suspect list. If you consider $2500 as your average unit of sales, then this means you will need approximately 100 customers in order to complete your sales goal. Working backwards from the formula security salesmen use, you need 400 prospects (a prospect is somebody who will submit to an interview and hear your sales pitch), and to obtain the 400 prospects you will need a suspect list of twenty times that amount or 8,000 names. These names can be obtained in several ways. First, you make a list of business and professional men in your own community or your own general area and total that up as your suspect list. As a rule, these people are investors in stock in one kind or another; and they have the available funds to invest in others. Next, you can contact a mailing list broker and get lists (costs of list of names) of known stockholders, investors, and speculators in your area. These will be obtained from compiled lists of subscribers to stock market information services, magazines such as Forbes, Baron's and other financial publications, buyers of books on investing and other such logical sources. You can purchase segments of these lists (and there are many of them), for your own area. This will flush out your suspect lists to the required number of people. Firms having investor lists are: Dunhill International List Co., Inc., 444 Park Ave., South, NY, NY 10016 . . . Investors's Information Service, 309 Main St., Great Barrington, Mass. 02130 . . . Market Compilation Research Bureau, 11633 Victory Blvd., N. Hollywood, CA 91609...Dependable Mailing Lists, 425 Park Ave., South, NY, NY 10016...National Association of Investment Clubs, 1515 E. Eleven Mile Road, Royal Oak, MI 48067.

ORGANIZING YOUR LISTS

When you have all your lists on hand, organize them into communities and neighborhoods so that when you start your telephone sales campaign you will be setting up appointments in small areas. This will make calls on prospects much easier.

Your lists will not have telephone numbers so that you will need to look up the phone numbers for all your names. The best way to do this would be to get a criss-cross directory from the phone company. A criss-cross directory lists telephone numbers by street addresses. Make up cards giving the name, address, phone number, and source of the name. Thus, when you are working your telephone campaign you will be able to tell which source of names is producing the most prospects. This will enable you to know which list to order more names from should you need them.

DEVELOPING THE SALES PITCH

When you obtain an interview with a prospect, you will have to have a definite, organized sales presentation in order to interest him in participating in your stock offering. In doing this, you will have to recognize that you will be talking to the stock trader. He is well informed about stock investing, recognizes risk potential, and his interest is simply in the growth factor of your company. In other words, he's interested in speculating in stock, not investing in it. In presenting your case to the trader, you will have to convince him that there is a good growth factor in your company and that the stock will be worth considerably more than he is going to pay for it in a relatively short time. You should recognize at the outset, he knows more about the market than you do and, therefore, you should stick strictly to the growth potential of your company, its market, and the methods of operation that are going to make it grow. Stay away from any discussion with him about further types of financing issuing convertibles, warrants, letter stock, etc. He will chunk in a pretty fair size of money if he is convinced the growth factor is there.

The second type of prospect you will be talking to is the accumulator. This is the individual who buys stock, but seldom sells it. He looks on his stock portfolio, like a stamp collector looks at his stamp collection. He is always interested in accumulating more, but seldom interested in trading or speculating stock. In talking to this type of investor, you will want to stress both dividends and growth. He is interested in both. A trader could care less about dividends, his direction is strictly speculative, but the accumulator loves to get those dividend checks in the mail. So you will tailor your presentation to him in terms of participating in company profits as well as in company growth.

The third type of prospect you will be talking to is the complete neophyte in stock investing. He may own some mutual funds, or have purchased stock in the company he is working for through an employee purchase program, but knows little or nothing about the workings of the stock market, understands nothing about growth, leverage, options, warrants, convertibles, etc. This type of individual has what is known as the "savings account syndrome." He looks on stocks the same way he looks at his savings at the savings and loan. He is interested in the kind of "interest" he is going to get for his investment. Thus, your conversation with him would be strictly on the potential of the dividend he might receive. It doesn't hurt to stress the fact that of course his stock will grow in value as well as received dividends, but with him you are talking strictly about security of investment and returns on it.

Now, there is a fourth type of prospect you will be talking with. And that concerns businessmen and professional men who could have a vested interest in the success of your company. These would be potential suppliers of goods and services, potential recipients of value from any payroll you produce, etc. With them, you strictly pitch the monetary advantage of having your company exist and grow. It doesn't hurt to stress the fact that the company is in a growing industry, has bright prospects, is backed by knowledgeable people, etc. But in the main, they buy because they expect to get something other than profits out of it. And while you don't say this directly, the inference is always there.

So, in general , you tailor your presentation to the type of individual you are going to be talking to. Each has different reasons for purchasing stock, and if you recognize these reasons in advance, your potential of making a sale is much greater.

When you have your sales presentation worked out and generally understand how you are going to approach the various types of prospects, you are ready to plan perhaps the most important part of your stock promotion program and that is publicity.

GETTING FAVORABLE PUBLICITY

The first step is to hire a competent man or woman who will help you plan and promote a public relations campaign that will coincide with your stock selling effort. Keep in mind that advertising is strictly limited to the name of your company, the amount you are offering, and that a prospectus is available. This is the rule of the SEC, and any flamboyant type of advertising where you are promising huge profits, get rich quick or anything of that nature, or even inferring that your company is in a great growth situation and a highly profitable investment will bring the SEC down on you like a ton of bricks. So, advertising is simply done to spread the word in the financial community that the stock is available, and serves little useful purpose in selling stock to the public at large. Therefore, your public relations campaign is really your only advertising campaign.

In getting media exposure, the first logical step is to hold an open house, grand opening or other type of function that will bring the press, cameramen and city dignitaries to your new factory, offices, headquarters, etc. This is usually in the form of a combined press and cocktail party in which invited guests can participate in the freebees and in so doing more or less obligate themselves to give you a generous amount of publicity.

In addition to the grand opening function, your P.R. man or woman will arrange speaking engagements for you or other officers of the corporation in front of civic and business groups in the community to spread the word about your new company. This gives you the opportunity of having additional exposure among prospective stock buyers, and, of course, adds to your own prestige in the community aiding in your stock sales.

You and the other officers of your corporation will be responsible for the most important part of the public relations campaign, and that is mingling with business and civic leaders of the community, participating in civic affairs, and becoming what is known as a good citizen. Exposure of this type opens all kinds of doors both for stock sales and other business benefits. So, plan a good deal of your time in the beginning to be circulating in the community and becoming well known.

Your major publicity campaign efforts would tie in precisely with the opening of your stock selling campaign. This puts your company name in front of the suspects of prospects you have listed, and makes it a good deal easier to obtain interviews for the purposes of selling stock. A skillful public relations campaign can really be the difference of a successful and unsuccessful effort in reaching your ultimate stock sales goal. So work very carefully on the plans and see to it that they are followed through to the letter.

INVESTMENT SEMINARS

One way to turn suspects into prospects in groups is to advertise a free seminar on investing in the particular industry you are in. Invite the public to attend and lure them in with free refreshments and a star attraction of some kind. The attraction could be a lecture by an author of a best selling financial book or somebody else whose name is known and recognized as being an astute student of the financial community. The lecturer won't tout your company or stock but will simply give his set lecture for a fee to the audience. Prior to his being introduced you can give a brief plug to your company, pass out literature and your prospectus concerning your stock offering at the conclusion of the meeting. One thing is absolutely necessary, and that is that everybody register with name, address, and telephone number. This gives you a prospect list which you can call and convert into sales interviews. Its advantage is that it creates some excitement and interest in investing in your particular industry, and this can be converted into selling stock in your company.

YOUR SALES PACKAGE

Your selling package should consist of your prospectus approved by the SEC and any letters of recommendations you can get as to the soundness of the business idea, picture, and other data on the products, services, etc., you are going to render, pro forma break-down returns on various sizes of investment, and if you want to go first cabin, some four color brochures that detail the operation prepared by a professional advertising agency.

You have to be very careful about not saying things that the SEC might question, and remember this: it doesn't hurt to be negative in the sense you admit there is a risk involved. It's the potential payoff at the end that interests the investor; he recognizes risk, so don't try and hide the fact. In fact, the risk is what makes it interesting to many investors.

THE TRANSFER AGENT

One important point, as you sell the stock and receive the money for it, you will have to have a transfer agent (usually a bank) who enters the transactions in a record book and records the stockholder of record. From any time on that the stock changes hands, the bank makes the necessary changes of ownership as they occur.

SALES METHODS

Once your sales package presentation and publicity campaign are organized and under way, you will have to set up a definite sales method program. As a rule, this will consist of taking lists of suspects, contacting them by telephone after they have been sent a prospectus, and trying to obtain an interview. As we noted before, you can expect about one out of twenty suspects to submit to an interview, once this is done they become prospects, and you make an appointment to see them at a convenient time. At this point, an account card should be written up for the suspect who has become a prospect. It gives names, addresses, home phone, business or occupation, business phone, family status, and other pertinent information. After the sales interview, the results are entered on the card. It is sometimes possible for another officer or salesman to re-contact the party and sell them when the original salesman failed. This is why it is important to keep these cards on file and re-contact them periodically during the campaign. Work should be done systematically, definite number of contacts made every day, and meetings held daily to go over results, listen to suggestions and get ideas for smoothing out the sales presentations, the telephone selling, etc.

TIME SCHEDULE

You will have to set up some type of time schedule for your stock selling efforts, as you start running the business as well. The best thing is to push it for all it's worth for 90 days, then keep up a steady sales campaign; but one that is almost automatic in operation.

The one advantage you have in a high-pressure, self- underwriting campaign is that there is little competition. Most brokerage firms and their salespeople live off the business they already have and few ever try to plow new ground. How many times have you been approached to buy stock other than routine letters from brokers, etc? Your effort can probably meet reasonable goals if you plan carefully and work hard. If you are successful , you will have opened up another door as well. If your first issue is sold successfully and puts money in the pockets of the buyers in a reasonable length of time, then when you decide to float another issue, you won't have to work very hard at all.

THE COSTS

Keep in mind it costs money to sell stocks. You will find you will be paying close to 20% (it should never be more) of your total income as stock selling cost. You will have to raise enough to cover the selling costs as well as the capital needed to get your venture started.

One final point, you are taking on a tough job and a risky one in floating a stock issue, and you should try all other avenues before trying it. But if all other doors are closed and you have the guts and determination to promote your venture no matter what, a successful self-underwriting of a stock issue can launch you into orbit in a hurry and prepare you for bigger and better things.

INCORPORATION FORMS

In the Appendix you will find two forms for Articles of Incorporation, a long form and a short form, a suggested set of rules for corporation bylaws; and the various notices that you will need to get your corporation forms.

In addition you will find the resolutions for forming both Subchapter S and Section 1244 Stock Plan

We reproduced here the Articles of Incorporation supplied by the State of Delaware, and these should suffice in most states.

CERTIFICATE OF INCORPORATION

OF

FIRST - The name of this corporation is -----------------

SECOND - Its registered office in the State of ----------

is to be located at ---------- the ----------, County of

----------. The registered agent in charge thereof is

------------------- at --------------------.

THIRD - The nature of the business and the objects and

purposes proposed to be transacted, promoted, and carried on

are to do any or all the things herein mentioned as fully

and to the same extent and natural persons might or could do,

and in any part of the world, viz:

Here should be stated, in general terms, the character of

the particular business to be carried on. Under Section

102 (a) (3) of the new law, the following may be stated

in lieu of the old purpose clauses: ''The purpose of the

corporation is to engage in any lawful act or activity

for which corporations may be organized under the general

Corporation Law of --.''

FOURTH - The amount of the total authorized capital stock

of this corporation is --------------- Dollars ($) divided

into ---------- shares of ---------- Dollars ($) each.

FIFTH - The names and mailing addresses of each of the

incorporator or incorporators are as follows:

NAME

MAILING ADDRESSES

SIXTH - The Directors shall have power to make and to alter or amend the By-Laws; to fix the amount to be reserved as working capital, and to authorize and cause to be executed, mortgages and liens without limit as to the amount, upon the property and franchise of this Corporation.

With the consent in writing, and pursuant to a vote of the holders of a majority of the capital stock issued and outstanding, the Directors shall have authority to dispose, in any manner, of the property of the corporation.

The By-Laws shall determine whether and to what extent the accounts and books of this corporation, or any of them, shall be open to the inspection of the stockholders; and no stockholder shall have any right of inspecting any account, or book, or document of this Corporation, except as conferred by the law or the By-Laws, or by resolution of the stockholders.

Who signed and executed the foregoing Articles of Incorporation, and they did acknowledge that they signed the foregoing and that the facts therein stated are true and correct.

HOW TO DEAL WITH PROFESSIONAL VENTURE CAPITALISTS

The Small Business Investment Act was passed in 1958 by the U.S. Congress. Its purpose was to set up venture capital companies to supply capital to small businessmen who were unable to raise money through normal channels . The object of the Small Business Investment Company (SBIC) is to supply long-term capital (minimum of 5-year term) and share in the ultimate profits of the venture. They will take greater risks, and therefore expect greater returns.

The capital raiser should understand this last point. It will cost more to secure capital from a venture capital firm than from a bank or other normal financial source. On bonds, or loans, they will take from 10% interest minimum up to whatever the traffic will bear. In addition, they will want warrants or convertible rights on bonds so they can share in the equity growth of a company they back.

THE VENTURE CAPITALIST

The operators of SBIC's or other venture capital firms are not kindly, rich uncles who supply funds to help entrepreneurs get productive enterprises started out of the goodness of their hearts. (Though this is the picture they often present to the public.) For the most part, they are hard-nosed, greedy and shrewd horse traders who are on a treasure hunt, looking for the "bonanza" in the business world. The new company that will sustain a growth rate of 20% to 50% a year for a period of time long enough to get the public interested in buying stock in the firm. They buy in for pennies and sell out for dollars. The welfare of the entrepreneur is always secondary to theirs, and they often cut and run at the first sign of trouble. There are no friends in a poker game or business deal, so disabuse yourself of any thought of altruism running rampant in venture capital firms. Greed is what makes the game go.

This is not to say they are all a bunch of bad guys (though some are), but rather to point out that you are going to be in for some very tough bargaining when you sit down to make a deal with them.

TWO TYPES OF VENTURE CAPITAL FIRMS

There are two general types of venture capital firms. You have the private venture capitalists who operate entirely on their own money. Then, you have the

SBIC's who get a large portion of their funds through the Small Business Administration and are controlled by the SBA in their dealings.

For the newcomer to this wilderness, percentage says you will get a better break from an SBIC than from a private capital firm, if for no other reason than the SBA puts some restrictions on how much the SBIC can take, while the private capital firm has only your bargaining ability to restrict them.

An example of this is the matter of taking a controlling position in a firm they finance. The SBIC cannot take over 49% in any firm they finance, that's part of the law they operate under. They can, and do, get around this in a number of ways, but essentially the entrepreneur retains control unless or until things start going badly. A private capital firm will almost always take either nominal or actual control. At the very least, they will put themselves in a position to take full control should the management of the enterprise severely displease them.

Another factor that works in favor of the entrepreneur in dealing with SBIC's is the right to buy back the securities issued for the capital at any time (or forcing the SBIC to convert debt securities in to common stock thus cancelling the senior debt). This, too, is part of the law, and it gives the entrepreneur a chance to make the investors fish or cut bait when he deems the time is right, not when they do. In private capital financing, you will find no such right offered. The SBA to some extent limits the interest rates an SBIC can charge on loans or bonds. A private capital firm can get anything you will go for, and since most states make interest on corporate debt in the range of 15% up to infinity, there are really no holds barred.

Many private venture capital firms are funded by banks, large corporations, wealthy families, etc., and they are interested in grooming new companies for acquisition bait. When it's to their advantage to have the new venture swallowed up by one of the conglomerate whales swimming in the financial seas, away you go. In exchange they get stock marketable on a national exchange, and what you get may be a lot of experience. The SBIC can go the same route, but by law, you have the out of taking back the bonds; and since they must allow you to retain control, you can, at least, fight back.

But either way you will be swimming in dangerous waters once your venture proves to be a big winner.

THE JACK POT SYNDROME

As we mentioned, the venture capitalist is a bonanza hunter. They want jackpots when they put their nickles in the machine . Few of them would be interested in investing in a venture that simply returned a fair rate of interest on an investment. They leave that business to the bankers and insurance companies.

Here are some published statements of venture capitalists. They will give you an idea of what they are looking for:

E. F. Heizer, Jr., Chairman of Heizer Corp...."we feel we should earn year in and year out, to be doing any job at all, a 15% compounded rate for return on our money. Our goal is actually 40% compounded"...

Charles B. Smith, Associate, Rockerfeller Family Assoc... "Our goal, like everybody else's, is to make wads and wads of money for the family four times (our investments) in three years, five times in four years, etc."...

Mark Rollinson, Vice-President, Greater Washington Investors..."We are looking for a compounded return on investment somewhere between 25% and 35% (annually)...We don't care how we arrive at it"...

B. G. Schmidt, Managing Partner, J. H. Whitney & Company... "should be able to at least double its money every four years" ...

These statements will clear up any doubts about the altruism of the venture capitalist...the least greedy among them wanted 15% a year compounded, and they are looking for 40%...Others like G. Stanton Geary, President of Inverness Capital Group says this..."there must be an opportunity to make ten times the original investment in five to seven years." The reasons for these kinds of returns are generally twofold. First, human nature. Get all you can. Second, the jackpots have to carry the washouts. Picking new business ventures is like picking horses. Often the best looking horse in the race is a dog, and the scruffy nag you wouldn't give a second glance to, runs away with it. No one has a foolproof way to always pick winners, so they've got to have jackpots to stay in business.

This jackpot syndrome poses two separate problems for the capital seeker. The first, obviously is to prove to the capitalist that you have the makings of a jackpot in your proposition. The second comes when it succeeds. How to keep some of the gravy on your own plate .

But, that is a decision that comes after the fact of finding a capital source.

There are some techniques and problems you should be aware of when you set out to find a capital source.

THE GOD COMPLEX

The God Complex is a problem you will run into almost instantly as you seek to get appointments to discuss your capital needs. It is an attitude that is common among people who are sitting in the "cat bird seat" so to speak. You find it in policemen, newspaper people, in TV it can only be described as "Super God," bankers, doctors, and anyone else who has people seeking them out for favors.

They develop a contempt for the seekers, and begin to assume that anyone who comes to them for help is trying to take advantage of them and really has nothing worth looking at. The only things they put any value on are the things they discover (or think they do) themselves.

Venture capital firms are deluged with people having "wizard deals" bound to make millions if they can just raise a little (or a lot of) capital. In 99% of the cases, the people are unprepared, know little of the realities of financing a business, and are simply eased out the door or ignored. The other 1% have to suffer because of the problem.

Many entrepreneurs have run into this problem without realizing what it was. They just never got past the front door, and assumed they had a bum deal to offer, where in reality they were just victims of the God Complex.

This complex, along with the pressures of time and on-going investments, make it very difficult to get more than a cursory hearing when you try the frontal (through the front door) assault on the bastions of money men.

THERE IS A BETTER WAY, THE OBLIQUE APPROACH

To get around the God Complex, you should try an end run instead of a line plunge. Catch them on the blind side, and you have a real chance. Instead of a letter or phone call, asking for an appointment, try getting an introduction (and if possible a strong endorsement) from a third party or parties who have a reputation the venture capital people know and respect. This gives your proposition the "aura" of discovery. They found you, you didn't come to them. In this manner, you get their full attention and interest. The key to absolute success is to have the third party arrange for the venture capital outfit to contact you about coming in for an interview, thus reversing the normal procedure.

How does one go about getting this type of recommendation? Simple, go and ask for it. All you need is to do a tiny bit of detective work to find out who to ask.

The first step would be your banker. Perhaps he knows the banker who handles the venture capital account, and he can find out if he doesn't. Lunch with the two bankers is one way to get the ball rolling. Perhaps your banker knows a businessman who is on the board of the venture capital firm or has some dealings with them. The banker can arrange for you to meet with the businessman and he can make the introduction.

The kind of person you are looking for in this situation is a "Mr. Ego." This is the gent to whom flattery is everything. If you make the comment that you wanted to meet him because "he is the shrewdest business mind in the area," you have a friend for life. Once you have shown the good judgement to recognize his great talent, obviously your proposition has to be worthwhile, and with a few more tugs at your forelock, you can have him taking you by the hand right into the inner sanctum of the venture capital vault.

If you can't find a Mr. Ego, then you have one ally you probably haven't thought about. Your friendly local congressman. This will be of particular interest if you are dealing with an SBIC. By contacting him, and arranging an appointment to meet him the next time he's home in the district (a strong pledge of political support usually turns the trick), you can get his help in this way. He can put some heat on the Small Business Administration to in turn put some heat on the SBIC to see you. You see the SBA gets its money from Congress, and the SBIC gets its money from the SBA. Chain of command stuff.

In choosing the venture capital firms you want to deal with, start with the one closest to your home. Then move out in a circle. You will find a list of them in the end of this section.

Get their phone numbers from information, and call and ask what type of ventures they prefer investing in, and what their investment is. Investment preferences change with the investment climate, so always check first. When you find one that is diversified (any old jackpot will do), you can start with them, assuming they can put up the kind of money you need.

If you are bashful about calling, then have your banker find out. But, start with one that has an area of interest that includes your proposition and can put up the kind of money you want that is imperative. Otherwise, you will be spinning your wheels working with people who are only curious; looking for an idea they can steal.

If you can't wait for the oblique approach to work for you, then when you find the one you are interested in, call them on the phone, ask for an appointment. Lay your cards on the table. If they say mail it, just reply you have to explain it in person, and you have a proposal ready to show them. Don't put off, hang in and stick by your guns, get through the door.

PICKING YOUR VENTURE CAPITAL FIRM

The VC's have varied interests, and some will only invest in one type of industry, but all of them will be interested in knowing about a "jackpot deal." If they can't handle it themselves, they will put you on to someone who can, and perhaps take a piece of the action.

Some VC's want no part of managing the business (except to protect their investment), others will want to be in on the almost day-to-day operations. You will have to decide whether you want to be left pretty much to your own devices, or you want lots of help. Both have advantages and disadvantages, and it pretty much hinges on what kind of manager you are. If you want to be your own decision maker, you'd best steer clear of the VC's who will take a controlling position in your firm, and have their own auditors, accountants, attorneys, etc., handling company affairs.

Some VC's will want all the interest they can get on their capital in the form of taking bonds. Some states allow corporations to be charged any amount of interest. If they can legally get 15% in a state they might want it, plus an option to convert or warrants. Others will be satisfied with an investment in common stock and perhaps a long-term note at reasonable interest.

The reason that common stock is interesting to some SBIC's is that dividend income to them is tax free. Other corporations are taxed on 15% of the dividend income. Thus, if the SBIC's take their money in dividends rather than interest, they have a tax loophole working for them.

The direct purchase of stock in the beginning by the VC puts them in a better position at jackpot time (when the venture goes public), as they can obtain more shares at lower cost than by using convertible securities or warrants.

These are things they won't discuss with you, but will have some bearing on their investment decision. As you can see, they are interested in a company that will be growing fast, having a strong price earnings ratio that will attract stock buyers.

NEGOTIATING WITH VENTURE CAPITALISTS

You have to be ready when they are. Your prospectus has to be complete, you must have all your facts and figures ready and proveable, and you must know exactly how you are going to use the capital, and save a reasonable projection of what return the capital will bring.

Don't try and con them by hiding information you feel might be detrimental to your case. Lay it all out, nothing is ever perfect; and if the good substantially outweighs the bad, you have a good chance of getting the money. If they catch you (and they will) hiding pertinent facts, they will close you out instantly.

When you begin to discuss the type of security you will issue for the capital received, try first to get them to take common stock. This relieves your capital from repaying loans (bond coupon interest) at the time it can be better employed elsewhere. If they are adamant, then your next best deal is convertible bonds. When you convert the bonds to common, you are off the hook on interest payments, freeing more capital from growth. While your equity is diluted by the conversion, assuming you have the growth situation you planned on, it will not hurt you that much. The third choice might be bonds with detachable warrants which are converted into common. If they want to go this route, you have the problem of never dissolving the bond debt till it's paid off, and still having dilution of your ownership through stock conversion. If the warrants are demanded, then make them fish or cut bait by having warrants expire within maturity date of bonds.

You will need some help here from a good accountant who can steer you through the deadfalls of esoteric corporate financing. Remembering this, they are going to try to get all they can, and unless you say stop, they will get more than they should. So, get competent help and fight back at the bargaining table.

When you are bargaining, you will note that interest rates are considerably higher than prime rates at the bank, and to be honest, this is fair because they are taking a longer risk than a bank will take. So, they deserve higher rates of return. But keep in mind the average is about 10% on loans, and anything over that on a reasonable proposition is to be resisted.

The maturity date of bonds or loans has to be at least 5 years by law by

SBIC's, and you may be able to get it extended. In practice, they do extend where conditions warrant, and in fact there is little profit for them in closing you out of it if you are unable to meet the deadline.

The question of repayment of the investment can be sticky. The demand may be for amortized payments over the period of the loan, which puts great pressure on you right at the start, or it can be for payment at the end of 5 years. In practice, they will probably do a little of both. Have you set up a a sinking fund for a portion of the loan and the balance due as a balloon payment at the end of the period, subject to renegotiation. One thing that helps here is they are not loan sharks and have no interest in putting payments on your back that will break it. They are interested in the jackpot, and not looking to kill the goose that's going to lay those golden eggs for them. So, they will generally be quite practical about this phase of the negotiations.

The subject of collateral might come up. A venture capitalist should not get collateral beyond the interest in the business. He gets rewards for risks, not for sure things. If you are dealing with a small VC, they may demand collateral. If so, then you pay a good deal less for the money than the full risk loan would call for. You should pay only close to prime rates, or even below if they are also getting a substantial interest in the venture as well.

The individual SBIC can only lend $500,000 maximum, or less if that amount is greater than 20% of their paid in capital, without the consent of the SBA. If needed, this consent is usually forthcoming, or the SBIC can form a consortium with another one and lend more. The private VC can put up any amount.

The SBIC equity stake in a company can run from 5% to 49%, but in practice it usually is around 20% to 30%. At the table try to keep the equity to them as low as possible, because if the jackpot comes, you'll be giving away tens of thousands of dollars you could have kept for yourself right here.

The big question to solve at the start is how to value the warrants or how many shares the bonds will be converted into. The SBIC will propose something, and you will have to decide if it's too much. Again, they want all they can get, so the prices they pay for warrants will be low, and the number of shares that they can convert into will be high. There is no need for them to have the total amount of the loan converted in equity, so they will try to have their cake and eat it too. Your job is to try and get the prices of convertibility high enough so that a major portion or all the loan is liquidated at conversion. In the case of warrants, a high enough per share price is paid to give you funds to retire some or all of the debt...and this will be the fulcrum of the teeter-totter.

The VC may rightfully require you to use some of the capital they supply to consolidate all your debts, so they can be your sole creditor. Any personal loans that have been converted into equity are into equity and not paid off by the VC's cash, you can assure yourself of that. If you cannot pull in all your debts, then they may want the terms extended to conserve working capital. This is only common sense on their part, and no big problem as a rule.

They will naturally put restrictions on your company for acquiring additional debt without their consent. This may not restrict you in normal activities (ordering materials and supplies, etc.) but will require their consent for major outlays for machinery, new product development, etc.

You will also be required to get their consent to any changes in ownership or major shift in top personnel. Also any new stock issues, options, executive bonuses, ... , etc., that might tend to dilute ownership or place a burden on earnings. They will be very nasty about increases in executive compensation until the footing is very firm.

They will also require that there be no dilution of their share of ownership without their consent. This means any further stock, bond, option, or warrant issues must be approved by them, and they will want first call on further financing of this kind.

They will want one or more of their people on your board of directors, and you probably will wind up with their accountants and attorneys, insurance brokers, and the like. This gives them a constant line of sight on your operation and avoids any dealings they won't be aware of.

Venture capital is a hard dollar and should be almost a last resort.

TAPPING THE FEDERAL MONEY MINE

The Federal Government not only has money to burn, it also has money to loan. By last count there were some 1400 individual programs operating within the Federal Government that passed out money to a variety of enterprises ranging from tap dancing to building oil tankers.

As in all government programs, they change in intent and amount of money available with political whim and the proximity of election day. The one thing they all have in common is that they all come wrapped in miles and miles of red tape.

Disabuse yourself of any idea that this money source is like Aladdin's Magic Lamp, just rub a politician and "Presto," the money is forthcoming. Also, don't believe that you can simply fill out one of their applications in triplicate and the money will be handed out. It's a good deal more complex than that. One firm in Washington D.C. makes pots full of money selling computer print-outs of available federal funds and helping the money seeker get through the red tape jungle to the cash drawer. The average application will be handled by some low-level bureaucrat, dutifully stamped, filed and forgotten.

Everything in government moves with the speed of influence. Influence in government comes from only one source...political clout. If you can get some on your side, the coffers of government are wide open; fail to have it, and you will be better off dealing with Scrooge before Christmas Eve.

Therefore, before you set out to tap this capital source, get some of that clout working for you. Your best starting place is through the office of your Congressman or Senator.

To get attention from them, you need another kind of clout. They operate at the speed of delivered votes. So, if you can get a local "Wheel:" who delivers votes (or money that buys votes) to recommend you to the politician, you have the making of clout. A letter, or better yet, a phone call on your behalf from this wheel, will bring you the influence you need to get favorable attention from the bureaucrats who guard the gold.

To get the wheel interested you must show him how much good your venture will do the community (and his particular section of the community). If you can show him how your venture will make a dollar for him, that's the best thing of all for the community.

Once you have arranged your clout, move fast. Get your application in, and if your political sponsor happens to be on the committee that ok's the funds for that particular operation, you will get quick action (if he's the chairman of the committee, you'll get it with the approximate speed of light). Remember, it will move with the precise speed of the influence of your sponsor.

Now, if all this sounds very cynical and slightly outrageous to you, then you are looking in the wrong area for money. Just believe that you will be better off using this method than you will trying it on your own.

What follows are the details of the various programs that can offer you some capital from government sources. As we write this they are current, but they can be changed, eliminated, expanded, or otherwise be altered at any time. Keep in touch with your congressman about new opportunities that congress might open up (particularly in election years).

Now, here's how the government puts it. Here is what the Small Business Administration puts out to instruct people in applying for loans. Of major importance here is the kind of venture they do not grant loans on under any circumstances.

Following the section on Capital Sources in Government you will find listings of addresses of all government offices who are possible sources of capital.

HOW TO APPLY FOR SBA BUSINESS LOANS

Small Business Administration business loans have helped thousands of small firms get started, expand, grow, and prosper.

Small manufacturers , wholesalers, retailers, service concerns, and other businesses may borrow from the Agency to construct, expand, or convert facilities, purchase buildings, equipment, materials, or obtain working capital.

One important restriction applies to all SBA loans. By law, the Agency may not make a loan if a business can obtain funds from a bank or other private source. You, therefore, must first seek private financing before applying to SBA. This means that you must apply to your local bank for a loan. If you live in a large city with more than 200,000 people— you must apply to two banks.

Applicants for loans must agree to comply with SBA regulations that there will be no discrimination in employment or services to the public based on race, color, or national origin.

LENDING OBJECTIVES

SBA, by the direction of Congress, has as its primary goal the preservation of free, competitive enterprise in order to strengthen the Nation's economy.

SBA's specific lending objectives are to (1) stimulate small business in deprived areas; (2) promote minority enterprise opportunity; and (3) promote small business contribution to economic growth and competitive environment.

WHAT IS A SMALL BUSINESS?

For business loan purposes, SBA defines a small business as one that is independently owned and operated, not dominant in its field, and meets employment or sales standards developed by the Agency. For most industries, these standards are as follows:

Manufacturing—small if average employment in the preceding four calendar quarters did not exceed 250, including employees of any affiliates; large if average employment was more than 1,500. If employment exceeded 250 but not 1,500, SBA bases its determination on a specific size standard for the particular industry.

Wholesaling—small if yearly sales are not over $5 to $15 million, depending on the industry.

Retailing and Services—small if annual sales or receipts are not over $1 to $5 million, depending on the industry.

In some instances, SBA uses other standards. Ask the nearest SBA field office which standard applies to your type of business.

GENERAL CREDIT REQUIREMENTS

A loan applicant must:
* Be of good character.
* Show ability to operate his business successfully.
* Have enough capital in an existing firm so that, with an SBA loan, he can operate on a sound financial basis.
* Show the proposed loan is of sound value.
* Show that the past earnings record and future prospects of the firm indicate ability to repay the loan and other fixed debt, if any, out of its profits.
* Be able to provide from his own resources approximately half of the total required funds if the venture is a new business.

AMOUNTS AND TERMS OF LOANS

When the financing is not otherwise available on reasonable terms, SBA may guarantee up to 90% or $350,000, whichever is less, of a bank loan to a small firm.

If the entire loan is not obtainable from a private lender, and if an SBA guaranteed loan is not available, SBA will then consider advancing funds on an immediate participation basis with a bank. SBA will consider making a direct loan only when these other forms of financing are not obtainable.

The Agency's share of an immediate participation loan may not, at the present time, exceed $150,000. Direct loans may not be available due to Federal fiscal restraints.

MATURITY

SBA business loans may be for as long as ten years, except those portions of loans for construction purposes which may have a maturity of 15 years. However, working capital loans usually are limited to six years.

INTEREST

Interest rates on SBA's portion of immediate participations, as well as direct loans, may not exceed 5 ½ percent. Within certain limitations, banks set the interest rate on guaranteed loans and its portion of immediate participation loans.

COLLATERAL

Security for a loan may consist of one or more of these:

* A mortgage on land, a building and/or equipment.[1]
* Assignment of warehouse receipts for marketable Merchandise.
* A mortgage on chattels.
* Guarantees or personal endorsements and, in some instances, assignment of current.

A pledge or mortgage on inventories usually is not satisfactory collateral, unless the inventories are stored in a bonded or otherwise acceptable warehouse.

INELIGIBLE APPLICATIONS

Because it is a public agency using taxpayer's funds, SBA has an unusual responsibility as a lender. It therefore will not make loans:

* If the funds are otherwise available on reasonable terms.
* If the loan is to (a) pay off a loan to a creditor or creditors of the applicant who are inadequately secured and in a position to sustain loss, (b) provide funds for distribution or payment to the principals of the applicant, or (c) replenish funds previously used for such
* If the loan allows speculation in any kind of property.
* If the applicant is a nonprofit enterprise.
* If the loan finances recreational or amusement facilities, unless the

facilities contribute to the health or general well-being of the public.

* If the applicant is a newspaper, magazine, book publishing company, radio broadcasting company, or similar enterprise.

* If any of the gross income of the applicant (or of any of its principal owners) is derived from gambling activities.

* If the loan provided funds to an enterprise primarily engaged in lending or investing.

* If the loan encourages monopoly or is inconsistent with the accepted standards of the American system of free competitive enterprise.

* If the loan is used to relocate a business for other than sound business purposes.

* If the purpose in applying for a loan is to effect a change in ownership of the business. However, loans may be authorized for this purpose if the result would be to: (1) aid in the sound development of a small business or to keep it in operation; (2) contribute to a well-balanced national economy by facilitating ownership of small business concerns by persons whose participation in the free enterprise system has been hampered or prevented because of economic, physical, or social disadvantages, or disadvantages in business or residence locations.

STEP-BY-STEP PROCEDURE

If, after carefully reading the first part of this pamphlet, you are not sure of your eligibility or about meeting SBA's objectives, credit or policy criteria, call or write the nearest SBA office for clarification.

If you believe you qualify and wish to apply for an SBA loan, follow this step-by-step procedure:

FOR ESTABLISHED BUSINESSES

1. Prepare a current financial statement (balance sheet) using all assets and all liabilities of the business— do not include personal items.
2. Have an earnings (profit and loss) statement for the previous full year and for the current period to the date of the balance sheet.
3. Prepare a current personal financial statement of the owner, or each partner or stockholder owning 20% or more of the corporate stock in the business.
4. List collateral to be offered as security for the loan, with your estimate of the present market value of each item.

5. State amount of loan requested and explain exact purposes for which it will be used.

6. Take this material with you and see your banker. Ask for direct bank loan and, if declined, ask the bank to make the loan under SBA's Loan Guaranty Plan or to participate with SBA in a loan. If the bank is interested in an SBA guaranty or participation loan, ask the banker to contact SBA for discussion of your application. In most cases of guaranty or participation loans, SBA will deal directly with the bank.

7. If a guarantee or a participation loan is not available, write or visit the nearest SBA office. SBA has 79 field offices and, in addition, sends loan officers to visit many smaller cities on a regularly scheduled basis or as the need is indicated. To speed matters, make your financial information available when you first write or visit SBA.

FOR NEW BUSINESS

1. Describe in detail the type of business to be established.

2. Describe experience and management capabilities.

3. Prepare an estimate of how much you or others have to invest in the business and how much you will need to borrow.

4. Prepare a current financial statement (balance sheet) listing all personal assets and all liabilities.

5. Prepare a detailed projection of earnings for the first year the business will operate.

6. List collateral to be offered as security for the loan, indicating your estimate of the present market value of each item.

7. Take this material with you and see your banker. Ask for a direct bank loan and, if declined, ask the bank to make the loan under SBA's Loan Guaranty Plan or to participate with SBA in a loan. If the bank is interested in an SBA guaranty or participation loan, ask the banker to contact SBA for discussion of your application. In most cases of guaranty or participation loans, SBA will deal directly with the bank.

8. If a guaranty or a participatin loan is not available, write or visit the nearest SBA office. SBA has 79 field offices and, in addition, sends loan officers to visit many smaller cities on a regularly scheduled basis or as the need is indicated. To speed matters, make your financial information available when you first write or visit SBA.

The following are sources for federal funds for specific purposes. These sources ebb and flow and are offered only as worth investigating, not as genuine sources:

ECONOMIC OPPORTUNITY FARM LOANS

Farmers Home Administration, Department of Agriculture.

Through the extension of credit and supervision enable low-income farm families to acquire and develop farm resources that will increase their incomes and assist them to increase their standard of living.

Who is Eligible: An applicant must (a) be legally competent and the head of a low-income farm family or a legally competent member of such family; (b) have experience or training in the farm enterprise sufficient to assure reasonable prospects of success; (c) possess the character, ability, and industry necessary to carry out the proposed operations; (d) be unable to obtain the credit needed from other sources on reasonable rates and terms.

How to apply: Applicant files Form FHA 410-1, "Application for FHA Services," at the local county office of the Farmers Home Administration. Certification as to eligibility is made by a local county committee of three persons.

For further information contact: (1) The County Farmers Home Administration office; (2) Farmers Home Administration, U.S. Department of Agriculture, Washington, D.C. 20250.

ECONOMIC OPPORTUNITY FARM LOANS TO COOPERATIVES

Department of Agriculture, Farmers Home Administration

Provides 30-year, 4 $\frac{1}{8}\%$ loans to cooperatives that furnish essential business services, supplies, or facilities to low- income rural families.

Who is Eligible: Cooperatives, if (1) 2/3 of members are from low-income rural families living in population areas under 5,500; and (2) they cannot otherwise get credit at rates and terms they can meet; and (3) the services to be supplied are not being adequately provided within the community.

For further information contact: (1) County FHA Office; (2) Farmers Home Administration, Department of Agriculture, Washington, D.C. 20250.

ECONOMIC OPPORTUNITY NONFARM ENTERPRISE LOANS

Farmers Home Administration, Department of Agriculture

Offer direct loans and repayable advances.

Enables low-income farm and other rural families to buy and develop nonfarm business enterprise that will increase their income and help to raise their standard of living.

How to apply: File FHA Form 410-1, "Application for FHA Services," at local county FHA office. Certification regarding eligibility is made by local county committee of three persons.

For further information contact: (1) Regional or local FHA office; (2) Farmers Home Administration, U.S. Department of Agriculture, Washington, D.C. 20250.

FARM OPERATING LOANS

Farmers Home Administration, Department of Agriculture

Offer direct loans and repayable advances.

Provides operating loans up to $35,000 and technical management assistance to farm families to develop and carry on sound farming.

Who is Eligible: (1) U.S. Citizen, living in rural area; (2) Adequate training or experience for proposed operation; (3) Farm background; (4) Demonstrable abilities for operation; (5) After loan is made, own or lease a family farm; (6) Cannot get credit elsewhere at reasonable rates.

For further information contact: (1) County Farmers Home Administration Office; (2) Farmers Home Administration, U.S. Department of Agriculture, Washington, D.C. 20250.

FRANCHISING AS A METHOD OF RAISING CAPITAL

Under certain conditions it might be possible to use franchising as a method of raising capital to expand your business. Obviously, franchising requires some prior experience in the field and the ability to package a business program so it can be operated by others successfully. The franchise method should only be considered where the capital seeker has a pilot project going, for at least six months to a year, in order to develop enough figures and information to organize a franchising package.

Franchising, in brief, is a system of distribution that grants distribution rights to a limited number of selected people. In effect, it allows you to expand the market for your product by using investment money supplied by others.

The main advantage of franchising is that it offers an opportunity to rapidly pyramid a venture into a nationwide, or even world-wide, operation in a very short time. It offers an immediate source of growth capital without diminishing your personal ownership of your company, such as would be necessary in going public and issuing stock. As a franchiser, your only limitations are those you set for granting the franchises, since investment capital comes from them.

Another obvious advantage of franchising is reducing management overhead. Instead of hiring area managers, branch managers, local managers, and having managers managing managers, you have the franchisee managing his own business under the loose supervision of the home office.

As the franchise grows, it also offers the advantage of customer recognition of the company name and/or product. So that customers moving from place to place would tend to shop at the local franchise outlet or buy the local franchise product or service because they had a favorable experience with it at their previous location.

Perhaps the most important aspect of franchising is that it provides a strong success motivation to the franchisee; he's got his time and money invested in the venture, and under normal circumstances will do his best to see to it that investment returns a good profit.

WHAT LENDS ITSELF TO FRANCHISING

In the franchise boom of the sixties, almost everything that the human mind could think of was packaged into a franchise deal. Every con man, soft suede shoe boy, and shady operator jumped into the field with both feet because it offered immense immediate returns, and what happened later was of little or no concern to them. Thus, franchising got a black eye from which it is only now starting to recover. However, franchising has been a successful business method of some of America's largest industries. The petroleum industry has franchised gas stations almost since their inception. The automobile industry franchises dealerships for their products and national TV and Radio Networks sell franchises to the stations to carry the material produced by the Networks. Franchising, in short, is a legitimate, sensible way of doing business if it is properly handled by both franchiser and franchisee.

The most successful franchise operations as a rule are those involving either a patented or otherwise protected product that cannot readily be duplicated by others. Coca Cola is an example; it gives franchises to local bottlers to bottle and distribute Coca Cola in their area. But, they manufacture and distribute the base syrup to the bottler, from a secret formula. Kentucky Fried Chicken is another example of this protected process that gives the franchisee a uniform product backed by national publicity in order to sell his product. Service franchises have been somewhat successful, but it is too easy for people to open service businesses in direct competition with franchise businesses; and since service, particularly to the nonbusiness consumer, is extremely difficult to promote in the sense that people will remember a brand name, the reputation of the individual serviceman is of far more importance than the fact that he represents a national chain of some sort. Such service franchises as "Duraclean" and other rug and upholstery cleaning franchise operations have been advertising for years to sell their franchises, and yet if you would take a poll among housewives you would find few, if any, recognize the name of any of these national service organizations. Franchises selling products or services to businesses are fairly common, and somewhat more promotable than those to a broad range of consumers. This is because you have a much smaller audience to work with.

In essence, the successful franchise represents something unique. If what you have is not unique, it will probably be very difficult to sell franchises.

THE PILOT OPERATION

The key to proving the value of the franchise will be in your operation of a pilot program at an average location using the same methods and techniques you will later sell to the franchisor in his package. As we said before, you will need at least six months to a year's actual business operating experience in order to properly develop the franchise package. Because of restrictions placed on franchise selling due to the excesses in the 1960's, you will almost be required to show a successful pilot operation before you will be allowed to sell franchises in most states.

The pilot operation will give you two things: figures you can use for future planning and setting your franchise package price, and assistance in selling the franchise package to franchisees. You can bring them to the pilot operation, allow them to see it working, and use it as a demonstration sales tool in order to sell the franchise package. It is important that the total franchise package be developed from this operation and that it include everything from the accounting system right on down to the number of pens and pencils there will be needed to get started. Such things as signs, trademarks, advertising programs, publicity programs, grand openings, anniversary sales, cash registers, other tools and equipment , hours of operation, days of operation, and every other detail of business operation carefully analyzed and developed in the pilot operation.

FRANCHISEES NEED HELP

When you sell a franchise to a franchisee, you are going to have to provide him with more than a location and the necessary furniture, tools, and equipment to operate it. He is going to need a great deal of assistance, because in most cases he will be inexperienced in the type of venture he is about to operate. It is in your own best interest to see to it that he is properly trained, guided, and instructed so that your franchise operations have the same level of efficiency and the same methods of merchandising wherever they are. This creates a customer following, and no matter where people go once they are used to trading with a franchise organization will automatically take their business to the location in a new locality should they move. For this reason, all franchises should be operated at as nearly the same level of efficiency and productivity as is possible. The methods of training, controls, and guidance will be obvious once you are operating your pilot program.

THE FRANCHISE AGREEMENT

The basis for providing all the things necessary for a successful franchise operation will be found in this franchise agreement. You will need to retain a knowledgeable and astute attorney to develop a contract that will be both saleable and protective of both parties involved.

One of your major concerns in the contract will be the right to terminate the contract should the franchisee fail to measure up to minimum standards set in the contract. Often these can be stipulated as failure to do a certain amount of gross business, failure to use the franchise name, trademarks and other pertinences properly, failure to keep records and send in reports that are required on the operation, failure to follow quality and control procedures as set forth to maintain a standard level of operation, and/or failure to generally abide by reasonable business standards in the operation of the franchise. This right of termination is necessary in order to protect all the other franchisees in the organization.

The second point will be the franchisee's right to sell or transfer his rights to someone else. Most responsible franchisers will assist a dissatisfied or otherwise unwilling franchisee to dispose of his franchise. It is in your interest to do so, because you can help get someone in who will be a successful operator and will also assist in rapidly getting rid of incompetent or unreliable people.

Mostly allied to the right of sale will be the right of termination. As a rule, franchises are granted for a period of years ranging from 1 to 100, depending on the initial arrangement. When the franchise comes up for renewal, you should have a right at that time to buy out or otherwise terminate an unsatisfactory franchise operation; but you should make it simple and easy for franchisees to renew as almost an automatic process.

One thing to be wary of is the so-called "directed purchases" program. This is the deal that got most franchisers into deep trouble in the 1960's. They forced franchisees to buy equipment, supplies, and other materials from them as the sole source of supply. The franchisee was not allowed to go out into the open market and shop for a price for supplies and equipment that he needed. This resulted in class action suits that cost franchisers many millions of dollars. It is ruled, and rightly so, as a restraint of trade. So in your franchise agreement, make it clear that the franchisee has a right to shop for competitive products or services (given the same standard of quality) and the right to buy them should he feel they are a better deal than you can offer. For this reason, it is not wise to base a franchise sale on hope for future sales of supplies, equipment, and other miscellaneous material.

Other items of the agreement are the agreements of the franchisee not to compete directly with you for a period of X years; a very important one is "protection against third party claims" in which the franchisee is contracted out as an independent contractor and is not an agent or employee of the franchiser. Have the lawyer draw this paragraph very carefully, because otherwise you can wind up with a big lawsuit as a result of a negligent franchisee. The franchiser should have some right in the contract to prevent the franchisee from carrying directly competing products, inferior products, or otherwise doing things to cause a lessening of the value of the franchise name. In stipulating prices the franchisee can charge, it is common practice not to direct specific prices be charged with specific items, but rather to set a maximum price which each franchisee can charge for a given item, product and/or service. This way the franchisee is free to reduce prices but cannot overcharge the public.

In short, in the agreement do what is necessary to protect yourself as the franchiser, but allow the franchisee enough leeway so that later you will not get into legal difficulties because of your really rigid restrictions.

PACKAGE

PRICING THE FRANCHISE PACKAGE

The price you will charge for the franchise package is generally based on two factors. First, how profitable the pilot operation has been and how profitable you can expect the franchised operation to be. Second, the cost of opening the business and carrying it to a break-even point.

In your pricing of the franchise, you are obviously going to put in a price for the value of the franchise package itself. This is over and above the actual hardware, buildings, equipment, and so forth that is involved. You are going to collect money for what you know and what you have learned in the pilot operation. This amount is your capital for future expansion. This is the sole reason for starting a franchised operation in order to expand your working capital. Therefore, as a rule of thumb, you could set this price at roughly five times one year's net profit to the owner. Thus if the owner makes $10,000 net profit after paying himself a reasonable salary for his services, the franchise package price is worth $50,000. While this might be subject to negotiation that is a fair price to offer for a business of that kind.

The way to capitalize quickly with a franchise operation and have net capital inflow is to sell master franchises for an area...You sell, say, California, Oregon & Washington with a projection of 50 franchised units to an individual or company for $50,000 ($1000 a unit), they in turn sell the individual franchisee and collect $12,500 on each unit sold plus 1% of gross of each unit.

The $50,000 is net capital to you as you have no commitment for hardware or inventory, and the sales program has no net expense to you.

If you are going to promote franchise sales, you will need the help of an attorney to clear the program with state laws and possibly the S.E.C....it's no longer the wheeling- dealing caveat emptor deal it used to be. But, create a good package, and you can go from zero to a million in a few months.

BIBLIOGRAPHY

Franchise System for Establishing Independent Retail Outlets. Davis J. Schwartz, Georgia State College of Business Administration , Atlanta, GA 30303. August 1959. 25 pp. Free.

Partners for Profit, A Study of Franchising. American Management Association, Inc. 135 W. 50th Street, New York, NY 10020. 1966. 128 pp. $6.75 ($4.50 AMA members).

The Franchise Boom—How You Can Profit In It. Harry Kursh, Prentice-Hall, Inc. Englewood Cliffs, NJ 07631. 273 pp. $7.95.

The Economic Base of Franchising, Louis P. Bucklin. (1970) University of California, Berkeley, Working Paper Series— Research Program in Marketing, No. 62.

Franchising : New Problems with an Old Concept, James A. Murphy. Bulletin of Business Research, Vol. 46, No. 6, June 1971, pp. 1-3, 5. Ohio State University.

A Model for Determining Cash Balance Requirements in the Franchise Operation, Marvin A. Jolson and Takao Hoshi. Atlanta Economic Review, Vol. 21, No. 9, September 1971, pp. 34-37, 46. Georgia State University.

A Perspective on Franchising: The Design of an Effective Relationship, P. Ronald Stephenson and Robert G. House. Business Horizons, Vol. 14, No. 4, August 1971, pp. 35-42. Indiana University.

Franchising, Richard K. Ransom. (1969) 9 pp. University of Toledo.

The Impact of Recent Antitrust Decisions Upon Franchise Marketing, Donald F. Dixon. MSU Business Topics. Vol. 17, No. 2, Spring 1969, pp. 68-79. Michigan State University.

The Nature of Franchising, Parts I and II, B. J. Linder and Wayne Lucas. Atlanta Economic Review, Vol. 19, No. 10, October 1969, pp. 12-14; No. 11, November 1969, pp. 18-21. Georgia State University.

The Scope of the Franchised Marketing, Thomas W. Speh. Miami Business Review, Vol. 40, No. 4, July 1969, pp. 1-4. Miami University.

ALTERNATIVE MONEY SOURCES

In addition to the major money sources we have covered thus far, there are additional sources of capital for methods of creating capital available to the entrepreneur.

FACTORING

If you have an operation that will be carrying heavy accounts receivable, and the length of time from sale to collection might cause a major strain on your cash, you can use factoring services to ease that strain.

If you are going to be doing business with large, or well-rated companies, the factor will buy your receivables at a discount, advance you the cash for immediate use, and be responsible for the collection of the accounts himself. The factor can do his billing directly to the account, or he can send the bills in your name , have them sent to a post office box which he controls, collect the checks when they come in, and be responsible for his own books and records. A factor operates on a notification, or non-notification basis. Notification simply means the factor lets the account know he is factoring the account and all monies should come to him. The non-notification system involves the factor billing in your name without letting the account know the accounts are factored.

As a rule, the factor charges anywhere from ¼ of 1% to 2% of the net invoice amounts for his services. Sometimes, he advances money against the invoices prior to the date the money is due from the firm billed; he requires interest on the funds so advanced. Thus, if you gave a $1000 account to a factor on the first of the month, he would discount it from $5 to $20; and if he advanced the funds at the time, you would pay interest on the money advanced up to the due date of the invoice (usually the 10th of the following month). This is in effect a capital investment in your business which can give you cash without giving up equity or incurring long-term debt.

Other factoring services are secured inventory loans (factor advances money to buy inventory which is pledged to him and released as sales are made), letters of credit (authorizations to make drafts on the issuer up to specified amounts), and on occasion will finance export shipments.

Still another form of factoring is called "drop ship factoring." In this system, the factor guarantees payments for orders from suppliers. This allows a company with no line of credit to order enough material to take advantage of price breaks on larger orders.

INVENTORY FINANCING

There are commercial credit firms who finance inventories in a similar way a pawnbroker operates. The inventory is hocked to the financer and released as payments are made by the borrower.

This system is often worked through public warehouses. The goods are placed in a public warehouse, and the seller redeems the goods from the warehouse as sales are made. As a matter of convenience, the inventory financing firm may set up "field warehouses." These are warehouses which are actually on the premises of the borrowing firm. The space is leased from the borrower and secured by the finance company and is often a common practice for the financing company to hire a member of the borrowing company's staff to man the warehouse and release the goods as required. This method of financing allows a company short on operating capital to maintain a substantial inventory without incurring a long-term debt.

CONSUMER INSTALLMENT FINANCING

Consumer installment financing is a form of factoring in that the finance company purchases the accounts from the seller and collects the money themselves. Banks and small loan companies often involve themselves in these types of operation. Most familiar are automobile loans, furniture loans, and other large ticket items where the bank purchases the account from the seller, issues a payment book to the consumer, and the customer pays the bank or finance company directly. In some large credit type retail operations, a consumer sales finance company may actually have an office on the premises of the seller. They run the credit checks, accept the accounts and handle payments there, and appear to the customer to be a part of the sales firm itself.

REDISCOUNTING

Rediscounting is where a small finance company gets funds from a bigger finance company to buy retail paper. It is often possible for a group of retailers to get together and form a rediscounting agency to handle paper in this fashion.

FLOOR PLANNING

Commercial finance companies often engage in floor planning arrangements. The sales finance company pays the factory invoice for merchandise that goes on a retailer's sales floor. When the merchandise is sold, the retailer pays the finance company rather than the manufacturer. As a rule, floor planning is part and parcel of purchasing retail paper. By putting the merchandise on the retailer's floor, the sales finance company generates loans. For this reason they will often charge a low rate of interest on money used to obtain merchandise for this purpose.

INDUSTRIAL TIME SALES

This is a service most often used in service trades and occasionally in retailing and manufacturing. It involves the purchase of capital goods by time payments. Thus, a service company in the janitorial field might need floor cleaners or expensive rug cleaning equipment and so forth and purchases them on a time sales plan similar to that they use to purchase an automobile or truck.

The dealer usually sells industrial time sales paper on a full recourse basis to the finance company. This means if the purchaser fails to make payments, the dealer agrees to buy back the paper from the finance company at full value, less payments made. There is also a limited recourse arrangement whereby the purchaser of this paper will limit the contingent liability of the dealer by periods of time. This means that should ten or twelve major accounts default all at the same time, the requirement to repay the finance all at once might bankrupt the dealer. So arrangements are made whereby the dealer will not become liable for more than a specified amount of recourse paper in a specified period of time. Another form of this type of financing is called the re-purchase agreement. This is where the finance company actually repossesses the equipment from the default buyer, and the dealer buys it back from the finance company. This is contingent liability but rather a straight re-purchase agreement.

In this field of commercial finance you will run across the "uniform commercial code." This is a uniform contract under which financing is made and was drafted by the American Law Institute and is effective in almost all fifty states today. In general it covers these areas.

Article 1. Covers the purpose and policy of the uniform code.

Article 2. Covers the sales of goods.

Article 3. Covers commercial paper, checks, drafts, notes, trade acceptances, or other obligations to pay money.[1]

Article 4. Covers bank deposits and collections.

Article 5. Covers letters of credit (import, export).[1]

Article 6. Covers bulk transfers—this covers legal problems that develop where businesses are sold without creditors being notified or paid.

Article 7. Covers warehouse receipts, bills of lading, documents of title—rights and obligations of issues, builders, and transferees.

Article 8. Covers investments and securities—stocks, bonds, and debentures.

Article 9. Covers secured transactions, sales of accounts, contracts rights and chattel papers, commercial finance and factoring laws.[1]

If you are going to be dealing in any kind of commercial papers, you should have a copy of the uniform commercial code and be familiar with it. One of the largest and most active commercial finance companies is the SIT Corporation, 575 Madison Ave., New York, NY; and if you write them on your business letterhead, they will send you a book of information about commercial financing services.

INVESTMENT BANKERS

The investment banker, as opposed to the commercial banker, is a supplier of long-term capital or a finder of long-term capital for companies who need it.

The investment banker is primarily interested in what is termed "private placement" of corporation stock. This means that a corporation will sell a block of its stock or will borrow money from an institution in exchange for a "kicker" in the form of stock options, convertible bonds, etc.

The investment banker may also decide to underwrite a new stock issue if he feels the market is right and the condition of the company warrants it.

The services of an investment banker are primarily used by companies with an operating business who have proven management, a solid growth picture, and are in an industry which has investment interest.

The investment banker would seldom be interested in a new venture.

If you feel you have an opportunity that would interest an investment banker in securing private placement stock in your company, or purchasing stock, or providing a long-term loan, you can get in contact with one through your commercial banker.

INVESTMENT CLUBS

One overlooked source of capital in your locality may be an active investment club. These are groups of people who are engaged in investing in the stock market and/or types of income producing investments. The opportunity to get in on the ground floor or a new enterprise, and particularly one that is local, may have a great deal of appeal to these investors. To locate one in your area you can write the National Association of Investment Clubs, 1515 East 11 Mile Road, Royal Oak, MI 48067. They can provide you with the name of an investment club in your area.

LEASING

One way to conserve capital in a start-up situation is to lease capital goods and equipment rather than purchasing it. There are many leasing companies who would be interested in producing long-term leases of such goods. Your local banker will have knowledge of those operating in your area.

Another approach to creating capital through leasing, is to form a leasing group of your own. These would generally be people in high-income brackets who would pool funds to purchase equipment and lease it to you for your manufacturing processes. They would, in turn, get immediate returns in the form of tax rebates for a tax credit on the purchase of new equipment, then could engage in accelerated depreciation of the equipment, and finally after it is fully depreciated they could sell it to you or lease new equipment for you. The advantage of this type of arrangement from the investor's standpoint is that the depreciation and tax credits are available to him as income tax deductions which he would not otherwise receive.

The type of people most interested in forming a pool of this kind are professional men with high taxable incomes and few deductions.

ISSUING COMMERCIAL PAPER

If your company will have a net worth of 1.2 million dollars and up, you may be able to sell commercial paper, which are short-term (a a few days up to 9 months), unsecured notes which are purchased by business and financial investors with surplus short-term funds.

To issue this paper, you must get a D & B rating. As a rule, firms with 25 million in assets get prime ratings, 5 million get desirable ratings, and 1.2 to 5 million get satisfactory. In order to successfully issue this paper, the issuer must have a line or credit equal to the amount of paper issued.

The market in commercial paper of smaller companies is regional, and dealers charge from $3/8$ to 1% for selling it.

This can be a less expensive way to raise funds than a short-term loan from a commercial bank which may require a somewhat high compensating balance. Obviously, this is no way for a new venture to raise funds, but you may keep this in mind after you are established. You can easily find out who deals in commercial paper in your area from your own banker. There are some in each region of the country.

CONSUMER FINANCE COMPANIES

One fact not well known is that consumer finance companies (whose interest rates run as high as 32%) have about 10% of their loan portfolio with small businessmen.

This, of course, is the court of last resort. But if you have some sort of security, some kind of income, and any kind of credit rating at all, they will make loans when no one else will.

INSURANCE COMPANIES

Insurance companies are sources of long-term loans for well-established business firms with a record of operating profits over a period of years. They are not sources of capital for "start up" situations however. They will consider loans as low as $250,000 and the sky is the limit. They like long-term arrangements, and 10 to 15 years is the term of their loans as a rule.

On some occasions, if you have a sound track record in your present business and want some long-term money for expansion, then the insurance company might take a flyer with you for an "equity kicker" on the loan. This means a convertible bond or warrants.

One way to get insurance companies interested in a deal is to have a real estate sale leaseback potential in it. That is, you buy a factory, office building or some other type of real estate, they (the insurance company) will buy it, and lease it back to you on a long-term lease. This gives you a capital inflow without reducing your equity or paying interest; and, of course, lease costs are deductable business expenses.

All in all, insurance companies are money sources only for the already successful business operation, and only then if the track record is highly favorable. Your best bet in contacting them is through an investment banker or other intermediary who will know who lends what for how much.

CAPITAL RAISING SYSTEMS

The idea of raising capital is to get the money you need on the most favorable terms possible. These systems offer capital on the least advantageous terms, but if all else fails may be a way of getting the money.

Perhaps the oldest method under the last-resort system is the U.S. Government bond method. You advise your investors that they can invest in your firm without risking the loss of a dime of their money. They invest $1000 in your venture, you purchase a $1000 U.S. Savings Bond in their name, take the difference in price (which is $250 since the bond costs $750) and put it in the venture, and give the investor credit for $1000. If the business fails, he'll be able to cash in the bond at maturity for his investment; if the business prospers, he gets both the bond money back plus the value of his investment. In effect, he can have his cake and eat it too. The problem is, of course, that you pay dearly for the funds, and the investor is on the hook for a long time either way.

The co-signer method is another way of getting people involved without having to put up any money themselves. You get them to co-sign notes at the bank or from a private party for the needed funds. It is a fact of life that people will co-sign notes who won't put up cash. This obviously is a system that can be used for limited capital needs. The best way to operate this program is a chain method. Get one person to agree to go along if you can't get a number of others. Thus, when you get agreements from a given number, you go back·for the signatures.

The sale leaseback method of getting money is also to be considered under this system. First, you have to have something to sell and take back a lease on. Real Estate with a building is the best bet. You find such a property and arrange to take an option on it. Obviously, you have to get it for less money than it will sell for to give you operating capital. The way to do this is to get the owner to take an interest in your venture for the difference or give him a note for the difference to be paid off at a future time. Then you arrange to sell the property and give the buyer a lease at favorable terms on it. This obviously takes some wheeling and dealing, but if you can get something in the $200,000 range, you can pick up anywhere from $25,000 to $50,000 in capital with that arrangement.

The double loan system. Let's say that you are only good for a $5000 loan and you need $15,000. You arrange with a relative, or group of them, to borrow the $15,000, and you borrow the $5000 yourself. Then you give them the $5000 to pay off the $15,000 loan for say 18 months, and you pay off the $5000 yourself. Then at the end of the year, you take over the $15,000 loan or re-finance it With another loan if you need more time.

The credit card scam is an unethical, if not illegal, method of getting money for a business, but it's been done. You arrange with friends or relatives to purchase something from you for the limit of their credit card liability the day after the due date on the cards. Thus, they won't get billed for 30 days and have another 30 days to pay...at the end of 45 days they return the merchandise and you give them credit on their cards for the amount. In this way you have the use of bank funds (who sponsor the credit cards for 45 to 60 days), and you can work it all over again if the bank doesn't close you out.

If you have a small corporation, you might work the letter stock loan angle. In this system you arrange for a private loan, and for a sweetner to make it interesting, you give the lender some letter stock, which is the right to a given number of those shares of stock when you go public with your corporation. Under this arrangement, you will probably have to set a date for the public offering, but this method allows you in effect to sell stock without SEC approval since it is only a promise, not actually shares. You can give the lender the option of getting back the loan with interest or taking the stock instead, so that you only have one obligation at the due date. This arrangement is often of interest to professional men and high-income people because they can qualify their letter stock for capital gains. To give you an idea of how lucrative this can be to the lender, if they lend you $10,000 and get letter stock for the right to 10,-000 shares of stock, when you go public at say $5 a share, they get $50,000 in stock value, which they can sell and realize $27,500 in net profit on their investment, and get interest on their loan as well. Of course, you lose the $50,000 to get a $10,000 loan, so it's costly.

The penny stock route is another way to go... By issuing stock at a dime a share, and keeping the financing to $50,000 or less you can go public without SEC registration...To sell penny stock you issue 100 share lots ($10 a throw) and then start the whole town trading in it...sell it at fairs, to businessmen, housewives, professional people, etc...almost everyone will take a flyer if they know about it...The key is getting lots of publicity.

The tax dodge method can be worked on occasion. If you have a fat loss on your books, you form a limited partnership with some high-income people at the end of the year. Let them take the loss from their incomes and put back half into your venture after the first of the year as investments...this way they are only risking government tax money, and you can get the funds for very desirable terms. Example, say you can show $100,000 loss. Get five partners to take $20,000 each of the loss from their income (a $20,000 bonus for them), then after the tax year is over, they can put $10,000 each into the business which would then be incorporated and stock issued.

There are variations on all these, but they are courses of last resort and the devices of desperation. Far better to plan your program and raise the capital on the open market so that you will have all the funds you need to profitably operate your venture.

TO SUM UP

There are ways for the small businessman to get operating capital, and raise money. We have outlined some of the best of them, and should you need money in the future for business purposes, it would be well to review this information because it has been used successfully thousands of times by small businessmen and particularly successful S.O.B. type small businessmen to get all the money they need whenever they needed it.

CHAPTER 4
HOW TO TURN OFF THE RED TAPE MACHINE

How To Turn Off
The Red Tape Machine

A vast army of piss ants, called bureaucrats, armed with paper clubs are swarming over the nation with a dedicated zeal to beating society to its knees.

Over 7,000 new bureaucratic regulations came out of Washington, D.C. alone in one year. They had state, city, county bureaucratic edicts in all 50 states, and you could total upwards of 50,000 new regulations introduced each and every year nationwide.

One of the chief victims of this mindless ant army is the small businessman. He is harassed by everything from Osha to a city sign inspector, from the IRS to the county assessor and city license bureau, from the FTC to local county business bureaus. He is having his ass kicked-in every time he stands up.

His options are few. But, he has one that can and occasionally does work. When hit by a bureaucrat with a regulation that is both ambiguous and debatable, he can try to change the game.

Instead of yelling obsenities or paining and grumbling about it, he can come back swinging with everything he's got. This counter offensive is something that bureaucrats are seldom quite ready for, and many times they will back away and the S.O.B. has won again.

In this chapter we will try to tell you how some of these techniques operate and why they allowed the S.O.B. to emerge victorious.

THE INTERNAL REVENUE SERVICE

The Internal Revenue Service came into being by the 16th Amendment to the Constitution, ratified February 25, 1913. It says, "The Congress shall have the power to lay and collect taxes on incomes, from whatever source derived, without apportionment among the several states, without regard to any census or enumeration.

When ratification of this amendment was being argued in the Virginia House of Delegates, on March 3, 1910, Richard E. Bird, speaking in the House of Delegates made a prophecy about what was to come.

"The 16th Amendment means that the state must give up a legitimate and long-established source of revenue and yield it to the Federal Government."

"It means that the state actually invites the Federal Government to invade its territory, to oust its jurisdiction and to establish federal dominion within the inner most citadel of the of the commonwealth."

"This amendment will do what even the 14th and 15th Amendments did not do — it will extend the federal power source to reach the citizen in the ordinary business of life. A hand from Washington will be stretched out and placed upon every man's business; the eye of the federal inspector will be in every man's counting house."

"The law will of necessity have inquisitoral features, it will provide penalties. It will create a complicated machinery."

"Under it, businessmen will be hauled into courts distant from their homes."

"Heavy fines imposed by distant and unfamiliar tribunals will constantly menace the tax payer."

"An army of federal inspectors, spies and detectives will descend upon the state. They will compel men of business to show their books and disclose the secrets of their affairs. They will dictate forms of bookkeeping. They will require statements and affidavits. On the one hand the inspector can blackmail the tax payer and on the other, he can profit by selling his secret to his competitor."

"When the federal government gets a strangle hold on the individual businessman, state lines will exist no where but on maps. Its urgence will everywhere supervise the commercial life of the states....I am not willing by any voluntary act to give up revenue which the state of Virginia herself needs, nor to surrender that measure of state's rights which was, and the construction of the federal courts have permitted to remain."

It is worth noting that Virginia did not ratify the 16th Amendment.

This prophecy has more than come true. This amendment has created a maze of laws and regulations consisting of over a quarter million words — 2,000 sections, 900 pages and even the IRS itself does not understand it. They now state they will not be responsible for any advice they give a taxpayer on taking deductions or preparing his tax forms. They reserve the right to give him advice, and then turn around and collect money from him contrary to the advice they gave. This is assininity, carried to the level of Alice in Wonderland.

When all of the business people who we've interviewed on the subject of the IRS and audits of income tax returns were asked, the consensus was that the best way to deal with the IRS in these matters is not to fool with them directly, but to either have your tax accountant, or preferably a lawyer familiar with tax matters represent you with the IRS.

The reasons for these are two-fold. First, the taxpayer is liable to give more information than he is legally required to do in conversations with IRS agents. Particularly if nervous or frightened, he waives many of his rights inadvertantly, and allows the IRS to delve into matters with which they were not originally concerned. The second reason is that he is not usually fully aware of his rights, and is often intimidated by the agent's statements as to what is or is not taxable, and inferences that there are heavy penalties unless full cooperation is given.

Most such intimidation can be put upon third parties, and you need not even be present while these discussions take place.

There are two types of audits conducted by the IRS, one is the civil, and the other criminal. As a rule, the agent is simply interested in civil matters, and collecting money for disallowed deductions or under paid income. The special or intelligence agent is involved in fraud cases, and if you are aware of such an agent investigating you, you must immediately go to a lawyer and say nothing more of any kind to the IRS.

Tax returns are selected for closer study by the IRS for several reasons. First, all returns are checked for accuracy of arithmetic, and whether the proper schedules and forms are attached.

Second, each return is given a computer analysis, which compares the return with standard models that have been set up to show which returns may be suspect, and enable the IRS to collect more dollars from.

Third, there are specific types of businesses and situations which the computers indicate are most often ripe for audit.

Fourth, the computer compares the taxpayers information concerning extra income received from second jobs, interest, fees, dividends etc., and if the information received by the IRS does not match that of the taxpayer, there is probably sure to be an audit.

Fifth, people who call attention to themselves by doing unusual things; file an extra claim for a refund; file an amended tax return; requesting a closing agreement on a previous year's taxes; offering a compromise settlement of taxes; requesting a tax rule or determination letter from the IRS about some investment or business venture; writing books on how to save taxes; and possibly writing strong letters of complaint about treatment from IRS personnel.

Sixth, tips received from informants.

Seventh, random selection to keep the troops busy.

YOUR LEGAL RIGHTS DURING AN AUDIT

Your first right is the fifth amendment right against self-incrimination. This states, *"no person. . .shall be compelled in any criminal case to be witness against himself."* Using your right under the fifth amendment, you do not have to give up any of your records if you feel the audit would in any way put you in a position of being found guilty of tax fraud or tax evasion.

The second right is to be represented in audits by the tax advisor. He or she must be a public accountant, CPA, attorney or enrolled in practice before the IRS, and can argue your case before the IRS through all the stages of initial contact and appeal. This individual can always be present with you during audit agents procedures. If you give power of attorney to your advisor, he can represent you alone without your being present. You have a right to be treated decently and objectively by the IRS agent. You are a citizen, and you can demand the IRS treat you in a courteous and respectful manner. They should operate within the laws, and apply the spirit of the law and make issues of any material matters where there is general reason for an inquiry being consistent with existing laws and interpretation of these laws. In other words, you don't have to settle for abuse or threats from an IRS agent during an audit.

Third, you have a right of appeal from any agent's decision. If you fail to come to an agreement over the issues, there are many appeal procedures within the IRS and in tax court you can use to try to get the verdict changed. That failing, you can go to the federal district court, and higher courts, with an appeal.

Fourth, you do not have to allow the audit to take place in your home or place of business. The IRS prefers to have their agents conduct their audits in your domicile or office, but you do not have to allow it. Instead, you can use the IRS offices or the office of your tax advisor or attorney.

Fifth, you have a right to prior notice of an audit. If an agent appears without an appointment and demands to conduct his initial inquiry or audit on your premises, you have the right to say no and set a definite time mutually convenient to you and the agent at his office or that of your representative.

Sixth, you have a right to obtain copies of past year's tax returns from the IRS. For payment of a small fee, you can request any year's tax return you require, and if the IRS has it on file they will send it to you. Just send a certified letter to the closest district director's office or an IRS service center. As a rule such returns are kept for individual and partnership returns at least seven years, and supposedly, all corporate income tax returns and estate or gift tax returns are kept indefinitely.

Seventh, you have a right to deny anyone the right to search your premises or seize your property without a warrant. Only when presented with a warrant issued on probable cause and supported by oath or affirmation are you required to yield your premises or property.

Eighth, you need not submit to constant and unnecessary re-examinations of your books and records. While this is a somewhat nebulous right, (the IRS can request an additional examination by notifying the taxpayer that such examination is necessary) the IRS is allowed only one inspection of the taxpayers books or accounts. But since further demands are made, you have a fifth amendment right to fall back on.

Ninth, you have an attorney client priviledge. If you have revealed your tax situation to an attorney, and given him books and records to explain that position, these are inviolate. They cannot be seized or attached due to the confidentiality of the attorney client relationship. But, this does not apply to tax accountants. Any records of yours they have on hand, can be seized by the IRS upon demand.

Tenth, all people subject to audit and given testimony under the Administrative Procedure Act, can request and are entitled to a copy of the transcript of such testimony. This includes anything a taxpayer may have said himself as a witness.

HOW A TAXPAYER SHOULD PROCEED WHEN FACED WITH AUDIT

You have a partial list of your rights as a citizen and taxpayer when faced with an audit. It is a personal decision about how you wish to proceed, but as we stated previously, most small businessmen who have faced this situation, feel that you are better off to obtain expert help in dealing with the IRS. However, should the amount be small and the argument over a single type of deduction, you may well want to proceed by yourself. If so, stick to the subject, and if the agent starts going on a fishing expedition asking about other non-related matters, you should back off at that point and tell him either you will discuss what you came to discuss, or get your tax accountant and lawyer to come into the proceeding. While you may have some hesitation in offending or making the agent irate, you are only doing what any prudent individual would do when faced with an unknown situation.

THE SMALL CLAIMS TAX COURT

If you are involved in a small tax case, in which the amount of the deficiency or the amount of the claimed over-payment placed in dispute does not exceed $1500 for any taxable year or $1500 in the case of estate taxes, you have a right of appeal to the small claims tax court.

This comes under Rule 172: election of small tax case procedure under Code Section 7463.

You file a petition (a sample of which you will find in the appendix), and if the court agrees it is a small case, you will be notified of the time and and place of trial, or preliminary hearings. There is a $10 filing fee, payable at the time of filing. The taxpayer must file his tax court petition within 90 days of the date on the IRS 90-day deficiency notice which is sent to him by certified mail. Failure to do this eliminates his right to use the tax court procedures.

There are two main advantages for the taxpayer representing himself in small tax court, first, it is an informal proceeding and virtually anything he has is admissable as evidence. Second, there is no appeal from the decision by either party. Neither the taxpayer nor the IRS can appeal the decision to a higher court, which gives a final solution to the problem once and for all. The higher tax courts can start a daisy chain of appeals either by the taxpayer or the IRS, clear to the Supreme Court.

If going to higher tax courts is necessary, then you need a tax expert to represent you.

BE ON THE SIDE OF THE ANGELS

If you decide you are going to resent or fight the IRS, be sure your are on safe and firm ground. So, if you are right, then attack.

HOW TO INTIMIDATE A BUREAUCRAT

One S.O.B. we talked to, related a hilarious story about a little act that he put on when summoned into the presence of some over-bearing bureaucrat to discuss some fuzzy regulation the bureaucrat felt he was violating.

His story went something like this: "When I received the summons, I looked it over and decided it was alot of bullshit. So I called the local college and had them send me a law student who wanted to make a few dollars for doing some research. He came to my office, and I gave him the letter I had received and instructed him to go look up legal precedence that would prove the law was both illegal, immoral and fattening. I instructed him to return these to me written in the deepest legalese he could summon, and gave him $20 for his trouble.

He allowed it would take him about a week to get the material together and typed up, so I called the bureaucrat and made an appointment for the following week.

I then called a friend of mine who was currently unemployed, but who was an imposing looking gentleman; tall, gun-metal gray hair, piercing blue eyes and one of the worst flakes I ever knew in my life. I had him dress up in his best dark blue suit, white shirt, conservative tie and well polished shoes, and got him an imposing looking attache case. Then I got my wife's baby sitter, who was barely literate enough to write her own name, and told her to come dressed for the office on the appointed day.

We drove to the building, and appeared in the bureaucrat's office at the appointed time. Upon being announced, we marched into his office, me first, my flaky friend second and the baby sitter third. We had provided the baby sitter with a note book and pencil, and told her to sit there and make marks that look like shorthand on the notebook.

Upon entering the office, without being asked, I arranged the chairs in a semi-circle around the bureaucrats desk with me on the left, my imposing looking flake in the middle and the baby sitter on the right. We sat down in unison, and I opened my brief case and pulled out a tape recorder and ceremoniously set it on the desk of the bureaucrat, punched the record button and announced, this recording is being made in the office of Mr. So and So, Commissioner of Such and Such, and gave the date. I looked him right in the eye and said, 'I am making a tape recording of this meeting in order that there will not be any misunderstanding later about what was said in this room.'

Then I leaned back in my chair, and looking at my flaky friend, 'are you ready, George?'

He nodded and pulled out a long yellow legal pad and a ball point pen, put the attache case on his knees and poised the pen over the paper ready to take notes.

I looked back at the bureaucrat who was sitting there with his mouth open, and said, 'now sir, state your case.'

You could see the red spreading above his collar, working its way up into his cheeks, as he stared at the tape recorder like a victim would stare at a cobra. Finally, he cleared his throat, and decided he would proceed, though obviously unsure of what he was doing.

He roughly stated his case, pointing out that I was a willfull violater of the first nine commandments, plus the regulation he was talking about.

When he ran out of breath, I stared at him and said, 'is that your case?'

He snarled a snappy 'yes'.

I turned to my flake and said, 'do you have our legal research there, George?'

The flake nodded, opened the attache case and pulled out the file the law student had prepared for me. I took the report, flipped through the pages casually, then tossed them on the desk in front of the bureaucrat. I said, 'are you familiar with these legal citations pertaining to the regulation you have accused me of violating?'

He picked up the report gingerly, and his eyes turned a little glassy as he attempted to translate the legalese into some sort of sensible information. His face got a little redder, and he laid the report back down and looked at me and said, 'I am not a lawyer."

'Well," I said, 'I happen to have a good one'. I looked meaningfully at the flake.

'Since you have accused me of a violation of a law, I must inquire as to your expertise in this field.'

I then looked at the baby sitter, and said, 'Miss Jones, take this information down'. She opened her steno pad and poised her pencil over the paper.

I looked back at the bureaucrat, and said, 'how long have you worked for this department?'

He mumbled something like seven years, and I came back with 'and what did you do before that?'

He mumbled something else, and I continued questioning him about his education, background, what legal basis he was accusing me on, etc. As I continued, he began to get extremely agitated, and snarled something about refusing to answer any more of my damn questions.

I then said, 'very well', got up and walked about the back of the chair to stand beside the baby sitter.

'Miss Jones', I said, 'take this letter'. I then proceeded to dictate a letter stating that I was being harassed and abused by this bureaucrat, that I considered this defamatory, that I considered him incompetent, and that I would prepare a suit against both him and his agency.

Then I looked at the flake and said, 'I think $200,000 would be about right, don't you, George?'

The flake nodded solemnly and wrote something on his yellow legal pad.

I then walked back to the desk, turned off the tape recorder and shoved it in my brief case, looked the bureaucrat in the eye, and said, 'if I hear any more about this, you will be hearing from my attorney, you have heard my letter, and I can assure you I mean every word of it.'

With that I snapped off the tape recorder, shoved it in my briefcase, and we marched out of the office leaving a very nervous and upset bureaucrat behind us.

Needless to say, I never heard another word from the bureaucrat about my alledged violation.''

Almost any bureaucrat would be completely overwhelmed by a procedure such as this, and you would certainly apply the breaks to any precipitous actions that he may want to take in putting the shaft to you. In every case, it is one definite way of turning off the red tape machine.

THE I DON'T UNDERSTAND LETTER

Here is a copy of a letter that you can send to almost any bureaucrat who writes you about non-compliance, inquiry, threat of action etc. It is a letter designed to set up a meeting such as we described previously, and one that is bound to attract the bureaucrat's attention. It goes like this:

Dear Sir, Madame or Ms.:

I have received your notice. I am impressed by the fact that the (U.S. Government, State of ------------------------------, County of ------------------, City of ----------------------- (insert one) has taken notice of me. I thank you for that.

However, since there are some 50,000 regulations, laws, edicts, proposals, dictums, decisions, misdemeanors, torts, felonies, controls, ordinances, injunctions, abeyances, orders and advisories that I am subject to, I must plead confusion.

Before attempting to deal with your problem, I must confess I find it unclear, nebulous, enigmatic, disengenuous, murky, puzzling, eversional, adamantine, unintelligible, foggy, metamorphical, nescient, and possible reductio ad adsurdum.

I suggest you translate, redefine, requadrate, repostulate, explain more lucidly, expand, expurgate the pleonams and the protean, pusillanimous propositions you have propounded.

I have the feeling I am dealing with a pompous pursuivant who is engaged in over-zealous obfuscation.

So, until I receive your answer I must respectfully stand on my Fifth Amendment Constitutional Right of not incriminating myself; my First Amendment Right of Free Speech, which also includes the right not to speak, my right against involuntary servitude, and my Seventh Amendment Right of Trial by Jury.

I shall look forward to receiving your answer.

Respectfully,

John Jones

By the time he looks up the meaning to all the words, he may decide the game isn't worth the candle. But, in any case, you are serving notice that in this particular ass-kicking contest he is not going to set the rules for the game.

FIGHTING BACK ON ASSESSMENTS

Assessments on personal, business and real property by a county assessor are at best nebulous guesses. The smart S.O.B. never accepts one of these assessments where increases are involved without using all the available procedures of appeal.

The first step is to discover which power buttons you have that can bring some influence to bear; the second is to learn precisely how to use the appeal procedure in getting assessments reduced; and the third is to assemble positive facts and figures when you present your case.

In matters of personal property and business equipment it is always wise to keep track of market prices on used equipment, and bring to bear this information when property is over-assessed. By being able to cite the specific facts and figures, show catalogues with prices and items listed, and from time to time call dealers in used equipment to come out and bid on your equipment, you will compile a dossier of facts and figures that will be hard for the assessor to refute. Using this type of technique, you can often get stated deductions without going through an official appeal. Once the assessor becomes aware that you know what you are talking about, these over-assessments become more rare.

In terms of real property, it is best to get professional appraisal from time to time, and keep track of two or three pieces of property quite similiar to yours and make a compact with the owner that each will tell the other what their assessments are. In this way, these can be kept in line with each other, and any sudden jump in one can result in a specific appeal showing that it was over-assessed in terms of like proprety.

The point is, never accept an increase in assessment without using all the weapons you have to force it down. Most small businessmen feel they don't have the time to fool with this sort of thing, but over a period of years it will put many hundreds and even thousands of dollars in your pocket you would otherwise lose.

DEALING WITH BIG BUSINESS

In dealing with big business, we treat it the same as dealing with any other bureaucracy. Big business is made up of levels of bureaucratic paper shufflers and regulation issuers who work for and by the book.

If you are buying equipment and supplies from big business, you are probably paying more than you should. The big business firms that maintain direct sales forces selling equipment, sell for prices far higher than the equipment is actually worth. What you are paying for is high sales commissions, maintenance and service facilities and a lot of sales management and other personnel who add nothing to the value of the equipment as far as you are concerned. You are far better off to buy the equipment used from a local dealer who can service it. You will wind up paying far less up front with much much lower maintenance costs than you would dealing direct with the manufacturing firm. The costs of service contracts or service man repair calls are absolutely ridiculous. Their charges for supplies are equally high for the same reason.

Their siren song is that they put the equipment out with smaller down payments and smaller lease payments, but the over all cost of the equipment, and their contract cancellation fees are exorbitant. If you are selling to big firms, don't get caught in the trap of putting all your eggs in one or two baskets. Often times a lucrative contract from a big business firm looks like Manna from heaven to the small businessman. But if he sluffs off his smaller customers, in order to satisfy the immediate whims of a big business customer, he could one day find himself in a position where they demand his product at a lower price than he can afford to sell it, or they will go somewhere else. Big business generally buys on price and service alone, and there is certainly no loyalty in those S.O.B.'s and their purchasing departments to a supplier. If they are offered a better deal they'll take it.

Some small businesses with a good product have laid themselves open to cheap takeover by allowing a major company to absorb their full production. Once this has been done the major company simply cocks the gun and sticks it to their head and says, join us at such and such a price or we'll pull our business.

When you get into conflicts with a big business over payment either by you or by them, you have to come on like gang busters. Once your problem gets into the bureaucratic maze, it is essentially unsolvable. You will never be able to find anybody who can give you a final decision, and you will wind up,if you owe them money, in court, or if they owe you money simply being told to sue.

So, the move is to get your lawyer to sue first. Then, if some two bit bureaucrat has been holding up your claim over some supposed company regulation, it will get shaken loose, he will get his ass chewed, and you will get your money, or they will settle with you on the basis of what you should pay and not what they say you should.

Just remember this, there are no nice guys in the higher eschelon in big business. They are all bastards, trying to become president of the company. Their only motivation in solving problems is to not make waves or make themselves or their departments look bad. So any attack on them should be taken from that angle, that when you sue or threaten to sue, you are making somebody in the organization have to explain to somebody else higher up why this action is being taken. In most cases they prefer not to have to do this, so your problem will get some specific attention and a settlement will probably be made.

One successful S.O.B. we talked to used this very effectively, by hiring a law student for $25, to research out all the citations on failure to honor warrantees, fraudulent billing, threatening letters, coercion in collection debts, liable, restraint of trade, and several others. He would then have his typist place these citations at the bottom of each letter as grounds for potential suit. This resulted in the legal department of the big corporation researching out what these citations referred to, and getting back to the credit department with a recommendation. This built a sizable delay into making payment, and resulted in a letter of opinion from the legal department after 60 to 90 days that they did not apply in this case, etc. He would then reply that this was a matter of legal opinion, which he would be happy to discuss in court. However, if they cared to negotiate maybe something could be worked out. The point is that the ass-kicking worked two ways in this situation. And he reported often as not he got a settlement and in some cases they simply walked away.

HOW TO BORROW MONEY FROM YOUR CREDITORS

Most small businessmen we talked to had difficulties when they were first getting started and having operating capital. The shrewd S.O.B.'s devise means of using their creditors as capital sources. They simply work out maneuvers to delay payment without injuring their credit standing so that they could use the money they normally would have had to pay suppliers to operate their business.

The first proposition is one where the small businessman has decided that particular creditor was somebody who he was no longer going to do business with, and there was a substantial amount of money owing. This was one who was preferably some distance away, and not a local firm.

Upon receiving the first bill, payable in ten to thirty days, he set it aside, and after that they had sent the second bill, wrote a bill of particulars up about why he was dissatisfied with their products or service, and wanted an adjustment on the invoice. He returned this letter with the original invoice, and sat back and waited.

His bill of particulars took some time for processing, and he had bought at least another 30 days before they finally got back to him with their answer. Usually somebody called him to discuss the matter, and when they found him unrelenting in his complaint, stated that the amount would stand. On occasion they would make concessions, and come down in the amount owed. At that point he told them he would calculate the amount he thought he owed, and send them that information.

He would buy thirty more days doing this, and then send them a check for an odd amount (say the bill was $2,000, he would send them a check for $963.27, and type on the back of the check, payment in full of all obligations due, and the name of the creditor). He would then send this check with his voucher giving the estimates amounts due, and sit back and wait for the results.

If the company was foolish enough to go ahead and cash the check, the war was over, but he was over $1,000 ahead of the game. If the check was returned to him, with a refusal to accept it as payment in full, which would give him another 15 to 20 days, he would put the check and his letter in the file and sit back and wait for the results.

This often took the form of more dummy letters, finally turning it over to an attorney agency, and finally the threat of a suit.

At this point he would reiterate his offer of settlement perhaps upping the anty by $100 or so, and watch what happened. He would not make this offer to the attorney, or collection agency, but direct to the creditor.

He had now used up 4 or 5 months of the creditors money, and if he decided he needed more time, would accept the initial filing of a law suit.

He would answer this suit himself, using a format similiar to this:**Appendix**

He would file the answer in the court for something between $12 to $25, after he had taken the full 30 days to give his answer. He was now six months their money, and as a rule it would take the opposing attorneys another three weeks to 30 days to file their first set of interrogatories. These are attempts by the plaintiff's attorneys to figure out your defense against the suit, so they can prepare for it. He would answer that interrogatory in a very vague manner, and return it to them, and file his answer with the court.

He would send them an interrogatory (a sample of which you will find in the appendix), but it would take them another 30 to 45 days to answer. He is now 7 to 8 months into the creditors money, and on the verge of going to court and probably losing, so then he would make whatever settlement was necessary, working out some easy terms on payment, for something less than the amount owed, so whatever interest he had to pay was less that he would have had to pay originally.

So, in effect, he had borrowed $2,000 interest free for 7 to 8 months to help his business over the hump.

In some areas, because of the overloaded condition of the courts, this could actually be stretched out to 18 months without endangering his business operation at any time.

THE DOUBLE PLAY SYSTEM

An offshoot of this system is to wait the full 90 days on a bill that is due, and then send a check for half or less of the total amount with a statement, "I have calculated the amount owed to be," and then whatever the amount is. This is then mailed to the creditor, and two days later another letter is mailed, stating that the calculated amount sent you in payment in full of invoice number so and so was $2.16 over the actual amount owed. "Please send an immediate refund."

This will throw their billing department in enough of a state of confusion to give him another 30 to 60 days before everything was straightened out, and he had to pay the bill or whatever portion of the bill was reduced.

CALCULATING THE INVOICE REDUCTION

Once you have decided that you are not going to do any further business with the creditor, you can follow the example of some smart S.O.B.'s who decide they don't want to get a reduction on the amount owed. They simply ignore the invoices, until a telephone call is made, at which time they tell the creditor that they are in dire straits, and on the verge of bankruptcy. But they appreciate the fine treatment that the creditor has given them in the past and if the creditor is willing to accept such and such an amount as payment in full they will forward the check. The calculation is that it is going to cost the creditor about one third of the amount to put it into a collection agency to collect. So by offering to pay 75% of the total, they pick up a 25% discount as the creditor would rather do that than put it through for collection and lose a third or more of the total amount, and if your story is true, the entire amount.

THE STOLEN CHECK BOOK PLOY

Another ploy used by a successful S.O.B. who needed about 60 days relief from paying bills, without losing credit, was the lost check book deal.

He sat down and wrote payments in full to every account he owed, and sent them by mail. The next morning he reported to the bank that his check book had been stolen, and that he wanted the account closed immediately before checks would be forged against the account.

He asked the bank for a letter stating that his checkbook had been stolen, and that they had closed his account, and that to avoid confusion he would be opening an account at another branch.

Instead of opening an account at another branch, he opened his account at another bank so that there would be no way that the bank could honor his check and then come back and slip it into his new account. This is something that banks will often do to cover their own error.

He made copies of the letter from the bank, and with a letter of apology wrote to all the creditors he had sent checks to, asking them to return the checks to him as soon as they received them, and he would write checks out of his new account to make them good.

IN GETTING EVEN PLAY

One successful S.O.B. we talked to, related the story of a supplier who he discovered had been overcharging him badly and when asked to make restitution flatly refused.

His current invoice with the company was $290.80. So he sent them a check for $29.80, and wrote only the number $29.80 on the check, leaving the portion blank where he would normally write in the number. He left a space for one digit between the nine and the figure 80 cents. The check routinely went through, and he was credited with a $29.80 payment against his $290.80 bill.

He then determined about the time the check would clear his bank, and on that day he went down and cashed his check for cash for $290.80. He redeposited the money in his account deposit the next day.

When he got his return checks he carefully put in the zero after the 29 and then wrote in $290.80 in the place where there was no figure in writing. When he got his next month's bill, he sent them back a photostatic copy of both sides of the check, and a photostatic copy of his bank statement showing the $290.80 figure having cleared, and since it was such a large company, they wrote him a letter of apology crediting him in full for his account and no more was said.

While this *may* be illegal and unethical, they had still gotten even with somebody that had been giving him the shaft.

UNSIGNED CHECKS

One way to get 30 days on most of your accounts with no appreciable difficulty, is to send out all your checks for one month unsigned. Most of those who receive them will send them back with a polite note that you forgot to sign, which will take a week to ten days, and you can wait another five days before signing and re-sending the check, and by the time it is received and cleared, you have gained the best part of 30 days.

This again gets you a quick loan ranging anywhere from $1000 to $10,000 for 30 days use with no interest. Obviously, it can't be used more than once or twice over a long period of time, but it is a simple way to get a quick, short-term loan.

THE DOUBLE STOP PAYMENT PLAY

Another way to borrow some money is to use a double stop payment play.

You send a check for a large amount which you don't want to have to pay for 40 to 45 days, and then go down and stop payment on the check. (When stopping payment on a check, be sure and get a receipt from the bank that payment was stopped, because then you have proof that the bank was wrong in case they let the stop payment slip too).

When the stop payment check is returned to the creditor, marked stop payment, you will either get an angry letter, or an angry phone call inquiring as to why payment was stopped.

Supplier will identify himself, and you'll listen for a moment, and then you say with an angry show, "Oh my God, I told my bookkeeper to issue the stop payment on Jones' Supply not Smith's Supply." Then you go on to order them to put the check back through immediately as you lift the stop payment order with your profound apology.

However, you do not lift the stop payment, and the check goes in and payment is stopped again, and an even angrier phone call or letter follows. You then erupt in an explosion of anger cursing the stupid bankers, and tell them you will go down personally to stop payment, and send them an immediate letter cerfitying that it had been lifted with a statement from the bank that it has been done.

This will mollify the creditor, and you do as you say, returning the letter to them, buying another five to seven days, and then the check clears.

TO SUM UP

In turning off the red tape machine, and playing ass-kicking games with bureaucrats, it is only necessary that you make it clear that it is not going to be a one-sided contest. Once the bureaucratic mind discovers this, like steam, it seeks the source of least resistance to escape.

The successful S.O.B. recognizes this, and plays the game accordingly.

CHAPTER 5
HOW TO TEACH LEGAL AND FINANCIAL VULTURES HUMILITY

How To Teach Legal And Financial Vultures Humility

TWO SUCCESSFUL PROS TO PULL YOUR WAGON

As society, particularly business, grows more complex, every smart S.O.B. will find a sharp lawyer and accountant to help pull the wagon.

Almost every successful S.O.B. we talked to started out with the idea that they didn't need or want to pay these professionals high fees to do things they probably could do for themselves. But, they learn very quickly that the fees they pay are often the best investments they could make.

As we said in the prologue, anyone is stupid who sits down to play in a game where they don't know the rules and can't understand the procedures. The game of law, accounting, and taxes is such a game. Therefore, you need professionals sitting in for you when that type of a game starts, and the only problem you have is finding the right one to do the job for you.

FINDING AN ATTORNEY

One of the great mysteries of commercial life is how to locate an attorney who will be interested enough in you and your problems to do what is necessary to keep you out of trouble, get you out of trouble when you get in it, and with his advice help you make a lot more money in deals you get into.

Lawyers, like cops, are professional cynics. They are constantly dealing with the seedy side of life. They know that every adversary in the court room is lying; they also know that in the vast majority of cases their own clients are lying to them, and like the cop, come to believe that all people are kinky. Two of the meanest bastards on earth are old cops and old lawyers.

Lawyers are naturally aggressive, are nit-pickers and fog-finders by nature, have a God complex second only to that of doctors, and practice the second oldest profession involved in screwing people for money.

So, the smart S.O.B. out looking for a lawyer, is essentially somebody who thinks like he does. Since this encompasses 90 percent of the legal profession, he must look for other qualifications to find the man or woman to represent him.

THE TIGER OR THE PUSSYCAT

In general terms , lawyers fall into two categories. First, the tiger, is young (but not too young), on the make, and he figures he is big enough, smart enough, mean enough, and cunning enough to kill anything in the jungle.

For the small businessman, he probably won't find this individual in a large law firm (the partners are smart enough to know that he could eat them too), but could well find him in a small law firm or practicing by himself.

It should be noted that this is the individual you want when you are getting started; you are going to need lots of help, lots of advice on what you can or can't do, you need somebody who can fight like hell for you when trouble erupts.

The tiger you're looking for is not a young man just out of law school getting started, but, someone who has some battle scars already, someone who knows the ropes, can pull little stunts like juggling cases to get them in front of the more sympathetic judge, has good contacts so he can get information about adversaries, etc.

A pussycat will generally be a senior partner in a well-known law firm (or one of the senior partners) who knows everybody. He is an integral part of the local power structure , represents the biggest and best individuals and firms in the area, and would never do battle against any of them on behalf of a small business client.

The value of the pussycat is, when you are big, he can become a power button to use in making contacts with the power structure. But, when you are small, if his law firm does take you on as a client, you will only be dealing with the junior partner, your work will be done by clerks in the back room and outside of ten or fifteen minute pats on the head from the senior partner, you get nothing for your money.

HOW TO FIND YOUR TIGER

The first way to look for a tiger is watch local elections. If you find a lawyer running for office, he is a tiger. It would be worth your time to give him a hand, or toss a check in his election campaign fund if you like his attitude. If he loses, you have an attorney, and if he wins, you have a power button.

The second way is to go down to the court and get friendly with the bailiffs and the court clerks; try to get their opinion about who is the best tiger in the local jungle. They see them all, and know who fights like hell for their clients, and who doesn't.

If you can't get next to these people, then have your wife (or go yourself a couple of days when you have some spare time), watch some of the lawyers operating in civil cases.

You will quickly discover who the tigers are, and when you see one you like, simply meet him outside of the courtroom and get his card.

Most of the books and other materials you read tell you to find a lawyer by asking around. No wonder it is a problem doing this, because people recommend their relatives, their friends, their own lawyers, and unless they are dedicated S.O.B.'s like yourself, you don't usually have the kind of lawyer you are looking for. Your best bet is to do your own hunting, and there is one other source that you might contact.

That is talking to the cops. They appear in court all of the time, largely in criminal cases, but quickly become aware of who the S.O.B. type of lawyers are, and who the pussycats are. They probably don't like the S.O.B.'s, but being a kindred sole, have a sneaking admiration for them.

As a note of passing, getting to know a local cop (a street cop or detective, not a part of the police bureaucracy), can be a good investment. They hear all the rumors, and know what is happening with everybody in town, and by getting friendly with one of them, you can get a lot of information other people don't hear about.

WHAT YOUR TIGER CAN DO FOR YOU

Your lawyer has two primary functions, attack and defend. Hiring a lawyer is something like owning a football team. You set up the game, he prepares the game plan and goes into action, and wins or loses.

If he's your man, he will accept the responsibility of playing the game for you, and give it his best shot.

He can tell you when to sign and when not to sign contracts and agreements; he can draw up agreements for you to have other people sign that are lopsidedly written in your favor; he can get any number of harassing bureaucrats and complainers off your ass; he can force settlements that you would otherwise be unable to make; he can collect money you would otherwise be unable to collect; he can help you set up deals that will be successful because of his legal knowledge that would have failed without it; he can get you out of trouble that might result in criminal prosecution if he was not there; and, finally, he can help you make a hell of a lot of money that you would not otherwise make.

There is one other thing that he does, and only people without lawyers understand. That is, when you get into difficulties, and the other party is represented by a lawyer, having your lawyer step into the breach puts the problem on a lawyer-to-lawyer basis. Lawyers understand each other and can make deals that are for their clients' benefit that no layman dealing with their lawyer could make for himself.

LETTING IT ALL HANG OUT

When you meet with your new tiger, and decide he is your man, and get all the cards face up on the table. Have him tell you flat out what kind of fees he is going to charge you, and while he can't give you a price when defending you for murder, or getting himself involved in a highly technical trial, he can give you hourly fees, and rough ideas of what certain portions of his service will cost. He knows exactly what the situation is, and if you have screwed somebody, tell him so, and let him work it from there. He is not interested in your morality or Christian charity, he is interested in representing you and getting the best deal for you that he can.

Don't call him up on the phone and expect free advice; be willing to pay for it. But use his services as liberally as you can afford, and above all whenever you are going to launch into something in a nebulous area, consult him first. Let him show you the pitfalls ahead, what can happen if trouble comes, and then you can decide if the game is worth the candle.

For one final note, cut him in on a few deals. Help him make money and make a buddy of him. If he is politically ambitious, help him meet some power buttons of his own, help him with his career, bring him some more clients, and do whatever you can to keep him 100 percent on your side.

Just remember that jungle out there is full of tigers, and if you are going to operate in it you want a tiger of your own that is just as big, just as mean, and just as cunning as the rest of them.

If you do this for your lawyer, he is going to jump into your harness and pull your wagon laughing and scratching all the way. But, if you try to chisel your lawyer, lie to him, give him a hard time, you are going to get exactly what you pay for...Nothing!

In making your decision about hiring this tiger, there is one little test that you can give that will help you make the right decision. When you first talk to the lawyer, tell him about some kinky deal that you got involved in, where in true S.O.B. fashion you screwed somebody with a clever move. Watch his expression and reaction. If he chuckles and gets a kick out of this, he is your man. If there is no reaction, and he simply does not change his expression or changes the subject, he is not the S.O.B. . you're looking for. So play it cool, and be sure you get the right man or woman before you start.

FINDING A C.P.A.

Finding an accountant is more or as important as finding a lawyer. The problem is somewhat different, because accountants are not tigers, and you wouldn't want one if you found him. Most accountants are rather un-imaginative, unaggressive people who are quite secure in their profession, but really don't have any way to show it such as a lawyer might in court.

In terms of finding an accountant, your best bet is probably to go to the biggest accountant firm in the town, or in the area, and have them take you on as a client. It adds some status to your situation, and even if you are a small business, most of them have a department that will start out handling you.

When you talk to the accountant who will be handling your affairs, you want to discover something about his state of mind. You are going to use him a lot to get advice on tax avoidance, and you are looking for somebody who appreciates good tax-avoidance angles.

So, you should use the same test you would use with your tiger, and tell him about a particularly unique, but not very moral tax angle, and watch for his reaction. If he is horrified, he is probably not your man; but if he is interested, he probably is.

In negotiating with a C.P.A. about fees, he can be precisely specific in this area and give you a pretty good idea of what his services are going to cost. Here again, there is no use trying to chisel one down, or whine about his costs; if you can't pay them, go some place else. But again, he is the individual who can help you make a hell of a lot of money if he does his job right and you follow his instructions.

Once he takes you on as a client, he will set up an accounting system for you, and you should follow it without question. Because once you both understand the system, his reports are going to be the most interesting reading you can receive. You will discover very quickly what kind of money you're really making in your enterprise, and what needs to be done to make even more.

The one thing to remember about the accountant, is that if you get bad news from him don't kill the messenger. He is simply reporting what has happened, and there's no use getting sore at him because your business isn't being run properly. So, when bad numbers come up, get together with him and see what can be done to change things so it doesn't happen again.

So choose your accountant well and your attorney well and you will have a team that is going to make you a successful S.O.B. if there is any chance at all.

CONSULTANTS

There is an old saying, *"when you fail at everything else, become a consultant."*

This pretty much sums up the field of small business consultancy. Any general consultant who is going to come in and show you how to improve your business, will be wasting your time. The only type of consultants to use are specialists. Advertising and promotion, publicity , specific production, merchandising, freight rates and shipping, and other specialties of your business. You can forget the rest of them, and use your banker, lawyer, and accountant.

CHAPTER 6
HOW TO BECOME A GEOMETRY BOOK OF TAX AVOIDANCE ANGLES

How To Become A Geometry Book Of Tax Avoidance Angles

HOW TO GIVE THE TAX MAN CONSTIPATION

Tax avoidance is the best game in town. Saddled with a tax law no one really understands, the only specific rule in the tax-avoidance game is, "make-em prove it." Your accountant can give you an opinion, and you can get some information by reading the manuals, but in many cases, it is simply a matter of opinion. So opinion being what it is, you have the choice of taking and using the tax angle, or not as you choose. But, in most cases, where there is doubt , the smart S.O.B. will take it and make them prove it.

CHOOSING AN ACCOUNTING METHOD

One of the first tax angles the tax man should consider is which accounting method he uses. There are four methods available; cash method, accrual method, hybrid method, installment method, preferred method, sales method, long-term contract method.

The cash method may be used by any tax payer who does not have inventories to reflect income. The tax payer must use it if no records are maintained or the records are not complete and it can be used in one business although another method may be used in another business.

The income under this method is taxed in the year the cash or property is received. The value is fair-market value.

Deductions on expenses must be taken in the year in which payment is made. Giving a note is not payment, and payment cannot be made with borrowed funds. There is some dispute about pre-paying certain items, some will be required to be spread over the periods to which they apply such as insurance premiums and rent. But as a rule payment for supplies bought in advance is deductible in the year payed for.

The advantages of the cash method is you don't pay taxes until you have actually received the income. You also can control each year's receipts and in pay-outs to even the income, over the years, and you can keep very simple records.

The disadvantages are that you don't always match related income and expenses in one year creating some distortions in your business picture. And there is some potential for not having full control over receipts, and income may pile up unusually high in a single year, forcing you into a higher tax bracket. And, finally, liquidation and sale of the business may create a high, sudden income due to payment for the business and all receivables having to be picked up at one time.

The accrual method is available to anyone except those with no, or incomplete, books of records. It has to be used if inventories are necessary to reflect income there are one of the more sophisticated methods we'll talk about later.

Income is taxed in the year it is earned, not necessarily the year it is received. You also cannot accrue contingent, contested, or uncollectable items under this item and pre-payed amounts or income when received, even if not yet earned.

Expenses are deductible in the year all events have occurred which fix the fact and the amount of your liability, regardless of when they are paid. In order to deduct contingent or contested liabilities, you may deduct it when you pay it, but if you get a recovery later it is income when recovered. There are some more specialized rules concerning this, and you would have to consult your accountants concerning them.

The advantage of the accrual method is that it matches income and related expenses and tends to even out income over the years.

The disadvantages are that there is less lee-way than a cash basis tax payer to defer or accelerate income or deductions.

The hybrid method is available to any taxpayer if the method clearly reflects income and is used consistently. The accrual method is used in respect to purchases and sales, while cash method is used for all other items of income and expense.

The method is simple, it is not necessary to accrue income items such as interest and dividends. And the bother of accruing small expenses is also removed.

The method is not entirely accurate, since it is a hybrid which does not reflect true income. If consistently used it gives a fairly good idea of how the business is doing.

The installment method is used by sellers in sales of personal property of more than a thousand dollars or of real property provided, in either case, no more than 30% of the selling price is received in the year of the sale.

The income is taxed each year that collections are made, and a proportional amount of each collection (equal to a percentage of gross profit on the entire sale) is picked up as gross income in the year collected. Expenses are deductible when paid, the same as the cash basis, or incurred, the same as the accrual basis. On casual sales, expense of sale reduces sale price, thereby having an effect of spreading deductions over a period of reporting the income .

The income is spread over a period of collections so you do not pay taxes on amounts not yet received, and if tax rates decline in the future, part of the profits will bear a lower tax.

The disadvantages are dealers who switch from accrual to installment basis may have to pay a double tax on some receivables unless they sell off all receivables before they make the switch. Also, tax rates may go up; in which case some of the profits will bear a higher tax.

The deferred sales payment method is available to any cash basis taxpayer on the sale of personal property, and any cash or accrual taxpayer on the sale of real estate.

The income is taxed at the time of sale, seller picks up cash and fair-market value of buyer's obligation. If total exceeds basis of sold property, the difference is taxable. In later years, his obligations are collected, the difference between amounts received and value at which obligations were picked up originally as taxable at time of collection.

Since this is used generally with casual sales, so the expense of sale reduces sales price and is spread out over the period of collection, which means that deductions are also spread.

The advantages are that it can be where installment sales reporting is not possible, such as where more than 30% of the sales price is received in the year of the sale. Its primary use is in speculative deals where the value of the buyer's obligation is contingent on future operations and there is little or no present value.

The disadvantages are you may be in for a long and costly argument with the IRS as to the value of the obligations, even though the original sale gave capital gain, gain on collections on the obligations in future years will be taxable as ordinary income.

The long-term contract method is available to taxpayers who have long-term contracts of more than a year to complete, usually construction contracts. There are two long-term contract methods; first, percentage of completion and second, completed contracts. IRS permission is needed to switch from one to the other.

The income is taxed when a portion of the total contract price is taken into account each year according to the percentage of the contract completed that year. Architects' or engineers' certificates are required for proof. All expenses made during the year allocable to that contract are deducted, with adjustments made for inventories and supplies on hand at the beginning and end of each year.

The advantages are that income from one long-term contract is reflected as earned, and income bunching in one year is avoided.

The disadvantages are accurate estimates of completion are difficult to make in many cases, and if expenses are irregular as compared to income, there may be distortion of income in the interim years, although the final total will work out accurately.

By looking over these basic methods of accounting, you may be able to pick one out that would reflect better tax savings for your particular operation. When you spot one you can talk it over with your accountant to determine the best possible application to your business.

Picking a taxable year. Under the IRS code (No. 441), there are three types of taxable years recognized. They are (Regulation No. 1.441-1):

1. *calendar year:* A 12-month period ending on December 31.

2. *52-52 year:* This is a fiscal year, varying from 52 to 53 weeks in duration, which always ends on the same day of the week, whicn, (a) occurs the last time in the calendar month, or (b) falls nearest the calendar month.

3. *short period:* A period less than 12 months (allowed only under certain special situations such as initial return, final return, change in accounting period, and termination of taxable year by reason of jeopardy, assessment.

The reason it is important to pick the proper calendar year is that a business may have its heavy income in the fall of the year, but the majority of its heavy expenses in the spring. A calendar year would be foolish in these circumstances because income would always be ahead of the expenses connected with it.

So getting together with your accountant, you should pick your calendar year to best reflect the best balance between income and expenses, times when inventories can be taken, and financial statements prepared most conveniently, or when business activity is at a low point and it is most convenient for your professional service organization to help you.

If your business operates in different areas, and has different sources of income, it is possible to have taxable years for each source of income that reflects the most advantage to you. This would be a situation where you had subsidiary entities, or separate business ventures.

If you wish to get permission to change your calendar year, nad do not have an accountant, you can request it on Form 1128, available from your IRS office.

OPERATING AS A CORPORATION

In today's economic situation, and with the new ruling allowing small corporations to earn up to $50,000 and pay only a 22% tax base, the small corporation is really the small businessman's best bet for conserving income and having the potential to handle rapid growth.

By initially heading up as a Subchapter S and 1244 Corporation (review those in the appendix), you have the best of two possible situations. First, you can decide at the end of your taxable year whether you wish to be taxed as a corporation, or have the income or losses passed on to the stockholders. You can also take all corporate losses from your personal income should you choose to do so in any taxable year.

The second angle that a corporation provides great potential for is acquiring a tax loss company as a method of preserving current income and possibly getting one that had stock out on public sale, so that you could go public by simply acquiring the tax loss corporation.

You will find many other advantages of the corporate structure in our discussion of corporations in Chapter 3.

GETTING ALL THE DEDUCTIONS

You should sit down with your accountant and prepare your year-end strategy well in advance of the time the forms must be filed, You will want to determine approximately how much more income will be received by year end;

how to project taxable income for the current year; how to apply projected rates; and how to defer as much business income as possible.

Here are some of the items you should discuss with your accountant concerning conserving business income. How to handle reserves; what to do about contested liabilities; audit your pay set up at year end to arrange the best tax break for the company and working stockholders; what steps to take to protect against double taxation; how to defer compensation; accelerating deductions for advertising expenses; making interest free payments; how to accelerate the purchase of repairs and supplies; pre-payment of bills or services; using losses to reduce income; the advantages of abandoning property rather than selling it; write down of inventories; advances to salesmen; be sure to take the short year for a new corporation at the $50,000 earning mark; testing the retention of accumulated earnings; whether it is better to pay the penalty than the tax for retained accumulated earnings; when and how to pay dividends; the advantage of distributing appreciated property; how and when and how much stock dividends to distribute; the timing of the dividend payment; the possibility of shifting dividend income to children in low tax brackets; re-paying stockholder loan; timing stock redemptions, twelve-month liquidation distributions and one- month liquidation; when to consider Subchapter S election; shareholder consent on investment recapture ; pension and profit-sharing benefit election; which election to take in face of next year's losses; or next year's big capital gains; and the 1244 decision.

Each of these decisions has specific tax-saving angles, and should be carefully considered when doing your tax planning prior to the end of your fiscal year.

For example, here is a method of getting a deduction from personal income on your own corporation's debt. You set up a separate business, say as a sales agency or manufacturing unit, to either make or sell the corporation's product. As sole owner or partner of the sales agency, you personally guaranty the notes of the corporation. If you have to pay these notes, you have a business bad-debt deduction from your sales agency. The reason is that you made the guaranty as a way to further the sales agency or manufacturing units business.

Another way of sheltering business income is setting up a bad-debt reserve instead of specific charge off. When business is good and income needs sheltering, a bad-debt reserve larger than needed can shelter some income, as long as it is left in the reserve (Gsell, 34, TC 41acq). Then, when losses are available you can pull the excess. Of course the reserve account must be maintained at a level within reason.

THE TAX DODGES

As in every society where the tax collector has become oppresive, the peasantry begin to look for ways to hide their income from the collectors. A whole group of potential tax dodges have grown up in recent years, ranging from the so-called legitimate loopholes to some that are more esoteric and probably borderline legal.

We shall delve into some of these, for your consideration, but strongly advise consulting attorney and tax accountant before seriously getting involved with any of them.

START A CHURCH

The constitutional right of freedom of religion, and a congressional mandate that religious organizations pay little or no taxes, has created a great interest in starting your own religious institution among taxpayers looking for shelters.

It is not that difficult to start a church, in fact, the Rev. Kirby J. Hensley, who started the Universal Life Church, Inc., has made it absolutely simple.

First, you can send him a couple of dollars, and he will make you a minister in the Universal Life Church. (Address: Universal Life Church, 601 Third Street, Modesto, CA.) You will get an ordination certificate making you a minister in his church, licensed to perform marriages and all other ministerial functions.

Next, you appoint a church treasurer and a secretary. They can be members of your family, a friend , or anyone else who is interested.

Third, you obtain a church charter. The Universal Life Church will send you a charter and keep it in effect for $2.00 a month.

Then,you hold a religious service at your church at least once a week (this can be in your living room) and you don't have to pray or hold any kind of a ritual (apparently you can sit around and play poker if you like) as what you do is up to you.

Then you can turn all or part of your wages over to the church. If you wish to turn over all of your salary, you must take a "vow of poverty," and so notify the IRS on the appropriate forms, and your income is tax free. You are allowed to donate up to 50% of your income to the church, the rest is taxable. If you are donating all of your income to the church, and your employer is deducting social security and income taxes, you can apply for a refund of what you have paid in, as it is tax free.

To do this you go to the IRS office and fill out the necessary eligibility forms for tax-exempt status.

You also fill out a form for relief from social security taxes on grounds that it is against your religion. Then, your employer will no longer have to deduct those.

Then, from the donations the church receives you take only a "modest living" allowance to support your family, plus a parsonage (your home), and enough to take care of your food, clothing, and other household expenses. The church can also purchase you a car, which you can use for church work and personal trips.

You can even figure out legitimate reasons for traveling to Europe or any place in the world, on church business, and have the church pick up the tax tab free.

Obviously, the Internal Revenue Service, Congress, and the other greedy bureaucrats are anxiously studying this situation because it is entirely possible for everybody in the United States to start a church, and pay no taxes. But at the moment, at least, the first amendment right to freedom of religion stands, and precludes the state from favoring one religious view over another. The Supreme Court noted in Everson vs. Board of Education, 330 US 202, 91 LED 711:

"The establishment of religion of the first amendment means at least this: neither the state nor the federal government can set up a church. Neither can pass laws that aid one religion, aid all religions, or prefer one religion over another. Neither can force or influence a person to go to or remain away from church against his will or force him to profess a belief or disbelief in any religion. No person can be punished for entertaining or professing religious beliefs or disbeliefs, for church attendance or non-attendance.

In a recent federal court decision which upheld the right of the Universal Life Church to its tax-exempt status, a U.S. District Judge, James F. Batten, of Sacramento, ordered the government to refund $10,377 in taxes paid by the church. In his decision, Judge Batten declared:

"Neither this court, nor any branch of this government, will consider the merits or fallacies of a religion. Nor will the court compare the beliefs, dogmas, and practices of a newly organized religion with those of an older, more established religion. Nor will the court praise or condemn a religion, however excellent or fantastical or preposterous it may seem. Were the court to do so, it would impinge upon the guarantees of the first amendment.''

So given that legal backing, the church, or any church, can be established for virtually any reason, and obtain a tax-exempt status.

THE DISAPPEARING CHECKS

In the U.S. vs. Miller, the Supreme Court ruled that the bank owns the depositor's records, and they are required to turn these records over to the Internal Revenue Service at any time without a warrant. Whatever information these reveal, the government can use against you in collecting back taxes or criminal prosecution.

Some people are turning to the use of foreign checking accounts to get around this invasion of privacy.

One move is to open a Canadian bank account which is payable in U.S. dollars. The Bank of Montreal offers a checking account called ''U.S. funds at interest.'' On funds deposited in the bank, interest is paid quarterly that runs from 3 to 10 percent when the maintained balance exceeds $2500. All accounts are insured up to $20,000 by the Canadian government, and the bank makes a flat 25 cent charge for each account cleared. For information on this account, you can write the Bank of Montreal, 50 King Street West, Toronto, Ontario, Canada.

The way to use this account efficiently is not to try to pay your U.S. obligations with it, (other than those you don't wish to have the IRS look at), but to set up an account in a local bank, keeping a balance of $100 to $500, and then simply cashing your Canadian checks at that bank.

If there are obligations you wish to pay, that you would just as soon not have the IRS know about, you can simply buy money orders, spreading your business out among many places, and pay that way. It is unlikely they would be able to trace down these money orders unless you were involved in a serious criminal violation.

ILLEGAL SEARCH AND SEIZURE

If you have some reason to not want the IRS to look over your checks, you can try this wrinkle. Write a letter similar to this:

"Your Town Bank Attention J. Banker, Manager:

Dear Mr. Manager:

I am a customer at your bank, and concerned about my rights of privacy. I am writing to remind you that the records you hold with regard to my accounts are my private property, and that you are responsible under law for protecting it potentially liable for damages for invasion of privacy unless compulsion by legal process exists.

I make no suggestion that you resist a lawful search warrant issued by a court of law and signed by a Judge. However, I do instruct you to disregard any administrative summons (such as IRS Form No. 2039-A, "Summons") or of any other regulatory body that is not accompanied by a valid search warrant issued by a validly constituted court of law.

I also require that you notify me immediately should you receive such a summons, so that I may have the opportunity to use my consitutional right to seek a court order in my own behalf.

Should you wish to take this matter up with your legal department, the following citations are offered as proof that my request is valid:

Burrows vs. Superior Court (1974) 13 CAL 3d 238; U.S. vs. Miller (Fifth CIR. 1974) 500 F 2d 751; Reisman vs. Caplin (1964) 375 U.S. 400m, 84 S CT 508; Donnelson vs. U.S. (1971) 400 U.S. 517, 91 S CT 534; U.S. vs. Bssceglia (1975) 95 S ct 919.

I fully intend to preserve and protect my rights under the U.S. Constitution, and your cooperation is urgently requested. Please sign and return the copy of this letter after having certified its receipt, and place this copy in my files for presentation to anyone seeking access to my account without a legal warrant." And then sign it and send two copies to the bank by registered mail.

You may want to discuss this with your laywer, but it is our understanding that if the IRS did obtain records in the face of this knowledge that this letter existed, and you were denied your constitutional right of legal intervention, that any evidence they seized would be invalid in a criminal proceeding.

But again, that is a layman's interpretation, and you should discuss it fully with an attorney.

HOW TO GET LUXURY ITEMS AT GOVERNMENT EXPENSE

If you would like to own an airplane, yacht, condominium at the sea shore and the mountains, or other such luxury items, you can work it out as the owner of a corporation so it doesn't cost you a dime. You can use all of Uncle Sam's tax money to swing the deal.

For example, you can purchase an airplane for corporation use in conducting business for say $100,000, you pay $10,000 down and agree to pay $9000 in prepaid interest for the first year of the contract and whatever sales and use taxes, etc., are applicable.

If your corporation is in the 49% tax bracket, you can deduct the first $10,000 directly from the sum of taxes that you owe as an investment tax credit.

It is currently 10% at this writing and varies from time to time. So this gives you the downpayment directly out of tax dollars. Secondly, the $9000 of prepaid interest is fully deductible from your business expense or $4320 worth of tax dollars may be deducted directly from your tax payment. Then, you can take 20% accelerated depreciation on the airplane of $20,000 or $9600 out of taxes owed. The prepaid interest, license taxes, and insurance, and your tax deductions from money you would have paid Uncle Sam comes to $23,920, or $1420 cash in your pocket plus ownership of the airplane, all out of tax dollars.

From that point on, the operating costs, payments, interest, etc. can be deducted as a business expense from the corporation, and the airplane is yours.

You can do this with yachts, property, and many other things as long as you can prove that it is purchased for business use, and not for personal use.

Now should you want to get more sophisticated with a proposition of this kind and use the airplane and other expense items owned by the corporation to shelter more income, you go to some place like the Cayman Islands (a British colony in the Caribbean northwest of Jamaica), and set up a leasing company. It costs about $50 to organize a company there, and a few hundred dollars more in fees and charges. Once this is done, you sell the airplane back to the leasing company for $90,000. The leasing company pays off the balance due to the original lender on the airplane purchase, and charges your corporation so much a month as a leasing fee. You make it a closed-in lease, where the leasing company bears all expenses of operating the airplane from insurance right on down to gasoline and changing the sparkplugs. Let's say that the operating expenses come to $1500 a month in this manner, and the leasing company charges $3000 a month for the lease. The $3000 is written off as a business expense, and $1500 of that is profit to the leasing company, which goes into the sing company as profit. Thus, you have sheltered $1500 additional a month as business expense, and if the lease cost is in line with what other leasing companies charge, there is little reason to be challenged on it.

Since there are banking secrecy laws in the Cayman Islands, there is no way for anyone to discover who is behind this leasing company, other than the agents who supply their names to corporations for those fees, and they are under penalty of stiff fines and jail sentences for revealing any information about their clients.

This is an out and out tax dodge, and should only be done with very careful consideration of the potential ramifications by consulting your lawyer and your tax accountant carefully. But it is not an uncommon procedure, and there are many layered corporations of this kind in tax shelters all over the world.

USING YOUR KIDS' SUPER TAX DEDUCTIONS

Another place many small businessmen can find a rich tax deduction, is in using their children and members of the family as workers in the business.

Your children can earn up to $2000 a year each—tax free. You pay them the $2000 to work in your business, and you can still take a deduction and an exemption if he's living at home. So you've got your cake, and you're eating it too.

There are many things kids can do in every small business, and as long as they are something that must be done by other members of the firm, or the owner, it is work that can be paid for. Check it out carefully with your accountant, but consider this while you're thinking about it. If you had five kids working for you at full capacity, each earning $2000 a year, you would have the same deduction as 17 exemptions. Now that is picking up $14,000 tax free. No gift tax and no income tax. So it is a proposition, if you have children old enough to work, that is worth examining very carefully.

THERE ARE MANY TAX HAVENS

There are many places around the world where excess money caan be sheltered in what are now come to be known as tax havens. There are places with no income tax of any kind such as the Bahamas, Bermuda, the Cayman Islands, Gibraltar, the New Hebrides, and others cropping up from time to time.

There are places that have no income tax on foreign sources of income; Hong Kong, Panama, and the Shannon International Airport in Ireland.

There are countries which do not tax foreign sources of income of companies which are owned by non-residents; Barbados, Guernsey, the Isle of Man, Jamaica, Jersey, Liberia, and Montserrat.

These tax havens in some cases have strict bank secrecy laws, some even more strict than those in Switzerland, where companies can be set up, goods sold, income received, with no way of any governmental source ever discovering who gets it, who pays it out, etc.

For the man with few deductions, and a high income, these tax havens are well worth investigating. Now it does not make good sense to publish whatever is currently available in a book, because these situations change almost monthly. New ones come into being, other ones change their rules, but small countries are finding these tax haven operations to be highly profitable, and are making them more attractive to people living in countries who are being taxed to death.

CHAPTER 7
HOW TO MAKE YOURSELF FAMOUS

How To Make Yourself Famous

One reason that small business stays small is they fail to develop any individuality for their business enterprises. They blend into a rather faceless mass of look-alike business ventures, and rely primarily on locations and price service advertising to develop new customers. On occasion, a small business operator will come along who will suddenly leap ahead of the pack and become a local institution, rather than a business, simply because they recognize the value of publicity and promotion as a method of building business.

It is very difficult to become well known in today's society. It is a rootless society, where approximately one- third of the people move every year, where mass media tends to capture most attention, and it is a rare individual indeed whose name you can mention to almost anyone on the street, and have it recognized. Outside of the President of the United States, famous television, movie, and sports personalities, and occasionally some infamous criminal who captures the public attention, few people achieve genuine public recognition.

You could walk down the street, and ask people if they recognize the name of the Vice-President of the United States, their state senator, their state governor, their representative in the Congress, state legislature, mayor, city councilman, etc. and find far less than a majority will give you the answer that shows they recognize the position the individual holds.

The reason for this is that there is so much clamor for public attention, that it's extremely difficult for people to recall names unless they are constantly thrown at them. The well-known television personalities such as Johnny Carson, Walter Cronkite, Mary Tyler Moore, Bob Hope, etc. all have high levels of recognition for a particular reason. They have almost daily or weekly contact with people through their television sets, and in the main they come across as friendly and exciting personalities. In other words, they give people pleasure to a great extent, and for that they are remembered. And that is a thing to keep in mind when developing character and image for a business. It should give people pleasure, it should not have any negative aspects to it or be considered a cold-hearted money-making machine .

Those entrepreneurs who have had the courage and the willingness to exploit a name and business image to the public have enjoyed great measures of success. In the late 1940's and early 1950's, few people would remember the name of the mayor of Los Angeles, but almost everyone who was in Los Angeles in those years would remember the name of "Mad Man Muntz." He developed an image as a cut-rate seller of television sets, and later automobiles, and his name was virtually a household word. It made him millions of dollars, and even in an area as large and diverse as Los Angeles, he achieved almost total recognition among the populace. He did it because he advertised himself with a Napoleonic hat set sideways on his head, and a cartoon indicating he didn't have all his marbles. People laughed at him, his competitors sneered at him, while he was laughing all the way to the bank.

The point is to develop a theme and a character for a business that people will recognize in a pleasurable way. In recent years we have seen the development of what is called the "theme" restaurant. We had a situation during the 1960's and early 1970's, where vast fast-food chains were building empires across the country where every unit was the same, the decor was routine schlock, menu exactly the same, and the building block of the business was to shove the food in a bag, stick it in the customer's hands, collect the money, and let him eat it in his car, or sitting on a bench outside, and so mechanize the operation that it could be run by children.

Then three fellows, who had gone to the Cornell University Hotel and Restaurant School, came up with a new approach to the restaurant business. They started a restaurant called "Victoria Station" which was housed in old railroad cars, decorated with early British artifacts. Business boomed, and they now have a chain of some 50 of these restaurants around the country, grossing nearly 50 million dollars a year. The idea was quickly copied, and you found restaraunts with the motif of World War I aerodromes, hanging plants, and foliage, and one is currently serving Chinese food that will be designed like the diner on the Orient express.

The success of these businesses is simply that they have a character, a theme, and of course serve good food. But here again, you see the value of establishing a specific uniqueness and character to a business to get public recognition of your enterprise.

THE RICOCHET THEORY

In planning advertising and promotion for your business, you should plan it towards getting ricochets from all the promotions and advertising you use. The ricochet is the theory where you hit the target, and your message bounces off and hits another target and bounces off and hits another target and so forth. In other words, one message is ricocheted to anywhere from one to fifty more people, giving you tremendous impact for your advertising and promotion, and helping you gain the kind of recognition you need to become the business leader in your community.

Now a good example of the ricochet theory is the sales letter you received to induce you to order this book. You probably have never seen a sales letter just like it before, and because it was unique, it has ricocheted off many of those who received it (who sent it to others), and resulted in more orders for the book that we would have otherwise received. So, by sending one message, and getting some ricochet value from that letter, we developed extra business at no extra cost, and that is the value of the ricochet method of advertising and promotion.

Using ricochet advertising and promotion, you develop the best possible kind of advertising you can get, and that you cannot buy for any price. And that is the "word of mouth" advertising, where one customer recommends you to another. So in developing the ricochet techniques, you want to analyze whatever you do, to see how it can be set up so that more than one person will be influenced by what you are doing.

To illustrate the point of ricochet advertising, there is a story told by Stanley Arnold, a really great sales promoter, about a promotion he put on in Cleveland, Ohio in his family's small chain of supermarkets. One winter they had a tremendous blizzard in Cleveland, and there was not a single customer in any one of his 15 stores, and he got an idea for turning a disaster into a bonanza He called all 15 stores and ordered them to close up, and that all the able-bodied employees were to go out in the parking lot, make snowballs , the size of grapefruit, and pack them in grapefruit cartons. He then called a cold-storage company and arranged to have some 7,000 snowballs kept at 20 degrees below 0 until he needed them. He then called the weather bureau to find out what the hottest week of the year was going to be, and found it was scheduled to be in July of that year.

So he set up a plan to have a "blizzard of values" sale in mid-July in his 15 supermarkets. The gimmick was, that every five minutes, in every store a cowbell would ring, and someone at a checkout stand would receive a free snowball packed in a cellophane bag, and a ticket to go over and draw a number to win a prize, The idea was so successful, that the Police Department had to call out special patrols to handle the crowds, and they turned what was normally a slack week in their business into the greatest sales record in the history of the chain.

Now this is a perfect example of ricochet promotion. Giving away snowballs in the middle of July got everybody in town talking about the promotion, and the result proved the point.

FIFTEEN RICOCHETS

Now I am going to give you about 15 ricochet-type promotion ideas, that almost anybody selling to the general public can use, and they do produce results.

CIVUS OPTIMUS

Civus Optimus is a Latin phrase meaning superior citizen. If you have a small advertising budget, and you want maximum ricochet value for your advertising dollar, then you can set up a civus optimus program in your community.

It works like this. Each week, fortnight, or month, you are going to make an award (it's the form of a plaque), to a superior citizen in your community. Now, rather than doing the obvious in awarding them to the mayor, the chief of police, city councilman, etc., you are going to reach down in the community and find little-known stories of good deeds one neighbor has performed for another as the basis of your award.

In order to do this, you set up an advertising program asking people to make nominations for your civus optimus award. They send you letters telling of good deeds others have performed in their neighborhood, and you choose the best one of these, to award your plaque. If you do it weekly, then each week in your advertising, you run a picture of the winner, and the description of what they did in order to be awarded the plaque. Obviously, you can get newspaper publicity at least on the first award, with the story about your program.

On the plaque, will be the words civus optimus presented by the name of your business, and it would be suitable for hanging on the wall, putting on the mantle piece, etc.

Now the ricochet value of this is tremendous. It gets other people talking about your program, about your business, you create new friends by awarding the plaque, both to those who earned it and those who nominated them, and the name of your business is beginning to be hung up on walls all over town. When friends and neighbors drop in, and inquire as to what it is, again your name comes into the discussion.

So you have maximum ricochet value here, community impact, and tremendous good will building for you every time you make this award.

CONGRATULATION PENS

Another way to attract public attention and get ricochet value from a promotion, is using the congratulatory pen program.

It works this way. You contact your advertising specialty representative, and have him sell you some top quality ballpoint pens from their line. On the pens you will have imprinted congratulations and the name of your business. Then, you watch the local newspapers very carefully for names of people who have accomplished something. This can be a promotion to a new job, someone who has just had a baby, done some civic service, etc. You clip the clipping from the newspaper , and attach it to a little folder on which the pen is inserted, and a little handwritten note from you stating congratulations, it's nice to live in a community with nice people like you, and sign your name and have your business name or business card inserted with it.

Now what does this do? In the first place, it almost always gets a response from the individual who received the pen. They will either come by and thank you, write you a note, or otherwise make it known to you that they appreciated what you did. It also has ricochet value in terms of them telling their wife, their business associates, or others about your little gift.

You can control the people you send it to, sticking primarily to business and community leaders if you wish, and build recognition in the power structure for your business. It is inexpensive to do, and it does have excellent ricochet value and business image building potentials .

SANTA CLAUS PICTURES

One man who started a small toy store, was looking for a method of building customer loyalty and image for his store. He came up with the idea the first year, of having all the children come to the store to visit Santa Claus, and having their picture taken with him. He offered to send the mother a free picture, if they would fill out a little form giving their name and address, age of the child, his birthday, and names of any other children in the family and their birthdays.

He advertised free pictures with Santa Claus, and got over 3,000 people to go through his store in the three weeks after Thanksgiving, and wound up with a mailing list of people who had children, and the name and address and birthdays of those children.

He sent the mothers the Santa Claus picture as promised, and saved all the negatives. He then set up a mailing campaign to be mailed to the parents about two weeks before the child's birthday, offering a list of suggested toys for that child's particular age. Now this gave him year-long business from parents buying birthday presents, and in that first year he had to enlarge his store twice.

Then, the next Christmas , he took all those negatives and had the post-card made from each, and mailed it out to all the parents offering them a special discount, in an evening of shopping for preferred customers only. Santa Claus would also be there to visit with the children of his preferred customers, and the store was swamped that evening.

He developed a reputation for having the biggest line of toys in the area, and the ricochet value of his mailing promotions to parents, brought other parents into register with him so they could be reminded of their childrens' birthdays and get gift suggestions from him. He developed a chain of these stores, and sold out for a net profit of over 8 million dollars, and his initial opening cost was under $5000.

There is another lesson to be learned from this in promotion as well as ricochet value. And that is identifying your specific target, and being able to zero in on it specifically to increase business at times when it is normally slack.

THE BUDDY ONE-CENT SALE

Another merchant used ricochet advertising in a most unique manner. He too developed a mailing list of his best customers, and twice a year he would hold a buddy one-cent sale. That is, the women could come to his store, and buy an item at a sale price, and the buddy could purchase the same item for one-cent (or a comparable item). Now this system of ricochet advertising resulted in his best customers bringing friends into the store, who were not his customers, and he had them register at the door in order to qualify for the one-cent privilege, and doubled his mailing list each time he had the sale.

Now this is another example of astute advertising that increases business, using already satisfied customers to bring in new customers.

THE WINDOW ART CONTEST

Another merchant who had a store on a fairly well traveled street, who was interested in stopping traffic and getting people into his store, set up a twice-monthly window art contest. He allowed painters, poets, sculptors, people with handicrafts, etc. to bring their work to his store to be put on display in his window. He would display art work of the same kind, and have a sign in the window that the public could come in and vote on that which they thought to be the best. The winner in each period would receive a $25 merchandise certificate from his store, and of course the material was on sale at prices quoted by the artist (if he sold any, he took a 10% commission), and he increased his floor traffic five fold with this little gimmick.

The artists, poets , handicraft workers, etc. were standing in line to get in on his window contest program, and the public, intrigued by the idea of being able to vote, came into his store and cast their ballots.

Now this had a fantastic ricochet value because everyone in the art community in town was talking about it, customers would mention it to their friends, people who dropped in off the street would talk about it, and his business benefited proportionately.

FREE CLUB BULLETINS

Another way of getting great ricochet advertising, is to offer clubs, small clubs, organizations, and churches in your community free club bulletins from your store. You set up a mimeograph machine, and supply free bulletin paper , and they come in with their stencils (which they purchase from you at cost), and run off their bulletins.

On the bottom of each bulletin you print: 'this bulletin donated by', your business name, your slogan, and the address and telephone number. Now here again is a ricochet value promotion, that costs very little money, has the members of the clubs and organizations talking about you and your service in a very favorable manner, plus gets you free advertising on every sheet that they send out.

FREE MEETING ROOMS

Another facet of the free club service program is to provide a free meeting room for small groups and organizations. If you have a back room, or a place in your store that can be set up with folding chairs for the group to meet in, you have an opportunity for another ricochet-type promotion that costs you nothing. Some banks and savings and loans use this consistently, and one of the special values of this service, is that every time there is an announcement in the paper, the name of your business is mentioned when the address of the meeting room is given. Again a ricochet value promotion with little or no expense to you.

FREE ADVERTISING ALL OVER TOWN

One of the cleverest contest promotion schemes, involves having customers put bumper stickers with your business name on them, in order to win a prize. The common way to do this, is to have a roving photographer take a picture of the back of a car showing the license plate with your bumper sticker attached, and award a prize each week for the owner of that particular car.

In this way you get people driving all over the community with your billboard on the back of their car, at no cost to you except whatever the weekly prize is.

Another excellent example of ricochet advertising, that does not have to cost a great deal of money, and can improve your community recognition tremendously.

T.V.—RADIO PANEL SHOW

This is one that is particularly good for professional people who can't advertise. The idea is to develop a community panel show, where community leaders and others come in and discuss community affairs with you as the moderator. The trick to getting it on the air is to get out and find a sponsor for it, (bank, savings and loan, shopping center, etc.), and take the package to your local radio or television station. With the time paid for, time can be made available, and you are sitting in front of the microphone or the camera every show, getting fantastic ricochet value from your appearance, and it costs you nothing but your time.

THE 'SET A RECORD' PROMOTION

The Guiness Book of Records has developed into a national past-time. Now a smart S.O.B., looking for some free local publicity for his business, can set up a program where some kids will attempt to break one of the records in the Guiness Book of World Records in front of the store (or in the store for that matter). This results in newspaper publicity, you can promote it in some of your advertising, and again have ricochet value by everybody talking about it, and the curious coming down to see how the new record setters are making out. You can arrange for radio bulletins announcing their progress, and of course, if they succeed in breaking the world record, get pictures and stories in the newspaper concerning it.

Another simple method of ricochet promotion, that builds community identity.

THE LOSS LEADER SPECIAL

Some businesses have succeeded in getting identity by offering a consistent loss leader special. This is commonly done in restaurants where coffee will be offered at three cents a cup; or a sporting goods store where a box of worms will be sold for six cents; a service station where the tenth gallon of gas is one cent; a jewelry store where you can get your watch cleaned for a nickle; or a stationery store where you can buy a box of paper clips for four cents.

This type of steady special, develops ricochet potential as people mention it to other people. It creates new traffic in a store, and builds customer and store volume on a slow but sure basis.

The key to it is to accept the loss on the item, and not worry about who is taking advantage of you and who isn't. The very fact that you will stand by it, and keep it up is where the ricochet value builds.

JUMPING ON FAD PROMOTIONS

One quick way of getting identity, and lots of ricochet value from a promotion, is to capitalize on a fad.

I once developed a promotion for a small store in a large city, which no one had ever heard of. The owner asked me to come up with an idea that would get him some quick community recognition for a sale he was about to have.

So, I looked in the newspaper and discovered that there was a lot of play on preparing for the first moon shot. So, I advised him to go down to the county clerk's office, and file as the owner of the moon crater at which the moon shot was being aimed. Then I told him to make a map of that crater, and sub-divide it up into 50 acre sections, and offer anyone who wanted, a deed on 50 acres of moon. He followed my instructions, and it worked even better than I suspected. The wire services picked up his application, and he gained publicity from all over the world. People were writing him from Switzerland, Afghanistan, and other faraway places to try to obtain one of his deeds.

The local paper, seeing it come in on the wire service, sent somebody out to interview him, took his picture, and needless to say his sale was a fantastic success, and his name became a household word in the community during that period.

Here again we have ricochet value on turning a news item of some interest into publicity for a commercial venture.

Now recently, there was a tremendous amount of publicity given out about pet rocks. How the man who developed them was becoming a millionaire, and people were paying four and five dollars for a box with a rock in it. Now, a smart merchant, could have capitalized on this by offering free pet rocks in his store. Developing a clever advertising theme, making up a little booklet on how to care for your pet rock (similar to that used by the original promoter), he could have capitalized on an event of national interest that people were getting enjoyment from, and gotten fantastic ricochet advertising for a relatively small investment.

So watch these fad situations, because they do offer fantastic ricochet value if they're promoted correctly.

THE GOOD NEWS SHOW

Another idea with great ricochet value, is to set up a telephone line, on which there is endless tape and an answering device, and let the people call up that telephone number each day, and hear nothing but good news. You can hire a couple of women in your own and nearby communities to operate clipping services for you, clipping nothing but good news out of the newspapers, and sending it to you. Then you can put that on tape each day, turn on the machine, and let people call the number to hear the good news. Here again is a fantastic ricochet promotion, which people will be telling other people about, and of course on the endless tape you will insert commercial messages, or other messages identifying you as the source of the information. Your only cost for this is the cost of the telephone, answering device, and getting the information

THE HOROSCOPE TELEPHONE

Another angle on this telephone service, and one that has been successful almost everywhere it has been tried, is to put daily horoscopes on tape, and have the ladies call in to get their daily horoscopes that day. In some communities this has absolutely swamped the telephone lines when it was installed.

You can get astrological predictions by simply going through the astrological magazines, and making up general predictions for each day for each astrological sign, and have them put on tape, and have a fantastically successful ricochet promotion going 365 days a year.

THE BIRTHDAY CLUB

Here is another ricochet promotion, that developed into a community institution. The businessman that promoted this one ran little ads in the newspaper stating that if you have a friend who lives in our county, who is having a birthday or anniversary, send us their name, address, and date of birthday or anniversary and we will send them a free gift in your name.

This brought in a steady stream of letters, giving the required information, and nice little gifts were sent free of charge to each name received, to arrive just before the date of the birthday or anniversary.

Now, what value did this have for this particular merchant? He was in the gift business. So, he built a list of people who were having birthdays and anniversarys, and approximately two weeks before each birthday, or each anniversary, he sent a notice to an individual in the family who would be interested in giving them a gift, suggesting gifts that he had on hand that would serve the purpose.

Then, in his little newspaper ad each day, he ran the headlines offering congratulations, and he ran a list of names on birthdays and another list of names on anniversaries.

People read this every day and it became something of an institution. He wound up owning one of the largest gift stores in the state

RUN FOR OFFICE

Now another method of getting fantastic ricochet publicity and community recognition is to run for a non-controversial public office. This way you're able to spend some money to spread your picture, your name, and say nothing but good things in your campaign, (you might even get elected), and gain much personal recognition from getting free contact with many future potential customers.

While it is time consuming for the individual either in business or in a profession who is looking for instant community identification, seeking political office is probably the fastest way to get it.

The thing you must avoid is some highly controversial situation, where you make as many enemies as you do friends. But if you keep your campaign on a high level, and don't engage in typical political windbagism , it can do you a great deal of good in your commercial enterprise.

HIRE A PUBLICITY AGENT

Another move you can make, that won't cost you anything until you get results, is to hire some local gal, who is a part-time writer and has some journalistic experience, to be your public relations agent. Her job will be to get stories in newspapers, on the air, and in local media about you, your business, and any of your promotional programs.

You arrange to pay her on per inch, per minute basis for everything that is published. Many young gals, are interested in working on a program of this kind, because it gives them experience, something to do, and a little pocket money to go along with it.

Now here again is a ricochet-type promotion, that you are paying for only when something happens, and a steady diet of little plugs and promotional pieces about you is going to build your community image, and improve your business.

TO SUM UP

Most small businesses have a serious problem in developing advertising and promotional plans. The entrepreneur becomes so involved in the daily operations of the business, and all the business detail, that they give little or no thought to the key to the whole thing. And that is how to get customers or clients so they can make more money.

The real key to success in this thing is to sit down everyday, at lunch, first thing in the morning, in the evening, whenever your adrenalin is flowing the highest, and make one specific move that day to get more business. And if you do that, and you're open six days a week you're making over 300 specific moves a year to get more business. This has an accumulative effect, that will increase your business every time it's done, and you will be amazed at the end of the year how much your volume and income have increased. Just one move a day, thought out and put into practice, can make your business from twice to ten times as successful as it is now. Think about it!

CHAPTER 8
HOW TO WIN AND WIN BIG IN BUSINESS

How To Win And Win Big In Business

The reason most business never become big businesses, is because they don't follow the same business procedures that the big boys do. The basic procedure that they overlook, is planning. Most small businesses are reactors, rather than actors. That is they take a punch in the mouth, before they hit back.

As a general rule, the guy that lands the first solid blow, wins the fight. And in business, this takes planning. You've got to know what you're doing, where you're going, and how you're doing while you're getting there.

THE MARKETING PLAN

The first step to take is to determine the potential market for your product or services, and then determine what share of the market you are now enjoying, and from that figure determine how much more of the market should be available.

The techniques we are going to use here are designed to prepare an advertising plan for a retail merchant. You can use the same system for a wholesaler, manufacturer, bank savings and loan or other institution.

On the next page you will see a target table that will give you a general idea of the potential market available both month by month, and annually for the merchandise your client is selling.

To use the table, you first determine the annual average sales per household for the type of business you are in. Then, from your post office of Chamber of Commerce, get the number of households in your trading area, and multiply that number of households times the total annual dollar volume indicated. This figure will give you the total gross volume of sales available in your trading area for the year.

Now let's take for example, preparing a plan for an applicance store. We look at the total gross sales figure of $89.13 given in the target table. This represents the total average household purchase of appliances for the year. Rounding it off at $90, we discover there are 10,000 households in the legitimate trading area of that store, and multiplying that figure by 90, we come up with roughly $900,000 a year in gross volume for appliances in that trading area. You discover that you are doing $150,000, and there are three other stores in the area. This means you are doing 17% of the total potential business, and your competitors are doing 83% of that business. It would indicate that there is room for you to improve your market share dramatically with a comprehensive advertising and promotion plan.

By finding this market share statistic, you are able then, to develop a definite plan for increasing market share by more careful attention to your advertising and promotion, and not by spending more money to obtain it.

use this market target table as a starting point in setting a sales goal

	APPLIANCE STORES	AUTO ACCESSORY STORES	DEPARTMENT STORES	DRUG STORES	FURNITURE STORES	HARDWARE STORES	LUMBER DEALERS	VARIETY STORES	JEWELRY & WATCHES	MEN'S & BOYS' WEAR	SHOES	WOMEN'S CHILDREN'S WEAR
JANUARY	$ 6.45	$ 3.98	$ 28.18	$ 13.65	$ 11.49	$ 3.45	$ 9.76	$ 5.61	$ 3.50	$ 15.07	$ 7.34	$ 26.14
FEBRUARY	6.37	3.79	26.07	13.34	11.11	3.13	9.47	5.90	3.07	12.03	6.37	24.20
MARCH	6.81	4.72	35.30	14.55	12.15	3.75	11.62	7.92	3.86	13.78	8.84	30.83
APRIL	6.29	5.28	34.26	13.87	12.32	4.43	12.54	7.04	3.86	16.37	10.54	33.94
MAY	6.64	5.59	37.28	14.55	13.27	4.61	14.34	7.99	4.72	15.94	8.73	31.61
JUNE	7.46	6.30	39.46	14.84	13.66	4.81	15.02	8.36	4.67	18.08	8.94	30.05
JULY	6.78	5.85	34.12	14.27	13.09	4.45	14.97	7.73	3.96	15.94	7.66	27.70
AUGUST	7.21	5.62	38.75	14.44	13.90	4.35	15.48	8.51	4.32	17.01	8.41	29.65
SEPTEMBER	7.89	5.49	39.41	14.34	13.68	4.32	14.73	8.43	4.03	17.44	9.69	32.39
OCTOBER	7.48	5.76	39.29	14.44	13.94	4.30	15.16	8.14	4.32	18.08	8.41	33.55
NOVEMBER	8.45	6.19	46.90	14.63	14.60	4.33	13.63	9.70	5.08	19.81	8.73	34.71
DECEMBER	11.30	7.04	71.76	20.63	16.26	6.08	12.17	17.96	12.93	35.74	12.79	55.39
TOTAL	89.13	65.61	470.78	177.55	159.47	52.01	158.89	103.29	$58.32	$215.29	$106.45	$390.16

Source: U.S. Department of Commerce

Black figures show average household purchases by store type. White figures show average household purchases by merchandise line.

Multiply these figures by the number of households in your area to get the approximate sales potential for your size market.

TAKING A POLL

Your next step should be to determine what type, if any, name recognition you have in the immediate trading area. To do this you select 100 names at random in the area, from the phone book, and have your wife, secretary, or other lady, call those 100 names and ask a set of 7 to 12 questions. The lady prefaces her questions by stating that she is not selling anything, and is simply trying to determine how local businessmen might better serve local residents by finding out the answers to some simple questions.

You want to bury your key questions in the middle of the questionaire, and not come right out and offer the true purpose of your poll. As you will note later, the questions can also be useful in preparing your advertising plan later on. Here is a list of 10 suggested questions:

1. Which newspaper do you read?
2. Which shopping center do you shop at most of the time?
3. Do you listen to a local radio station, if so, which one?
4. Did you buy your automobile from a local dealer?
5. If so, which dealer?
6. Did you buy your appliances from a local dealer?
7. If so, which one?
8. Could you off-hand name a local appliance dealer other than Sears, Wards (name of any major department store in the area).
9. Do you own your home or do you rent?
10. How long have you lived in the area?

Now from this poll you have learned several things. First, you have learned which newspaper is probably most read in the area. Second, you have learned which, if any, local radio stations are listened to. You have learned which shopping center is most preferred. You have discovered where most people are buying their appliances locally. And you have discovered whether you have any immediate name recognition among a random chosen audience.

This information is valuable, because it gives you information you need to determine exactly how the advertising plan should be prepared.

For example, you have little or no name recognition in a random poll, the first job is to get that recognition and make people aware that you are in business, that you do sell appliances, and then, and only then, can you begin to increase your market share.

Now, with that poll out of the way, you will want to take a second poll of past customers of yours. You get the names of 100 people who have purchased appliances from you over the past three year period. You then call them up and ask these questions:

1. Which newspaper do they prefer?

2. Which radio or TV station do they watch?

3. From which stores have they purchased the appliances they own?

4. Were they satisfied with the purchases they have made?

5. Would they buy again from the same store or stores?

6. If not, why not?

7. What brand of refrigerators, dishwashers, (whatever other items you carry) do they prefer?

8. Do they own or rent their own homes?

9. How long have they lived in the community?

10. Are they planning any appliance purchase in the near future?

Now from this poll you will find out something more specific. Which newspapers, radio, T.V.s, etc. are most likely to reach present customers. You will also probably discover that several of their appliances were purchased from competitors of yours; business you lost that could have been yours if the customer had expressed satisfaction with what they purchased from you. You have also discovered which brand of merchandise they prefer, so that you can target sales information to overcome brand resistance if necessary. You learned something about their economic status from whether they are homeowners or renters, and how long they have lived in the community. You have also learned how many are thinking about buying new appliances, so you can immediately begin a direct mail campaign to all customers, to get them in the store to see the new merchandise.

Now by carefully analyzing your poll information, you are able to come up with some ideas about what needs to be done in order to increase the market share.

With this information in hand, you will then need to get some additional information. You will want to determine by percentages month by month how much of the total gross business you do in any given month. You will find charts for most retail stores on the following pages giving month by month ratios of businesses done. For example, in checking appliance stores   you will note they did 2% of their business in January and 12.7% in December. If you are operating at a proper level, figures should pretty well match those of the national average. If there are extenuating circumstances due to locality for example, severe bad weather in the winter months, when a little slower traffic can be expected, they should be adjusted accordingly. But, in most areas, these averages should hold pretty well true if you are doing business at a normal level.

If you find any severe variations in these figures, then you will have to determine why this is so, and arrange your advertising plan to bring up total sales where they are down in given months.

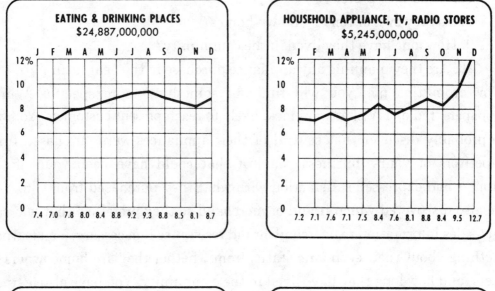

EATING & DRINKING PLACES
$24,887,000,000

7.4 7.0 7.8 8.0 8.4 8.8 9.2 9.3 8.8 8.5 8.1 8.7

HOUSEHOLD APPLIANCE, TV, RADIO STORES
$5,245,000,000

7.2 7.1 7.6 7.1 7.5 8.4 7.6 8.1 8.8 8.4 9.5 12.7

FAMILY CLOTHING STORES
$3,586,000,000

6.1 5.4 7.9 7.1 7.4 7.8 7.1 8.6 9.1 8.4 9.3 15.8

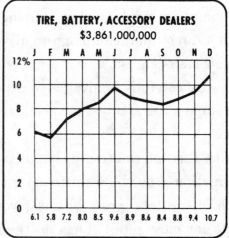

TIRE, BATTERY, ACCESSORY DEALERS
$3,861,000,000

6.1 5.8 7.2 8.0 8.5 9.6 8.9 8.6 8.4 8.8 9.4 10.7

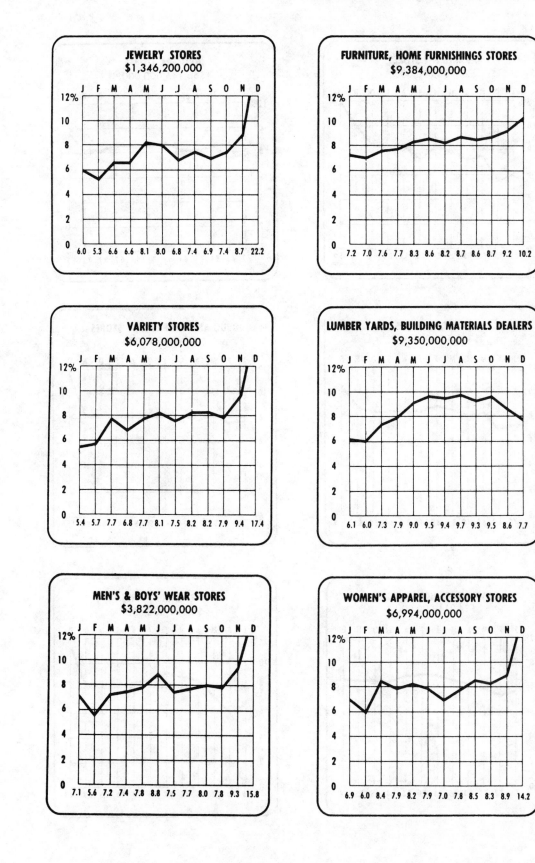

JEWELRY STORES
$1,346,200,000

J F M A M J J A S O N D
12%
10
8
6
4
2
0
6.0 5.3 6.6 6.6 8.1 8.0 6.8 7.4 6.9 7.4 8.7 22.2

FURNITURE, HOME FURNISHINGS STORES
$9,384,000,000

J F M A M J J A S O N D
12%
10
8
6
4
2
0
7.2 7.0 7.6 7.7 8.3 8.6 8.2 8.7 8.6 8.7 9.2 10.2

VARIETY STORES
$6,078,000,000

J F M A M J J A S O N D
12%
10
8
6
4
2
0
5.4 5.7 7.7 6.8 7.7 8.1 7.5 8.2 8.2 7.9 9.4 17.4

LUMBER YARDS, BUILDING MATERIALS DEALERS
$9,350,000,000

J F M A M J J A S O N D
12%
10
8
6
4
2
0
6.1 6.0 7.3 7.9 9.0 9.5 9.4 9.7 9.3 9.5 8.6 7.7

MEN'S & BOYS' WEAR STORES
$3,822,000,000

J F M A M J J A S O N D
12%
10
8
6
4
2
0
7.1 5.6 7.2 7.4 7.8 8.8 7.5 7.7 8.0 7.8 9.3 15.8

WOMEN'S APPAREL, ACCESSORY STORES
$6,994,000,000

J F M A M J J A S O N D
12%
10
8
6
4
2
0
6.9 6.0 8.4 7.9 8.2 7.9 7.0 7.8 8.5 8.3 8.9 14.2

DEPARTMENT STORES
$27,703,000,000

J F M A M J J A S O N D
12% 10 8 6 4 2 0
6.0 5.5 7.5 7.3 7.9 8.4 7.3 8.2 8.4 8.3 10.0 15.2

GROCERY STORES
$66,146,000,000

J F M A M J J A S O N D
12% 10 8 6 4 2 0
7.7 7.5 8.4 8.1 8.1 8.7 8.5 8.4 8.7 8.1 8.3 9.5

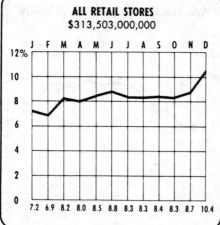

ALL RETAIL STORES
$313,503,000,000

J F M A M J J A S O N D
12% 10 8 6 4 2 0
7.2 6.9 8.2 8.0 8.5 8.8 8.3 8.3 8.4 8.3 8.7 10.4

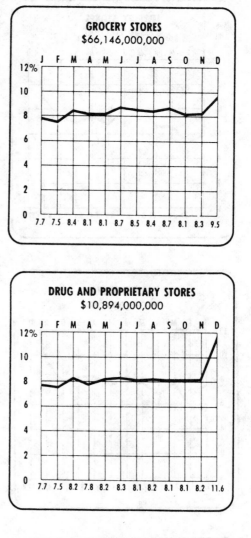

DRUG AND PROPRIETARY STORES
$10,894,000,000

J F M A M J J A S O N D
12% 10 8 6 4 2 0
7.7 7.5 8.2 7.8 8.2 8.3 8.1 8.2 8.1 8.1 8.2 11.6

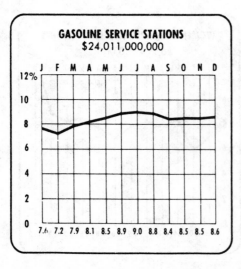

GASOLINE SERVICE STATIONS
$24,011,000,000

J F M A M J J A S O N D
12% 10 8 6 4 2 0
7.6 7.2 7.9 8.1 8.5 8.9 9.0 8.8 8.4 8.5 8.5 8.6

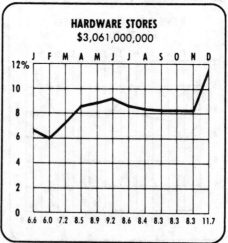

HARDWARE STORES
$3,061,000,000

J F M A M J J A S O N D
12% 10 8 6 4 2 0
6.6 6.0 7.2 8.5 8.9 9.2 8.6 8.4 8.3 8.3 8.3 11.7

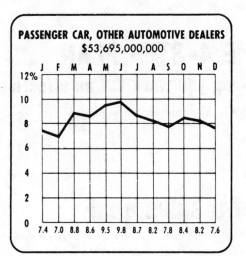

SETTING REALISTIC SALES GOALS

Once you have this information in hand, you know the national averages, you estimate how much increased market share you should get, you can sit down and give a month by month estimate of what the realistic sales goals for the next 12 months should be. Using the chart on the facing page, taking into consideration any expected increases (or decreases) in population, a horse back estimate of business conditions, you should be able to show in black and white figures how you can improve your business.

HOW TO PREPARE YOUR CAMPAIGNS

There are certain steps that you should be aware of in preparing an overall advertising plan, and should consider in developing your month by month advertising schedules.

THE 4-STEP PLAN
to help you work out an effective program for your store

(The following six pages demonstrate how to plan your advertising for next month.)

1.

set a sales goal

Write down the sales figures for next month last year—for the whole store and for each department.

Then, in view of this performance and your own knowledge and judgment of this year's picture, rough in sales goals for next month. Use the profit pointers at right as a reminder of the factors to be considered in making your sales goal realistic but challenging.

PROFIT POINTERS

- Your sales last year
- Population, income, employment levels
- New and expanded departments
- Tie-ins with merchandising events
- Current prices and stock on hand
- What competitors are doing, getting
- More aggressive selling and advertising

NEXT MONTH IS _____

DEPARTMENT OR MERCHANDISE GROUP	MONTH'S SALES LAST YEAR	MONTH'S SALES GOAL THIS YEAR
_____	$ _____ (%)	$ _____ (%)
_____	$ _____ (%)	$ _____ (%)
_____	$ _____ (%)	$ _____ (%)
_____	$ _____ (%)	$ _____ (%)
_____	$ _____ (%)	$ _____ (%)
_____	$ _____ (%)	$ _____ (%)
_____	$ _____ (%)	$ _____ (%)
_____	$ _____ (%)	$ _____ (%)
_____	$ _____ (%)	$ _____ (%)
_____	$ _____ (%)	$ _____ (%)
_____	$ _____ (%)	$ _____ (%)
_____	$ _____ (%)	$ _____ (%)
_____	$ _____ (%)	$ _____ (%)
TOTALS	$ _____ **(100%)**	$ _____ **(100%)**

Newspapers—You will have to determine which newspapers present you with the best coverage, both classified and display, and determine which is the best rate schedule you can obtain in the quantity of advertising you are planning on running.

Radio-TV! In your random polls, you have come up with some idea of who listens to local radio stations, which stations they listen to, and by perhaps taking another poll at random of say 250 to 500 selected people, you can quickly determine which local radio and/or TV station might have the best potential for you.

Direct Mail! Direct mail should be a definite part of your plan in soliciting business from past customers. There should be at least 4-6 mailings a year to all customers, announcing new lines or having special pre-dated customer sales, where when you put a lot of merchandise on sale and you invite the customers down to a special non advertised sale the day before the sale announcement breaks in the paper, to give them a chance to get first crack at the bargains. This is appreciated, brings in store traffic from old customers, and retains customer loyalties.

In Store Signs! You will have to coordinate all your sales programs with in-store signing. All sides, all special events, all new lines of merchandise should be appropriately signed. Window signs, particularly signs large enough to attract the attention of passing automobiles are a vital factor in creating additional store traffic and more business.

Window Displays—You will have to tie in your special promotions with special window displays if they are available. If the entire store is the window display, it should be arranged that the featured merchandise is predominantly displayed and spotlighted inside the store, so passers-by may see it.

Advertising Specialties! The use of calendars, and other specialty items is also an important customer loyalty builder, and one that should not be overlooked, but carefully planned for. All old customers should get an annual calendar, and possibly such things as pot holders, yard sticks and other specialty items to retain customer loyalty, store identification and building of good will.

Miscellaneous Advertising! You will run across the problem of purchasing advertising in local school books, club directories, fraternal publications, etc., which are all really charitable contributions. These should be gone over carefully and a small budget set aside to take care of them. None of them should be looked on as having any advertising value, and should simply be considered as charitable contributions, considered and handled as such. They should be budgeted for, and politely declined, asking them to send a letter so they can be considered in next years budget. Reserve Promotion Fund! And finally, not every dollar should be committed. You should hold something in reserve to take advantage of special opportunities, special purchases made that will build terrific store traffic if properly promoted, opportunities to tie into publicity and other events which should be taken advantage of.

PUBLIC RELATIONS

You should include in the advertising program, a public relations budget. This is to pay for the pictures that could be submitted to newspapers, radio, TV, etc., to gain favorable mention for your business because of any civic activities you have participated in, and special awards that have come your way, etc. Public relations are an important part of doing business, and should be a definite and planned part of any overall advertising and promotion campaign.

CO-OP MONEY

And finally, all co-op money available from manufacturer's or distributor's should be carefully included in the advertising budget. All co-op offers that are available should be taken advantage of, and the money should be available to use to the best advantage of the store. Rather than simply throwing in an ad, because it is more or less free, the co-op advertising dollar should be carefully worked into the overall budget and used at the most effective time for the store. Make sure that you note all co-op offers, so that you can integrate them properly in the advertising plan, and not have them simply be forgotten and not taken advantage of.

ADVERTISING FORMAT

When you sit down to design the advertising, the first step should be a recognizable logo. The logo is the store signature which appears on advertising, signs, packages, trucks etc. It should be distinctive, and always displayed on all promotional and advertising material to gain instant store identification.

The advertising layout should reflect a definite style. By keeping your advertising always in the same style, you gain reader identification. Once they see that style of ad they recognize immediately its source.

Too often, the advertising layout is left to the retail ad salesman of the newspaper, or the writing of radio commercials is left to the time salesman. You should sit down and analyze the type of store it is, develop an advertising layout format that fits the personality of the store, and once established, stick with it to gain reader identification.

All your ads for promotional things should be ready thirty days ahead of time in terms of layout and basic merchandise. Spaces can be left open until the last minute 1) to include merchandise that may not have yet reached the store, or 2) changes at the last minute; because there isn't enough to warrant advertising. But the layouts, the, plans, the sizes etc. should always be ready at least 30 days in advance, and all signs, radio spots, other allied and promotional material ready, properly timed for release so that the total advertising program works in harmony and combines to do the best job.

COMPARE RESULTS

With your sales target figure set down, you should then each month, compare the results of your estimates with the actual results you obtain. You might as well recognize in advance, not everything you plan and promote is going to work. Because of weather, economic conditions, or simply bad choices of merchandise some of your campaigns are simply not going to work as well as they should. But over all, by carefully planning and developing your advertising program you should be able to reach or exceed your target every month. By doing this, you convince yourself that your advertising services are worthwhile, and the money you are paying is well worth it.

compare your sales and advertising (month by month)

1. Write in monthly sales in the first column below. Then total.

2. Find what percentage each month contributes to annual sales by dividing annual sales total into each month's sales. Write in percentage figures. Round off to total 100% for the year.

3. Do the same for your advertising. Write in advertising used each month (either in dollars, column inches or lines). Then total.

4. Divide this total into each month's figure to get monthly percent. Again round off to total 100% for the year.

5. Plot the monthly percentages of sales and advertising on the graph below. Compare your sales and advertising. Wherever sales and advertising lines don't run close, you're missing selling opportunities with advertising that's too early or too late.

Note: If your store figures are not readily available, you can use the "typical store" sales patterns on pages 44, 45, 53.

	1. SALES LAST YEAR	**2.** % OF YEAR'S SALES	**3.** ADVERTISING LAST YEAR	**4.** % OF YEAR'S ADVERTISING
Jan.				
Feb.				
Mar.				
Apr.				
May				
Jun.				
July				
Aug.				
Sept.				
Oct.				
Nov.				
Dec.				
Total		100%		100%

PRICING RIGHT

The second reason that small businesses often fail to grow, and often fail, is the people running them simply don't understand the art of pricing. It is vital that a small business have a firm pricing policy, and one that reflects all the costs of doing business, adequate returns, an adequate gross profit, an adequate net profit, and a return on investment. Pricing is both an art and a science, and one that should be reviewed at least every three months in these days of rapid inflation. All pricing in the business should be kept at a level that reflects the necessary operating margins to keep the business profitable.

The problem of over-pricing is not as prevalent as under-pricing. Over-pricing is quickly reflected in loss of volume, and failure to grow as rapidly as one should. As a general rule, it is easy to determine over-pricing by simply checking the competition. There are seven general points that can reveal over-pricing.

   1. Competitors' prices are lower.[1]

   2. The gross profit percentage is growing.[1]

   3. There are many customer price complaints.[1]

   4. The number of sales is declining.[1]

   5. The clerks or salesmen receive many price complaints .[1]

   6. There are complaints about quality and returns of merchandise which are often price complaints in disguise.[1]

   7. There are more people asking the price and walking away, or asking for bids and not buying, than there should be.[1]

A much more common and serious problem is that of under-pricing A firm that is under-pricing probably has a high cash flow, and business seems to be good. But there are clues to determining the proper pricing, and they should be noted carefully, because many businesses can unknowingly fall into an under-pricing situation and be bankrupt before they realize what the problem is.

The things to watch for in under-pricing are:

1. That the growth profit margin is getting smaller.[1]

2. The net profit margin is getting smaller.

3. The prices are generally below those of the competition.[1]

4. Customers do not complain about pricing.[1]

5. Prices have not been changed for a considerable length of time.[1]

6. Increases in business and cash flow do not result in increased net profit.[1]

7. People are buying without haggling, and there is an increased number of orders without asking the price.[1]

8. Many new customers.[1]

9. A smaller bank balance.[1]

10. A sudden upsurge in business for no appreciable reason.[1]

11. Few quality complaints and few returns.[1]

12. Where labor and material costs have been raised without prices being raised.[1]

If you are using a good accountant , he should be able to quickly determine from analyzing your financial statements, whether you are engaged in under-pricing . While it is true, under-pricing makes selling easier, it doesn't make surviving easier. You have to work harder to sell at competitive prices, but the end result is success as opposed to failure.

In the appendix you will find a series of computations on how to arrive at proper retail prices. They are devised so that you can use the formulas immediately on your calculator, and by using them you can quickly determine the proper prices to charge to arrive at your needed income goal. If you will use these charts to check your pricing, you may surprise yourself.

HOW TO PRICE YOUR SERVICES

If you are performing a service for profit, or are planning to, the key question is, "How do I price my service to be sure I'm making a fair profit?"

Here is a report written by Alfred A. Cox and Rowe M. Meador, Professors of Business Administration, showing you how to put a fair, and more importantly, a profitable price on your services.

Often, small marketeers who sell services rather than commodities find it hard to establish prices. Those who deal in one standard service can sometimes overcome this difficulty fairly easily, but the problem is more complicated for small marketeers who sell multiple services—for example, a drycleaner who sells cleaning, repair, and laundry services. Additional problems are faced by those who sell services and goods, as in the case of an automobile dealer.

PRICING ELEMENTS

Most often, these small marketeers run into trouble because they are not aware of the elements that go into making up a selling price. The three elements are materials and supplies costs, labor and other operating expenses, and planned profit margin.

This explains a logical method you can use to determine your price for services. The method is based on your total cost for the service. It considers a fair price to the customer and income to you, including a reasonable return on your investment.

GROUND RULES FOR PRICING SERVICES

As you examine this method of pricing, keep three rules in mind.

1. Each service you sell should contribute to the profit position of your firm. Don't unintentionally allow one to subsidize another. Don't deliberately operate one service at a loss to promote the success of another unless you are sure that such action will increase your overall sales and profits.

2. Be sure that you have an accounting or bookkeeping system that accurately reflects all operating expenses and the cost of all materials you use in providing the service. (If you sell both goods and services, be sure that your records keep the two separate.) You need these facts in order to determine various bases for allocating costs and expenses.

3. Know the difference between direct and indirect costs. This is important when you use the cost method of pricing. Direct costs are expenditures you incur because you do a specific service for a customer. If you eliminate the specific service, you eliminate the labor or material you would need to perform it.

Therefore, you do not need to seek a base for allocating direct costs. You can easily charge the direct cost against the specific service.

However, with indirect costs the story is different. They will go on even though you eliminate a specific service to the customer. For instance, you will still have to pay your rent, your utilities, your fees for professional services.

One problem connected with indirect costs is that you have no precise way of determining how these costs benefit the customer. In other words, indirect costs exist primarily because of all the services you are offering. Your goal is to find some basis that will allow you to distribute or allocate indirect costs to each service in order to determine the total cost of a unit of service.

ANALYZING YOUR SERVICE COSTS

After you have the three ground rules operating in your firm, you are ready to use the cost method of arriving at prices for the services you sell. The cost method involves five steps.

1. Determine your indirect cost per unit of service.

2. Determine your direct cost per unit of service.

3. Add the indirect cost and the direct cost to obtain the total cost per unit of service.

4. Determine the percent of net operating profit you want on your total sales. Subtract this figure from 100 percent (your total sales in dollar volume). This difference is your "cost complement."

5. Divide the total cost per unit of service (from step 3) by your cost complement and multiply by 100 to get your unit selling price.

For example, suppose you are selling three different services. Each of them is standard. Your account ledgers are limited to the costs and expenses listed in the cost analysis table shown in the back. These figures apply to a 30-day month with 26 working days, or 208 working hours.

Service No. 1 is actively producing 80 percent of the time; Service No. 2 produces 70 percent of the time; and Service No. 3, 90 percent.

USING YOUR COSTS TO SET PRICES

After you know what it costs you to produce a service, you can use these costs to set your price. Using the cost analysis as an example, suppose you want a 10 percent net profit on your service sales. In this example, it may be that you have learned from your trade association that an average firm of your size gets approximately 10 percent return on sales.

In determining this percentage figure, be sure to consider the value of your own creativity and experience. As one consultant says, "many service businessmen who came up through the trade sell themselves short. They take their design and craftsmanship abilities for granted."

But, getting back to the example of using a 10 percent return on sales, if you use a 10 percent net profit, your cost complement would be 90 percent. In order to determine your selling price for an hour of each service, use this formula: Cost of service per hour-cost complement x 100 (selling price per hour).

For the three services shown in the cost analysis table, the selling prices per hour are:

Service No. 1: $9.62-90 x 100-$11.00

Service No. 2: $10.68-90 x 100-$12.00

Service No. 3: $5.82-90 x 100-$6.00

If an average unit of service for Service No. 1 requires 2 ½ hours of work, your price for that unit will be $10.69 x 2.5-$26.73.

Suppose that in your business the materials used by each service vary from customer to customer. In this case, you figure the cost of material used plus a reasonable markup to determine your selling price on a specific job.

USING THE MULTIPLIER METHOD

Sometimes you may be able to use the multiplier, or factor method for pricing services. It is particularly useful if these conditions exist.:

1. The amount of service varies from customer to customer.

2. The cost of labor is the most significant item in the selling price.

3. The hourly wage does not vary greatly among the production workers.

You get the multiplier, or factor, from an analysis of your operating statements over a period of several years. (You can use only one year if you are sure that your sales volume and profit margins in that year were what you want them to be.)

Suppose, for example, that an analysis of your operating statements gives the following 5-year averages:

Total Sales:....................$125,000

Total Production labor cost......$50,000

When determining your total production labor costs, do not include office or supervisory wages. Include only employees who are directly connected with the customer service. In this example, you compute your multiplier as follows:

Total Sales ($125,000)-Total production labor cost ($50,000- 2.5

Now, look at this formula in action. The problem: to set t the price for a service job that takes 3 hours of work by the service worker. You are paying $2.50 per hour. Your service selling price would look like this:

Worker's hourly pay....................$ 2.50

Worker's time (hours) on job.............x3

Cost of worker........................7.50

Your multiplier..........................x2.5

Selling price......................$18.75

When you use a multiplier, you should remember that your multiplier represents an average and therefore must be kept up to date. Plan to check your multiplier from time to time to make sure that it reflects conditions as they are at present.

ADJUSTING TO PARTICULAR SITUATION

Some firms are limited in using these pricing methods because of particular situations. In some cases, price schedules used by competing firms may mean that you have to use prices they have established. Other situations to which you might have to adjust are the limitations of a franchised dealer arrangement, prevailing practices or customs within certain service groups, and so on. For instance, practices or customs may dictate that you charge a specific fee or commission related to the value of the job.

In still other cases, local service associations may limit you. Perhaps they adopt price schedules, within the legal possibilities, that may serve as a pattern for your own prices.

Finally, it may well be that the quality of your service is the most important factor in shaping your price schedule. Many customers are willing to pay above-average prices for above-average service. If your customers feel this way about your services, you are ahead of your competitors.

UPGRADING YOUR PROFITS

One of your main goals in determining prices for your service jobs should be the upgrading of your profits. Increasing your profits does not always mean raising your prices. It often means improving your operating efficiency—cutting the cost of your service jobs. Of course, the level of your costs will be determined to a great extent by local prices for labor and materials. But even so, you can often get a competitive edge by improving your operating efficiency.

Some small service firm owners improve their operating efficiency through adequate planning and scheduling of jobs, and by providing for the easiest possible handling of rush jobs.

Your revenue is a condition of your price schedules and your ability to build sales volume. Consider your market area. In what income category are your customers? Are they able to judge quality of service? Do they demand and appreciate superior service—delivery, promptness, personalized attention, friendliness, credit, and so on?

Can you build volume with advertising and promotion? How many competitors are serving the same market area? To what extent can you build greater volume by selling supplementary services related to your main service?

The answers to these questions will help in determining your price structure. To upgrade your profits, continue to expand until your marginal costs equal your marginal revenue. In other words, you should continue to incur an additional dollar of cost so long as you receive in return more than an additional dollar in sales.

Even if your basic prices have been established largely by custom and competitors, you can still use the cost method to advantage. When you know exactly what it costs to produce a service, you can check on the reasonableness of the prices forced on you by outside factors.

ANALYSIS OF EXPENSES AND COSTS PER SERVICE PER PRODUCTIVE WORKING HOUR

	Total per month	Service No. 1	Service No. 2	Service No. 3
Indirect expenses:				
Rent	$200	$100	$50	$50
Manager's salary	600	150	300	150
Clerical wages	200	50	100	50
Other overhead	300	100	100	100
Direct expenses:				
Labor	1,300	500	400	400
Advertising	600	300	150	150
Material	1,200	400	600	200
Total costs	4,400	1,600	1,700	1,100
Productive working hours per month		166.4	145.6	187.2
Cost per productive working hour		$9.62	$10.68	$5.88

HOW TO GET INFORMATION

One thing every businessman should know is how to quickly get information about things he needs or needs to know about. The way to use specific commercial directories, to locate information about products, people, sources of supply, companies, financial information, etc., should be acquired by every businessman.

HOW TO CREATE MILLION DOLLAR IDEAS

The man with the ideas, is the man that is always ahead of the pack. The ability to sit down and create an idea, and implement it, is the key to getting to the very top of the heap.

In this section, we're going to go into the methods that you can use to create new ideas that can make your business and your personal life more successful.

We are going to show you the techniques that are used by professional think-tanks, and professional idea creators in developing new ideas. By reading this, and using the system or systems best suited to you, you can literally turn your mind into an idea factory, coming up with suitable ideas whenever you need them for any purpose.

CREATING NEW IDEAS

Creating ideas is obviously a mental process. It is what the philosophers call, "Creative Synthesis."

This means taking a combination of things, and so arrange them to create a new whole. Edison did not create the electric light out of new substances or new ideas. Everything he used was known. He simply arranged them in such a fashion that when the natural force of electricity was applied to them, a steady light glowed. It is a classic example of creative synthesis.

The psychologists have a set of rules outlined to explain how this process develops in the mind of the innovator. They are called the "The Laws of Association." This law postulates that when the thinker thinks of A, this will call to mind, B. Thus when you think of an egg, you will bring a chicken to mind, because they have a familiar relationship. This is a prime member of the Laws of Association, and is called "The Law of Contiguity."

The second Law of Association is called the Law of Causality. This refers to thinking of A, as an unrelated subject, but it brings to mind B, as a possible connection. Thus you are trying to think of a perfect container, and it brings to mind the egg.

The third law is called "the Law of Similarity." You think of A, and it brings to mind B, because they are similar. Thus you think of an egg, and it brings to mind a football because of their similar shape.

A summation of the Law of Association was put in these terms by W. James; "When two elementary brain processes have been active together or in immediate succession, one of them, on recurring, tends to propagate its excitement to others."

So, in effect, your mind is creating a chain reaction, one segment of your brain, excites the next and the next etc. This will produce a stream of cogent thought about a specific subject, drawing on the information you have stored in your mind.

The stored knowledge in your mind is capable of developing almost an unlimited number of combinations of bits of knowledge that you can use to create whole new concepts.

There is an old saying, "there is nothing new under the sun" . . . This refers to the known phenomena that no one can create anything new out of thin air. Everything they think of must be something they know. The newness comes when the combinations of what they know develop into something heretofore unknown. Every invention and innovation is the result of that process. One has only to look around them to see the products of that process. Everything from the pin to the spacecraft that took men to the moon is such a result.

So, you see, ideas are not the result of random inspiration, but are the result of natural laws at work in the mind of every human capable of thinking and reasoning. Your mind is fully capable of creating ideas that can make you rich.

To give you some idea of the value of that computer that you carry in your head, here's an estimate made by an engineer who builds them. He estimated that to house a computer that would perform the same functions, at the same speed your brain is capable of (in the area of reasoning), it would require a building the size of the Empire State Building, stuffed from top to bottom with electronic equipment, and all the power generated by Niagara Falls to run it.

So, you have the most valuable instrument on earth at your command. The human mind. Use it, and it can do whatever you wish done.

John Dewey outlined five steps in the act of problem solving;

(a) a difficulty is felt, which rational man

(b) attempts to define and locate;

(c) suggestions of possible solutions occur to him,

(d) from which he will make logical deductions or which he will try out experimentally, and then

(e) accept or reject accordingly.

Your mind works exactly that way, and so does the mind of all humans. To give you an example of how easy, and quickly this process takes place, let's assume you are in a restaurant reading the menu. You note there are three items on it that have potential appeal to you, so you must choose (step a). You note that Stew, Chicken and Steak are the three and you check the prices (step b). Stew is $1.00, Chicken $2.00, Steak $4.00. You would enjoy steak the most, and stew the least, (step c). But, cost must be considered, you decide steak is more than you want to pay, but you would rather have chicken than stew, and deduce the difference in price is worth the added enjoyment (step d), so you order chicken (step e).

So, you have engaged in a series of connected thoughts to arrive at a conclusion. You have done the one thing only man on this planet is capable of, you have engaged in the POWER TO REASON. You made a rational choice after weighing the alternatives, and in effect used the precise series of steps that Dewey outlined to do so.

Your mind does this for you everyday. You think, you reason automatically, so you have the power to take that process into the area of creative thinking to produce worthwhile ideas if you wish.

If we have an organized mental idea factory at our disposal why is it used so little by most people? For two basic reasons. First, laziness. Concentrated thinking is hard work. Researchers have discovered that more of the blood sugar is used up in concentrated thinking, than in digging ditches. Second, people are afraid to tackle things they don't fully understand. They shy away from unfamiliar terms and procedures, though they would be fully capable of comprehending them if they would apply some rational thought to them.

START A MENTAL TRAINING CAMP

The first step in building mental agility, is to toughen up your mind. Train it, discipline it so that it will respond at full power on command.

The mind is a muscle, and the harder it's worked the sharper and stronger it gets. To put your mind into training, first concentrate on your memory. In creating innovations, the ability to recall information is vital.

The mind can store immense amounts of information. Some say that everything you have ever seen or heard is stored for possible recall. That may be stretching the point, but there are indications that we do have far more information stored than we realize. For example, music offers some proof. How often have you heard a tune that you hadn't heard for years, and your mind moves ahead of the music you hear. You know what notes are coming next, words come to mind, and in effect you are remembering it without realizing it. The notes you hear trigger release of the notes coming in your mind. That is the key to building a powerful memory. Having keys that will release information on command.

The people who put on shows with memory acts use this technique. They organize a set of keys in their minds, and then each thing they want to remember is visualized with the key. The recall of the key recalls the information. The keys are symbols, or visual pictures with which they couple the information to be remembered.

For example, you commit ten keys to memory. They can be anything you choose. Random visual pictures of a boat, train, ship, car, horse etc. Or you can use the rooms in your house as keys. You can use any sequence it would be easy to remember to build your mental keys. Just commit them firmly to memory, in exact sequence. Let's try an example, we'll put ten in this order;

1. sailboat
2. freight train
3. passenger train
4. steamship
5. Cadillac
6. horse and wagon
7. sled
8. airplane

9. bicycle

10. pogo stick

Now, we have these keys committed to memory. We then pick out, or have someone else call out ten words at random. Let's say these are the words:

1. fracture
2. baloney
3. misanthrope
4. pussy willow
5. buffalo
6. trunk
7. eskimo
8. spaceship
9. chocolate
10. money

The job is to remember those ten words. Here's how you do that, using your keys. When the word fracture comes up, you visualize your sailboat (the first key) being fractured, visualize it in a splint, like a broken arm. Make outlandish visual pictures with your keys, so that recall will be vivid. Next, the word baloney. Visualize huge slices of baloney packed between the cars of your freight train, like a sandwich. Misanthrope for passenger train. If you don't know the meaning of the word off hand, use it as a name (Miss Ann Thrope) and visualize her ordering dinner on the train. Connecting a pussy willow with a steamship, visualize the steamship with a big bunch of pussy willows sticking out of the smokestack; a buffalo and a Cadillac, visualize a buffalo pulling a Cadillac, or sitting in it, and so forth.

The keys, and the words you want to remember will be vividly recalled when you need them. Just think of your memorized key, and the word you want to remember will pop up instantly.

If you work on this program a little everyday, you will be developing mental agility and building your brain muscles at the same time. Soon, you will be able to store bits of information you read and hear as they occur, and be able to do some amazing things. Things like meeting a roomful of strangers and remembering all their names. If you play bridge, have instant recall of each play of the cards, so you remember which cards are still left, thus can play a championship game. And, more importantly, you will be developing your mind to think in creative terms by mixing and matching stored information.

SEEING THE TREES INSTEAD OF THE FOREST

The next step in developing mental muscle for use in creative thinking, is to look beyond the obvious at everything. This requires mental training and toughness.

For example, everyone assumes that the "golden rule" is the perfect rule to live by. Do unto others as you would have them do unto you. Can you think of anything possibly wrong with that statement? Remembering, that there is no such thing as perfection in human affairs, let's apply it to a masochist (people who enjoy having others hurt them in some way). If the masochist applies the golden rule to his friends and neighbors, he's going to be a very unpopular person. The point is this; for every platitude, every so called rule, there are exceptions. The exception is always the place the creative thinker looks.

As a potential creative thinker, looking at a potential idea, ask yourself these questions first:

What is taken for granted here?

What is silently and unconsciously presupposed?

What are the assumptions made that are not always valid here?

What are the exceptions, and how may they be applied here?

Is there a better way?

If you look at each idea you are considering, each product, service or system you come in contact in that way, you will be amazed at how much we tolerate in shoddy, half baked products and services because we "take them for granted." No one really examines them, or comes up with a better way of solving the problems.

So use the techniques of memory building as a mental exercise to force your mind to work and strengthen itself, and then use the mental power you create to look past the obvious to discover the better way of solving the problems we all have.

GETTING RID OF LABEL THINKING

The first problem we all face is to stop becoming label thinkers. To examine the label, and see if it's not really a sham.

Here is a perfect example of label thinking. A very select and dogmatic group of people, highly active in political affairs, were given this statement to read, and to state whether they agreed or disagreed with it.

The statement was ostensibly made by a politician they all knew. The group was divided in half, and remember they were all of the same political persuasion, and all damned sure they were on the side of the angels.

Here's the statement they were given to read: "It is obvious I think, that each American Citizen has the inherent and basic right to hold any position in this land to which he aspires; that all of us may live in the manner and place we choose without asking the consent of any government or group; that we may enjoy the freedom guaranteed by our citizenship, and we may, without fear of penalty or reprisal, say and do as we please as long as we do not harm or inconvenience our neighbors.

Now the first half of the group was given that statement signed by the late Senator Joe McCarthy. The second half was given the statement signed by the late Adlai Stevenson.

Each half was then asked to comment on the statement, and whether they accepted it or not. In the half given the statement signed by Senator McCarthy, all but one, vehemently condemned it as the ravings of a demagogue. In the half given the one by Adlai Stevenson, everyone of them praised it as the statement of conscience of a great statesman. Now the statement was a paraphrase of the opening lines of the Declaration of Independence—All men are created equal, and have the right to life, liberty and the pursuit of happiness.

Label thinking. Put a label on it and you get an emotion. The emotions rule the mind, and people will simply not examine the contents if the label does not appeal to them.

The human being is ruled 80% of the time by his emotions, and only 20% of the time by logic. That is why so few people can be successful gamblers. They simply can't think logically, enough of the time, to manage their money properly.

To think creatively, and use your brain power to the maximum advantage you must avoid label thinking, and pre-supposing. Accept nothing at face value. Consider tha alternatives and you will start to think in creative terms.

PUT IN UNDERSTANDABLE TERMS

Too many of us will not examine a subject because we feel we are not mentally capable of grasping it. Therefore, we avoid it, and perhaps lose a great opportunity.

For example, solve this problem in one minute. It is a problem in space engineering that requires a quick and correct solution.

Get the sum of the variances in this capsulation of a digital thrust coelostat to get a Westphal balance.

Capsulation coefficients	variances
7 Staflic sensors @ .603 degrees	.70
3 Whirl stanchons less .066429	.69
3 cahode promuscators average 3.2 vector	.01
1 orbicular pyrometer @ 6.11 logotherm	1.40
2 Hydro frames, dual Vbs 7.49	0.27
5 flinch pins, tooth spacing @ 1.15	.43
Westphal variances major total	_____
Less 2% of Westphal variance total	_____
New total variances	_____

If you solved it in one minute you are already a breakthrough thinker, if you simply didn't understand it, then you have to examine your mental processes.

The problem was a very simple one, but couched in terms that are unfamiliar. In fact they don't even exist, because I made them up. I don't know any more about space engineering than you do. Probably less. The key word above in the instructions is sum. This means add, so you simply add the totals, and you get the answer. Deduct the percentage and you get the final answer.

The creative thinker would use one of two methods to solve the problem. Either he will carefully analyze the instructions and come up with the method to be used in solving it, or he will transpose the terms into understandable language. Let's try it. We'll substitute some terms that are understandable in place of the space age double talk.

One thing we are all familiar in dealing with is food. We note that the totals in the problem are in decimals, so they could easily be replaced by dollars and cents, rather than just decimal sums. With that option, let's look at the problem transposed into familiar terms.

7 cans of beans @ 10¢ each		70¢
3 heads of lettuce		.69
1 box of matches		.01
1 pork roast		1.40
1 bottle of catsup		.27
5 onions		.43
Total		3.50
Less 2% discount on total		.07
Net total		$3.42

Now, if I gave you a minute to solve that problem, you would think nothing of it. Add up the total, take the discount, and you've got it. It's something you do all the time.

So, when you approach a problem where you'll be dealing with unfamiliar terms, try substituting familiar terms to get a better idea of potential results or relationships.

WE THINK IN CONCEPTS

Another problem we have in creative thinking is dealing with concepts. It comes from experience and observation, and we tend to think in conceptual terms about things, and thus get in a rut of thinking that often leads in the wrong direction.

Let's take the example of flight as a case in point. When we think of flying, we think of birds. Man envied the bird his air since he first saw him. All efforts to create flight were based on bird observations. The airplane today is a copy of the bird, except in the power plant. Why? Because that was the concept we dealt with. Is it true, for example, that something must be aerodynamically sound in order to fly? No, it is not true. Put enough power on your house, and it will fly. Insects fly, fish fly, pollen and dust fly, rockets fly, rocks and bullets fly, balloons fly, snow flies etc. Aerodynamics supply efficiency in the framework of the airplane, but it does not alone, create flight.

So the concept that in order to fly you have to have something whose wings flapped, (and that was the early premise), was wrong. So, the concepts we have of flight have evolved into rockets and air boats that move through the air without birdlike configurations.

When you are thinking about a problem, examine your concepts. Are they necessary? May there not be an entirely different concept that would do the job better? Don't chain yourself to a single line of thinking based on just one concept. Move around mentally and try something else entirely unrelated and see what happens.

The worst concept we use, is that an idea can't be good because it is so obvious to us. Surely others have thought of it before. It may be they have, but it may also be they did nothing with it, or it was ahead of its time. Always put the idea to the test, by checking around to see if it is a new one. Hold its feet to the fire until you are sure it is nothing new. There is a great deal of lost motion in the idea business by creating what has already been done, but it's a problem that goes with the territory.

I always remember the story Alexander King used to tell about the winter he spent in a tiny hotel in the Swiss Alps with an old hermit. It was just after World War II, and the old man was the secretive type. It seems he had a great invention, and was about ready to let the world in on it. The old boy didn't read, or write, had no radio or telephone, and hadn't been out of the village in 35 years. So, one night he agreed to show King his great invention. They struggled up the mountain to the old man's barn, and there was a huge wooden machine the size of a small house. When the old man pounded on a lever with his fist, it rose up and struck a billboard size piece of paper, printing a letter of the alphabet on it. The old man had spent 30 years inventing the typewriter.

So, you can be a day late and a dollar short with your ideas, but there are always lots more where they came from.

Remember, concepts can defeat us if we fail to recognize them. Columbus didn't believe the earth was flat because he saw the masts of ships first over the horizon. He didn't accept a concept because everyone else did. We currently have a concept that nothing can move faster than the speed of light. That is a concept that is based on our ignorance, rather than unimpeachable data. Since all we know is that information we have been able to collect on this tiny speck of dust in the universe, we are only dealing with a smidgen of the total knowledge available. Never accept a concept because it is held as universal truth, until you have examined all the possibilities that it is not true . . . Do this, and you will be a creative thinker at all times.

Now, don't let this refusal to accept the obvious turn you 180 degrees in the opposite direction and become a negative thinker. You refuse to see potential and possibility in anything. You reject it all out of hand as nonsense. Remember this, encouragement and optimism are the fertilizer that makes people grow. Negativism and constant criticism are the weeds that choke growth to death. In other words, always be curious, always be skeptical, but never be closed minded.

In the words of Charles Kettering, one of the greatest innovators and creative thinkers of all time we have this. "Research is nothing but a state of mind—a friendly welcoming attitude toward change—The research state of mind can apply to anything, personal affairs or any kind of business big or little." . . . and from Charles Evans Hughes, this: "A determined soul will do more with a rusty monkey wrench than a loafer will with all the tools in the machine shop."

SYSTEMS FOR CREATING IDEAS

There are systems for working up ideas. They provide you with an organized format for your thought processes to work in. They are used in one form or another by every creative person. The successful innovator will learn to use one or more of them in logical and organized fashion when he has a creative problem. They are valuable in not only creating new ideas, but also in improving and evaluating existing ideas.

There is no one best or worst system, as individuals differ in their psychological makeup and therefore one method that works well for a Thomas Edison might be a total loss for someone else. The best way to find the one that does the job for you, is to try them out on a problem and see which method produces the most headway.

BRAINSTORMING

This is probably the most ballyhooed form of creative thinking. It usually consists of "group think" in an atmosphere of emotional stimulation. The Law of Association is the prime mover here, where people in the group are supposed to stimulate connective ideas from others. The group comes together in a room, and usually starts discussing the problem, ideas are asked for, and people are told to shout them out as soon as they think of them. It doesn't matter how far fetched or ridiculous the idea might seem, it is yelled out, and one person writes them down on a blackboard. The list grows and the excitement grows and more and more people participate in the action.

The advantage here is the stimuli provided by the group. One becomes lost in the excitement, and starts yelling out anything that comes to mind. The excitement and gamesmanship of the method produces a vast range of ideas (when the group starts moving), and supposedly there will be some wheat among all the chaff.

However, it is a scattershot method, with no real controls or direction, and it has been discovered after a good deal of research, it rarely produces anything of real worth. In most places where it was used and touted as the greatest thing since sex, it has been abandoned.

You can try brainstorming alone if you'd like to give it a try. You need first to concentrate on your problem, get your mind actively working on it. Then put some rousing music on your phonograph, turn on a tape recorder, then pace up and down, as ideas occur, shout them out. Pay no attention to order, sequence or even being on the subject. Just yell out whatever comes to mind. Get excited, keep moving, keep hollering, and the ideas will come, almost like a dam has broken. Later you can play back the results of the session and see if there was anything you could use.

The brainstorming technique can be of value in getting you started on a problem, on getting a series of ideas and possibilities to evaluate, and later, in calm, rational thought you may be able to find the germ of the solution you were looking for.

THE GORDON TECHNIQUE

This is a method of creating the germ of an idea for a solution to a problem using the indirect approach or the panorama approach. You approach the problem at a tangent by discussing a related subject, usually one of broad scope that can bring an idea that would not be possible to obtain by directly discussing the problem.

For example, you want a new kind of bicycle lock. So, you bring a group of people together of normal intelligence, but without any expertise in the lock field, and start them off by discussing a generic subject such as inhibiting. If we want to inhibit people from taking a certain action, what should we do. None of the people in this discussion have any idea that you are interested in a new bicycle lock, they only know they are there to discuss ways to inhibit people.

Now, with a broad discussion under way, and people talking aimlessly about the subject, discussing things and ways they were inhibited from doing something, or how they inhibited other people, animals etc., you begin to look for idea germs. As the discussion starts brushing into the area of locks, you can then start localizing it, getting into that specific area, and again waiting for the idea germ to develop.

This technique is particularly useful when you decide that you have been working down the wrong street, and what is needed is a whole new approach to the problem. A new area of search to be found. By getting the group together, and talking about the panorama the subject falls in, you may find a whole new line of inquiry that may solve the problem.

It is obvious that this method will fail far more often than it will succeed, but if the problem seems tied in a Gordian knot, this approach can often be useful in cutting through it.

ATTRIBUTE LISTING

This is the method based on the premise that everything starts from something else (the basic Law of Association). A new idea is simply an old idea to which something has happened.

It works like this; choose something to improve; list the essential parts of the object or subject; list the basic qualities, features or attributes of the parts, and or, the whole product. Then, systematically change or modify the attributes to better satisfy the original purpose or to satisfy a new need.

To give you an example of how this might work, let's take a cigarette lighter as the subject. We list the parts:

1. Fuel Tank
2. Flint
3. Striker Wheel
4. Spring (wheel)
5. Wick
6. Spring (Flint)
7. Screws (Flint and fuel retainer)
8. Case
9. Top
10. Top Hinge

Now we set down the purposes the product serves.

Product Use

1. Produces flame
2. Is portable
3. Generally malfunction free
4. Refillable
5. Can be styled nicely
6. Inexpensive
7. Quite safe to carry
8. Can be made for table-desk use.

Next we consider the problems that lighters have from time to time. This is the area we can look for improvement ideas in terms of performance, handling, packaging, durability etc.

Problems

1. Loss of fuel
2. Loss of flint
3. Messy refilling
4. Failure to light
5. Loss of wick
6. Getting lost

Then you note some potential improvements that you see as a possible solution to problems.

Potential Improvements

1. Better ignition system
2. Simpler refilling system
3. No need to refill
4. Positive lighting
5. Lifetime wick or no wick
6. Positive attachment so it won't be lost.

There we have the product, the problems and some general ideas for solving them jotted down. This opens up two areas of potential investigation. First, to improve the product as it is. Second, to solve the problems by creating a new product that serves the same purposes.

For example, areas of investigation might be in the fuel for creating the flame (or enough heat to light a cigarette). Sun power, make it disposable, fuel cartridges carried as spares inside the case? This process would in essence create a new product.

For improvements: locking in the flame and a small built in stand to make a tiny stove; use a self charging battery to provide heat; snap in fuel cartridges; injector flints like lead pencils etc. As you note these ideas, others will occur (Law of Association at work) and finally a concept that can be reduced to practice.

This is perhaps the most commonly used form of organized thinking about a problem or product, and one that produces many potential solutions. It's one drawback is that it often creates so many potential ideas the thinker becomes unsure of where to start.

INPUT OUTPUT

This is a device used to solve dynamic systems design problems, where one phenomena is used to produce a desired result.

The input system is force. Explosion; water flow; magnetism; wind; sound; sunlight etc. The output will be controlled energy. It will turn wheels, lift, bend, pick up, put down, rotate etc.

The problem is to develop a system that controls and channels the force at the input to do the desired job at the output. Example, is a water wheel that grinds wheat through system of gears. Wind as the input drives a pump to pull water from the ground. Explosion produces rocket flight, or drives a piston engine etc.

We have a good deal of thinking in this area during the energy crisis. How to use a cheap source of input to produce desired energy to accomplish heating, motion, cooling etc.

The creative process involves channeling the force through a system, and the creative problem is designing the system, getting the force from A to B with minimum loss, and enough impact to do the desired job.

Solar heating, more efficient windmills, lasers all fit into this category, and the jobs they can do are only limited by the systems that can be designed for them.

THE CATALOG TECHNIQUE

This is encyclopedia technique. It involves intensive research into the state of the art. Everything that is known about the subject is cataloged and organized, just like an encyclopedia. This material is then winnowed to separate the wheat from the chaff, and the kernels of ideas are picked out of the remaining material, and worked into suitable form.

This is a system that is best suited to large R & D organizations who have the manpower and the time to do the research needed to properly organize the program. For the average innovator it would probably result in finding out more than he wanted to know about the subject, and result in more confusion than clarification.

FREE ASSOCIATION

This is the ladder system for creating ideas. You jot down a number, symbol, word, sketch, picture, formula, measurement, etc., that is connected to the subject. Now, make a connecting notation to it, then another suggested by the first two, and add on until the basic idea emerges.

As an example, 1. a lighter; 2. produces flame; 3. uses fuel soaked wick and spark; 4. portable; 5. carried out in inclement weather; 6. hard to light in wind; 7. needs protection against wind; 8. a protective, perforated gate that can be raised and lowered as needed . . . and there's your innovation.

This system of course will produce many false starts, and you'll go back several steps, and have to start over, but it does lead to the associative thinking, and eventually will produce new and useful ideas.

FORCED RELATIONSHIP

It is a more esoteric and introspective way of developing ideas. The basic premise is that you isolate the elements of the problem at hand. Then you find the relationships between and among these elements. Similarities, differences, analogies and cause and effect. You put these relationships down in organized fashion on 3 by 5 cards. Now, you compare the record of relationships to discover patterns for overlooked ideas or innovations.

If the problem is to find a method of creating a paper that cannot be photocopied, you would put down the elements of the problem something like this. First, photocopiers can now reproduce every color of ink, and make useable copies from any color of paper. Next, you put down the basic processes used in the photocopy process, and the reasons they can copy all types of paper and ink. Next you research all types of papers, paper coating (photographic paper included), and all types of inks, and substances that can be added to other substances such as ink to make them light sensitive. When you have isolated all these processes and products, you proceed to match cards, change relationships until investigative ideas appear in these forced relationships that are well worth pursuing. Eventually you may discover an entirely new relationship of elements to give you the desired result.

TRIAL AND ERROR

This is the sweepstakes method of idea creation. The most often related example of this method was Edison's tireless search for a filament for his electric light. It took thousands of tries before he hit the right combination of a carbonized thread.

You try something, if it fails, discard it and try again. You rely on your own intuition and general subject knowledge for the ideas, and hope you hit. It is the most wasteful and failure prone method of working on new ideas.

MORPHOLOGICAL ANALYSIS

This is a method of systematizing the forced relationship method. It was developed by Dr. Fritz Swicky of Cal Tech, and is designed to provide all possible combinations of potential solutions to a problem.

First you state your problem, then you figure out all the variables in the problem. Then you list all the potentials in the variables. As an example, going back to the cigarette lighter, you put down as variables, fuel system, ignition system, case utility as the four variables. Now, under each category of variables you list all potential methods of doing the job. Under fuel system you can put lighter fluid, butane, electricity, sunlight, and all other combustible combinations you can think of. You put these on a strip of paper in little boxes about an inch or two square. You do the same for the other variables. Now you take a strip of cardboard and cut a window to fit the size of your boxes on the variable strips, and staple it on the ends to another strip of cardboard. You will have a cardboard carrier with four windows in it. Now, place the strips so they can be pulled to expose each variable box through the window. In this manner you can mix and match all the variables by changing the writing exposed in the boxes, and create ideas or suggestions of ideas by examining each possible combination of variables.

The idea is to make sure you have all the variables, and all the potential solutions to each variable on your strips. If so, you will have every potential combination of variables exposed, and possibly create a whole new approach to the problem.

THE CHECK LIST

This is a simple system where you simply make up a laundry list of everything involved and go down it point by point looking for ideas you can use. The most creative way to use the checklist is with the free association technique.

BIG TIME OPERATOR APPROACH

Take the idea that you are working on, and build a mental fairy tale around it. Put it to work in your mind doing the most fantastic job that it is possible to do. Visualize it doing this great job, and see what it looks like, how it works etc. Keep on thinking about it in this context, and you may suddenly discover how it can be done. Perhaps the best known invention created out of whole cloth this way is Gillette's safety razor. He reported that he visualized the razor complete, just as it was initially made. This is also useful in creating a product looking for a problem. You begin by visualizing something that doesn't exist, but that you would like to have, and then you begin to see it as a reality. For example, suppose you hate to fly, but would love to travel without being in the air. You dream of an air bullet that travels a thousand miles an hour in a vacuum tube three thousand miles long. You see yourself inside, you hear the noise, feel the vibrations, note the construction. As you think more about it, it becomes real. You can actually build a model, you go from there to find propellant etc. If you succeed you go down in history with Edison, Fulton and the Wright Brothers etc.

So these are systems you can use to develop ideas, or improve on those you already have. Try some out on your problems, and see if they don't increase your ability to find new solutions that have escaped you before.

THE IDEA STIMULATOR

Here is a check list to help you get your thinking off the ground, and on to a million dollar concept. First, a checklist for product thinking, second, one for thinking about services.

PRODUCTS
1. How can it be improved?
2. Bigger, smaller, make it mobile?
3. Make it stronger, thinner, lighter, fold it, adjustable?
4. More attractive, new package, color, design?
5. Make it cheaper, faster, less labor, fewer parts?
6. Easier to use, replace, fix, reuseable.
7. Do extra jobs, different jobs, attachments?
8. More durable, quieter, less expensive to operate, replace?
9. Combine it, add on, rebuilt.
10. Easier to transport, store, kit form?
11. Easier to maintain, clean, adjust, lubricate?
12. Disposable, portable, self contained, less power/no power?
13. CAN YOU GUARANTEE IT?

SERVICES
1. How can it be improved?
2. Do it yourself, all or part?
3. Less time, effort, energy?
4. Cut costs, labor, material?
5. Make it more pleasant?
6. Safer, surer, cleaner, faster, slower?
7. Do it on premises?
8. Combine it, automate it, make it permanent?
9. Teach it faster?
10. Make it cheaper, more convenient?
11. Extra benefits at no extra cost?
12. Is there a easier way?
13. WOULD YOU BUY IT?

MORE SPECIFIC

To enlarge on some of these thought lines, here are more detailed thoughts to work with:

ADD ON—Personalize it—electrify it—filter it—Add convenience (handle, latch, legs, non-skid etc.)—safety feature.

SUBTRACT—Remove odor—heat—cold—fire—weight—bulk—example: sugar from candy, tubes from tires, noise from typewriters, vibrations from cars, malfunctions from kitchen appliances etc.

MULTIPLY—Two for price of one—double sockets—twin headlights.

DUAL FUNCTIONS—Clock radios, ping pong pool table—calendars to watches etc.

ALTER—Easier to use—control—carry—snap-on—button down.

CONDENSE—Capsulize—hand held—pocket size—bite size—digest size—transistorize etc.

ENLARGE—Jumbo—king size—taller—wider—faster—inflatable.

ACCESSORIZE—Plug in—stack on—change blades, bits, needles—add light, heat, cooling, sound etc.

CONTRAST—Fat to thin—tall to short—wide to narrow—square to round etc.

EASIER TO USE—Quicker—one button to push—washable—portable—battery operated—disposable—rechargeable—adjustable—cleaner.

ANIMATE IT—Moveable—revolves—swings—flies—rolls—jumps.

REVERSIBLE—Coats—table cloths—sofa cushions—rugs—etc.

ADD SOUND OR SILENCE—Music—buzzers—bells—chimes—etc.

Next you will want to give some consideration to the problems of production of the product. As you have it planned, will it be best when you apply these tests?

MATERIAL APPROPRIATENESS—Is it the best for intended use? Can it easily be fabricated? Is it a familiar material to buyers? Will it adapt best to related materials used in product?

STRUCTURAL ADEQUACY—Can it endure production stresses? Will it operate best in temperature and climatic conditions it will be used in? Will it ship, store and handle well? Does it meet all legal requirements? Will it take the knocks, impacts etc. of hard usage?

AVAILABILITY—Is there an adequate supply, from a reliable source? Are prices stable? Are competitive supplies available?

PRODUCTION—Can product be produced on available machines and with normal skills? If not, can existing equipment be modified, and an adequate supply of skilled people trained? If not, has new machinery been designed, tested (i.e. skilled workers). Have assembly techniques been developed? Are components to be used? Are components in good supply at fair prices? Can they be mass produced?

DESIGN—Does design create any major production, assembly etc. problems? Is design most convenient for use? Does color and finish lend itself to the marketplace? Is nameplate compatible? Does it create any special packing or shipping problems?

PACKING, SHIPPING—Is shipping container needed? Can standard containers be used? Can package be reused? Is there a disposal problem? Are containers safe? Does container store easily and safely?

HAZARDS—Have the potential hazards been eliminated? Mould, vermin, light sensitive, bacteria, oxidation, corrosion, pilferage, water vapor, fading or running, odors, fragility, leaking, warping, heat or cold sensitive, loss of aroma, flavor, sedimentation, dehydration, evaporation, conductivity etc.

It might occur to the inventor these are problems for the manufacturer to solve. But, you will find the more answers you have ready to solve potential problems, the better your chance of sale, and the more you will receive when you do sell.

THE CREATIVE WORKING PROCESS

The process of creative thinking has its ups and downs. The resulting elations followed by disappointments and depression give every inventor problems. To avoid this roller coaster psychology, we have set down a set of simple rules the creative thinker should follow to keep his efforts on a more productive and less emotional scale.

1. Don't close your mind. Don't insist what you hold to be true must absolutely be true. Consider all possible alternatives in the approach to your problem. The same old approach may be only in your mind, not on your workbench.

2. Don't deny a fact. When it becomes clear that something is so, accept it. When all variations have been tried, all possibilities exhausted, then rest the

line. Don't beat a dead horse, set it aside and wait until a new line of potential crops up.

3. Keep your mind working. Think! Assemble, observe and evaluate data. Constantly look for keys, ideas for new lines of approach. Use different creative techniques to find them, make your mind constantly pick at the problem, and you will be amazed at the results.

4. Try another set of eyes, and another brain. If you are stuck, try some help. Go to universities, industry, other inventors and get their ideas. They may be able to see some trees in your forest you missed.

5. Break the problem into segments. Take one at a time. Go slowly, work your jig saw puzzle carefully so all the pieces fit, and suddenly what was a complex problem is clear when taken one piece at a time. Otherwise it may not be mentally manageable.

6. Ease up when frustrated. When the solutions literally slip through your fingers, then stop before you get too angry and bitter. Let the field lie fallow for awhile, then come back with a fresh mind and new determination.

7. Put your goal in sight. Know where the goal line is, and know your position on the field. Then you know what is needed to cross it. It also gives you a progress report, a point of reference. As you get nearer your resolve will strengthen.

8. Forget your false pride. Pride in creativity is the vice of fools. Admit mistakes, admit fallibility, admit failure. Don't try to rationalize your mistakes and failures. Accept them, they are also part of your success. Babe Ruth holds two records. One for home runs, one for striking out. It's no sin to strike out, it's only a sin to alibi it. Keep swinging, the home runs will come.

9. Don't seek total perfection. When you have done the job, and created a useful innovation, don't try to make it perfect. Nothing is. When you have crossed the goal, collect for your score, and don't worry about some small flaws.

10. Finish what you start. Don't be a grasshopper. Stay with a project till it's go or no go before starting something else. Better one completed project than 100 started and nothing finished.

These are only common sense, but as anyone involved in creative thinking knows, they are hard to live with. Just try and stay with them, work intelligently and steadily and your success will come.

TO SUM UP

If you will use the techniques, and these are the techniques big business uses successfully, to develop a merchandising plan for your business, to be sure that you are pricing competitively and for profit, to learn how to locate quickly information that you need and how to create ideas that you can use, you have all the ideas to run far ahead of the pack that are now competing with you.

These are the techniques big business uses successfully. If you use them to develop a merchandising plan for your business, to ensure competitive and profitable pricing, and to learn how to quickly locate information and to create useful ideas, you will run far ahead of the pack that are now competing with you.

CHAPTER 9
HOW TO BUY UGLY DUCKLINGS AND SELL SWANS

How To Buy Ugly Ducklings And Sell Swans

At some point, you may wish to sell your business. In fact, you may have to. When you reach that point, there are several things that you can do, to increase the price of the business considerably that won't cost you a dime.

THE BUYERS ARE EAGER

One thing you must remember about the 90% of the people out looking for a business, is they are hot to trot. They are eager to get started in a business, they have the bug and the urge to move in and get going. All they are looking for, is something they feel has a future.

And that word future, is the key to selling a turkey for filet mignon prices. Almost everything you hear and read about selling a business, revolves around the profit and loss statement, the balance sheet, etc. A business sells for X times its gross volume, X times its net profit, etc. Bull shit! A business sells for the same reason anything else sells, because the buyer feels it is worth what he is paying for it on the terms and conditions that it's offered.

Therefore, when you decide that you want to sell your business, you sit down and make up a business plan projecting that plan into the future. That plan will show how it is possible for business to be doubled, tripled, increased 1000%, by simply following a set of procedures. Now the reason that you haven't implemented this plan, is because you are sick, don't have time, don't have the capital, or that your wife won't let you. Whatever the reason, it doesn't have to be particularly logical, all it has to be is said.

Then with this plan, and your operating business , you can sit down with the eager-beaver buyer, and fill the sky full of pie for him, and he will eagerly jump at this fantastic opportunity, that he is getting at a bargain-basement price.

The point is, you sell the business on the volume you will be doing two or three years into the future, not the volume you are doing now. When you have sold this idea to a ready-to-go buyer, he is not going to listen to his lawyer, his accountant, his wife, even the Supreme Court judge couldn't convince him that he isn't getting in on a tremendous proposition.

So, keeping in mind that businesses are purchased on an emotional basis to fill a need that the buyer has, and not always them on a hard-nose return on investment analysis of the current business operation.

By the same token, when you run into somebody selling a business, who is painting the picture for you, zip up your pockets , pack up your bag, and run don't walk, to the nearest exit.

HOW TO BUY AND TAKE OVER GOING BUSINESSES

The first decision to make is your area of interest . . . all businesses are peculiar to themselves, yet must be managed about the same way . . . remember this . . . you can hire management . . . you can't hire the desire to succeed.

1. Area of Interest . . . Always choose what you know best and enjoy doing . . . if you don't enjoy a business, *you'll probably fail.*

2. Decide whether you wish to buy or start from scratch yourself . . . it will make your search easier.

3. The "cost" of buying can be less than starting . . . but it can take longer to turn a bad business around than build a new one to success in competition with a bad one.

4. If you find a poorly managed, but overpriced business with an obdurate owner . . . then consider starting a business in competition with him.

5. Remember, all businesses that are advertised in newspapers, or listed by business opportunity brokers are either overpriced or have a serious problem.

6. No really good business for sale will ever have to be advertised. If it's really good, competitors, suppliers, accountants, attorneys and relatives will know about it, and it will be snapped up through these sources first.

7. As a top limit . . . a business is rarely worth more than 5 times its net profit.

8. Businesses for sale are like any other investment. In boom times they are way overpriced, in recessions they go for next to nothing.

9. Timing is therefore important . . . buy when it's a buyer's market . . . start one when it's a (boom) seller's market.

10. Example: In 1960 a small aerospace manufacturer would sell for ten to twenty times earnings if one were for sale . . . in 1970 you could buy the same company by agreeing to take over their building lease. *Timing is the key.*

11. Try and stay out of crowded, highly competitive businesses that can be started by garage operators if you are buying. Things like rug cleaning, printing, appliance repairs, cleaning agencies, handicraft shops, boutiques, etc. Better to start one.

12. Never, never buy a franchised operation. If the franchisor lets it go in the open market, it's a real dog.

13. Service stations are bad investments. They are at the mercy of oil companies who treat the operators like serfs . . . if business gets really good, they'll open up another station two blocks away.

14. To find out what a prospective business is worth, have your banker get a Dun & Bradstreet report on them.

15. To determine net profit, get income tax returns from the owner for the previous 5 years.

16. *Goodwill* . . . small businesses for sale have substantial sums listed as goodwill . . . it's negotiable, usually highly overpriced. Big corporations now usually list it as $1.00 on their balance sheets.

17. In highly personal businesses, beauty and barber shops, professional practices, advertising art services, public relations firms, etc., goodwill is worthless to a new buyer . . . the customers buy the personal services of the owner, and when he leaves, so might the customer.

18. Turn-around opportunities . . . a business with a small share of a large market where competition comes from "out of town" is an ideal turn around

candidate. The usual failure is in selling effort. Organize a strong sales program and often the value of such a business can be doubled in less than a year.

19. Marketing Beachheads . . . another situation is where a large firm controls a large marketing area, and having a virtual monopoly has become arrogant . . . this is common in businesses such as stationeries and office supply, restaurant and automotive supply firms, swimming pool supply, garden supply and nursery, newspapers and appliance sales and services. Picking an area, starting a business to serve that area with better service and possibly lower prices establishes a quick beachhead . . . and immediate volume.

20. In marketing beachhead situations the big competitor will seldom react quickly enough to be a serious competitor in your chosen area . . . to establish accounts quickly, sell key items at cost as account openers . . . this builds an account base before the big firm can effectively react.

21. *Finding a business for sale!* Rather than starting with newspaper ads and brokers, pass the word to your banker, lawyer, look up accountants who do work for businesses and tell them (offer finder's fees), see wholesalers, manufacturer's reps, salesmen calling on businesses and send letters out to business owners whose businesses might appeal to you. This will give you a shot at a good business that will never reach the open market.

22. *The Business Broker* . . . he is handling the businesses that have to be sold, no one in the know wants to buy them. The best broker to deal with is one who specializes in a type of business. You will usually find them with listings in trade magazines of the business or industry involved.

23. The general broker, who deals in everything, or is a real estate agent with a business broker's license, is usually not worth your time. If you see an ad from such a broker in the local paper, send a friend to find out about it; then if it's worth looking into, you can deal directly with the owner.

24. The specialized broker knows his business and the in's and out's of the businesses he sells. He's a good man to cultivate because by picking his brains, you can learn much. If he knows you are a "buyer" and not a "shopper," he'll contact you with new listings as they come in.

25. Commissions on business sales are varied depending on the state. In New York they are stepped by amount (8% on first $10,000; 6% on next $90,000; and negotiable over $100,000); in California they are a flat 10%. In practice, the

broker takes what he can get, and it is usually a lot less than the authorized commission.

26. If you live in a large city, check business opportunity brokers out through some of the banks. They know the good ones.

27. When answering ads for business opportunities to blind box numbers, use a friend as a front. Have him locate the business, get some of the details, then if it's any good you can enter the picture. This keeps your name from being shopped around and a lot of wasted time following up worthless leads.

28. Many box number ads are brokers, and they rarely have much truth in them. Example:

For Sale
Well established manufacturer of
furniture and wood components for
the industry. New modern plant
located on large fully improved
industrial site with unlimited
potential. Principals only please.
Box 380SIN, The Sunday Special, SF

This ad is typical . . . question: What size is the company? What kind of money required? This is probably a broker's list builder ad . . . collecting potential manufacturing buyers' names . . . if it's the owners, they won't tell you much when you answer . . . they want to keep the fact they are selling a secret.

29. *Super Confidential* . . . the reasons owners play cloak and dagger games when selling may be good or bad. Good would be to keep customers from finding a sale is contemplated to avoid them from starting to look elsewhere. Bad would be to keep suppliers from finding out because they owe them a lot of money, and the suppliers would rush for payment. Good to keep valuable employees from hunting for jobs. Bad because they have labor problems and a sale might bring them to a head.

30. When the sellers play secretive games, it is your job to find out why. It may be to cover up serious problems, and you'd better know what they are.

31. Talk to suppliers, bankers, customers before you buy. Find out what is

going on. It's not your responsibility to keep their secret; you need facts.

32. When you approach the seller, you might as well put all your cards on the table. Give them a complete resume, a financial statement from your banker, and such other references as are pertinent.

33. By doing this, you can establish a frank relationship . . . since you have leveled with them, you can demand the same treatment and cut through the hyperbole to the hard facts.

34. The same situation is true in dealing with good brokers . . . lay your financial and personal facts on the line, and he will respond with proper listings . . . be secretive and vague, and he'll forget you . . . the bane of the broker is the "forever looker" who never buys, and they are vague and secretive most of the time.

35. The proper time one should spend on looking for a business can run from a week to three years. The average is six months to a year.

36. Don't pressure yourself, but time is money. And if you go beyond a year without finding something, better sit down and analyze yourself. It is possible that you don't want a business, but rather are just playing games with people and yourself. A successful businessman must be decisive above all things, and the first decision must be to get going.

37. Why do business owners sell? Understanding the basic reasons can give you a "looking point" as reasons for selling. The most obvious one is the business is losing money.

38. If it's losing money, the key question is why . . . if it's bad management, that can be corrected. If it's bad products, that's fatal . . . if it's poor location, that's correctible . . . if it's up against sharp, well-financed competition, that's fatal too.

39. If the reasons are personal, that's better. It may be the owner wants to cash out his equity at capital gain tax rates rather than pay higher and higher personal income tax rates.

40. The business has outgrown the capital available to the owner. This is often the case in sales agencies, wholesale and manufacturing. The owner does not want, or know how to raise the needed capital . . . this is often a real sleeper.

41. Partnership disagreements often cause a sale. Neither partner has the money or is willing to pay what the other asks. This can also be a sleeper, par-

ticularly where there is bitterness between the partners who want out at the first reasonable opportunity.

42. *The Estate Sale*. One place to keep your eye on is the obituary column for news of the death of business owners. Some successful brokers employ clipping services to get this information. The estate sale can often be a real bargain as heirs want quick cash.

43. The theory of finding an old man with no heirs running a highly successful business who will take in a younger partner for little or no investment who will gradually take over the company, paying for it out of profits . . . *is a fairy tale* . . . every business opportunity broker has standing orders by the hundreds for this situation. One broker who has handled over 5,000 sales says he's seen just two such situations in 25 years.

44. Finding a business that isn't on the market. Every business is for sale if the price is right . . . there may be many owners who haven't put their businesses on the market, but would be very interested in an attractive offer . . .

45. Have your banker (or a friend at the bank) look in Dun & Bradstreet's big book for businesses in the category you are interested in. (They are listed by state, city and standard industrial classification numbers. The S.I.C. number will give you the category you are interested in.) Look up the business, and pay to have them pull a report (which gives credit rating, volume, etc.) on the business.

46. Thus, for around $15.00 a look for the Dun & Bradstreet credit report, you can shop the best businesses in the field and the area you're interested in.

47. If your bank won't cooperate, try a stock broker, big wholesaler, an attorney, etc.

48. When you have your shopping list, send a letter to the owner with your resume and financial statement, telling him you are interested in buying his business. The results may surprise you.

49. Disabuse yourself of any idea that you will be able to buy a profitable business on the cheap side.

50. No good businesses are for sale for little down, and payments out of profits.

51. Some bad ones are . . . and if they have turn-around potential, they are potential gold mines.

52. Forget any idea that you can buy a business in January for $25,000 and sell it in February for $50,000. There will have been too many smart people ahead of you, just to grab these "one in a million" deals.

53. The 1929 collapse of the stock market looks like a minor dip compared to the way prices of small businesses fluctuate.

54. A business can be offered for $100,000 in January and by the end of the month be down to $5,000.

55. The owners first price is often anywhere from 50% to 5000% too high.

56. Anything over 5 times net profit, including fixtures and exclusive of inventory, is suspect. If a business grosses $5 million but nets $2,000, its price isn't worth much more than $10,000, regardless of volume.

57. Many businesses are offered for sale on a purely fraudulent basis. There may be products about to be banned or changes ordered by regulatory agencies that will cost an inordinate amount of money to change . . . or a location is about to be wiped out . . . a new product is about to kill the company's product. Law suits are possible against the company due to defective merchandise . . . an on the road business doomed because of a new freeway . . . etc.

58. The point is, put the deal in an escrow and check everything, and particularly the "market position" of the company and any projected changes in it.

59. The first contact with the owner should be away from the business, in a relaxed setting. Let the owner do the talking as he is, at this point, a salesman for the business.

60. What you are looking for at this time is the eagerness of the owner to convince you, any contradictions in his pitch to the facts you already have, and his reluctance if any, to touch on the real reasons for selling.

61. The next step is to look over the physical plant . . . the fixtures, inventory, etc. You should have the list of each item, its value as stated by the owner . . . by an eyeball check you can discover if this list is inflated in value.

62. The financial information should consist of an "audited" balance sheet, a profit and loss statement, and the income tax statements of the owner or owners for the past several years.

63. Never accept the statement (to cover inadequate records) that, "I keep these records for tax purposes," "I really made X thousand more." . . . demand an audited statement of his true financial picture. The man who says this is confessing a felony, by the way.

64. *The balance sheet test* . . . take current assets (cash on hand, cash in bank and securities), accounts receivable, and weigh them against current liabilities, notes payable, etc. . . . they should be 1.5 to 1 or better in favor of assets.

65. Accounts receivable . . . if they are a big portion of current assets, you'll want an aging report. How many are current (30 days or less), how many are 60-90 days, and how many over 90 days (probably uncollectible or will have to be turned over for collection at 50% or more loss from face value).

66. *Acid test ratio* . . . cash and net receivables to current liabilities . . . a sound business is at least 1 to 1 . . . or put another way, it has the cash on hand to meet current liabilities.

67. *Working capital ratio* . . . this takes cash, cash related items (securities, notes receivable, etc.), accounts receivable, inventory and inventory items (raw materials, goods in process, etc.), add them together and subtract them from current liabilities, the remainder is working capital . . . money available to expand business operations . . . a test of business success is to examine each segment of the total ratio . . . divide the total of current assets into cash (i.e., if $100,000 is the total, cash is $10,000, ratio is 10%) receivables are $50,000 ratio is 50%, inventory is $40,000 it's 40%) to get the cash ratio . . . check a statement 3 to 5 years back to see how these ratios have changed . . . if cash goes up, good. If receivables or inventory go up and cash goes down, look out!

68. Net worth to debt . . . owner net worth and surplus to total liabilities . . . an excess of net worth over total liabilities, if guaranteed by audit, indicates a healthy business. The reverse would indicate the real reason for selling. They owe more than they've got.

69. If you take the ratios and put them down for a three year period, it's the honest business history in terms of improvement or regression.

70. Questions you can answer from these figures: Is the working capital situation improving—are the ratios of "quick assets" (the acid test) to current liabilities improving?

Are receivables rising or remaining about the same to total current assets?
Are receivables rising in relation to sales? Note: This might indicate high credit risks are being taken to improve sales figures.
Is the inventory turnover getting better or worse?

71. One figure bankers are most interested in (in granting loans) is the ratio of fixed assets (machinery, land, buildings, fixtures, etc.) to net worth. A high ratio with low working capital and "quick asset" ratios indicate an overinvested position in equipment. You can recheck this figure by taking fixed ratios to net sales figures. A rising ratio of fixed assets indicates overinvestment is a problem.

72. Finally the bottom line figure, net income to net sales ratio can easily be checked against industry averages (you can get these averages from your banker). The ratio of net income to net worth will also show whether the present owners are leaving anything in the business for future growth.

73. This information will give you the story of this company's performance in the marketplace . . . and it offers something else . . . a way to estimáte the potential of future earnings based on new management and capital.

74. If you get the balance sheets, profit and loss (income) statement, a record of purchases for the last 12 months (by monthly volume), record of sales, the aging (how old they are), report of accounts receivable and payable, your accountant can make up a pro forma (estimated) income statement. If you estimate a $25,000 infusion of capital, it will raise gross volume by 25%. Accountants taking available figures can project this into terms of potential increased profits. It might well show that such an increase in volume might double the net profit.

75. By using the aging reports he can predict your cash flow, and show you how much more working capital would be needed to sustain the higher receivables increased volume would bring.

76. If it turns out you don't have the working capital to sustain the company for the first year during the increased sales, his figures can be used to get a line of credit at a bank to carry the company through its working capital shortages until working capital ratios are built up to handle the new volume.

77. In estimating prices for a business, you have four to work with: Liquidation price, market price, investment price, and asking price.

78. The liquidation price is what it would bring piecemeal at public auction for whatever tangibles, inventory, fixtures, equipment, land, buildings, etc., it owns. Nothing for the operating business. This is the "book value" price.

79. The market price is the price that comes from usual industry practice. For example, a weekly newspaper will sell at its one year gross volume, a sales

agency or franchised business for one year's net profit, a bakery will go for ten times its weekly gross business; supermarkets 5% of sales plus inventory, a manufacturing firm receives appraised value of machinery, cost of raw materials, packaging, shipping and processing materials, cost value of finished goods and 50% to 100% of one year's net profit; service businesses $20 to $30 for each dollar of weekly net plus appraised value of machinery; softwear (ready to wear) 25% of fixtures, 50% to 100% of inventory cost and no goodwill; most common retail stores go for 25% to 50% of fixtures, 50% of inventory, and no goodwill. It's too easy to open up a store of your own, and customers are transitory . . . restaurants, replacement value of fixtures, food inventory, plus 1/2 of annual net profit. These are rough, rule of the thumb "market price" estimates business opportunity brokers use. They have one for almost every business . . . they are not gospel, but simply places to start estimates.

80. *The Investment Value of a Business* . . . is the value it has to you . . . this has nothing to do with the other prices, but takes two primary things into consideration. What you are worth as an employee, and what kind of return you can get on your investment in the business. First, there is your worth as an employee. What are you earning now, or could earn working for someone else. You may be willing to employ yourself for less, but how much less is your first decision. You should be paid your honest worth . . . second, the return on your investment. You can make 5% in a savings account with no risk . . . up to 12% in real estate mortgages with little risk . . . your money has earning power, and your business should pay as much, preferably more, given the risk it's taking as you could get elsewhere. So, the investment price should be predicted on how much you earn in wages for your work, and the return on your invested capital that is fair for the risk involved.

81. The asking price . . . this is the opener, and it is probably too high, in most cases much too high . . . but it's a starting point in your negotiations.

In the final analysis, you will want the "investment price," as it's the only fair price to you.

82. The key question? If you like the business, and have the capital, could you really do better starting on your own, particularly if the business is weak?

83. Finally, what kind of offer are you really prepared to make and stick to. The price above which you won't go . . . this is a very important and necessary decision, because it gives you a base price to work from. It removes indecision, and puts you in a firm bargaining position.

If you decide on a price and are willing to proceed further, then you must be ready to pick up all the loose ends and really check the business out in detail.

84. *Inventory* . . . From Dun & Bradstreet get an industry average on inventory turnover. Take inventory listed on balance sheet, and divide it into gross sales to get a ratio of turnover, and see how it compares with industry average.

85. *Efficiency* . . . Divide gross sales into number of employees, and compare with average volume and average number of employees to get an employee per volume of sales ratio to test efficiency.

86. From income tax statements you'll want withdrawals from the business declared as income as the key figure to profits retained by owner.

87. Compare this earnings figure for the only true test you can have in evaluating most small business, because they simply do not have the records to show how other income was used or applied.

88. Do your own personal analysis first with the initial meeting behind you, some figures to examine, and an idea of what you are going to be up against.

89. First, honestly answer this—Would you be comfortable in this particular business? Would you enjoy operating it?

90. Do you have the necessary knowledge, training and temperament to make it go?

91. Can you really handle this financially, or are you going to be working on a shoestring and praying for a break? Remember, there is one you can handle somewhere . . . don't go in on the shorts.

92. If you have the capital, will it help this business really grow, or are you just buying an income . . . a job?

93. What are you really buying here? Are there actual physical assets fairly priced? Is the inventory valuation really honest? Have you checked this out with suppliers?

94. *The market* . . . First you'll want to identify the customers. Who they are, where they are, their purchasing power, stability and future potential.

95. What do they buy? What do they like and dislike about the product, store, service, etc.? You should spend a day or two on the premises observing, seeing the problems, hearing the customers, the suppliers, the employees, etc.

96. Check outside the company with suppliers, customers, competitors about the business. Don't show your hand as a buyer . . . one of the best covers is to pose as a free lance writer for a business magazine . . . if you don't want to compromise yourself should you buy, hire someone to do the job for you. This approach can turn up some hidden problems you couldn't discover any other way.

97. The product or service . . . is it in common use? Is it a steady seller, or is it being phased out due to new technology? Has it a successful history elsewhere? . . . product or service acceptance is the keystone of future potential.

98. One thing to check carefully in trade publications and talks with people in the trade is the product susceptible to cheap foreign competition?

99. Is there anyone who can stay in business by consistently selling a comparable product or service cheaper due to better equipment, sources of supply, or other reasons?

100. Who are the major competitors going to be? Large firms who can still grow or small firms who can be beaten in the market place?

101. The distribution . . . How does the customer get this product or service? If there are middlemen between it and the end user, who are they, how do they like the product, how are they compensated? Is this in line with industry practice? How stable are they?

102. Can this method be improved upon? Is it a method that can create future growth? Is this system common trade practice?

LOCATION-RETAIL-SERVICE

103. Is the community large enough for this business and existing competition? Is the location convenient and likely to remain so to present customers?

104. Is the physical appearance attractive by contemporary standards, and if not, how much will it cost to make it so?

105. Check parking, public services, utilities, shipping and receiving facilities, transportation.

106. How about the lease? What are the jokers, if any, if so . . . have it checked by your attorney.

107. Is the labor pool sufficient? Are there any union problems?

108. Is it in a deteriorating or improving area? Is the community going up or down?

LOCATION-MANUFACTURING-WHOLESALE

109. Is the building adequate? Will it support growth? Is it in a properly zoned area with no prospective changes?

110. Are wage levels such that you can compete? Will the community support growth of your company, or is it one that fights growth?

111. How close are you to sources of supply, adequate transportation, supportive services, the biggest market?

112. How efficient is the plant layout?

113. One thing that required your own judgment more than research and investigation is your ability to evaluate this flow of information intelligently. Obviously, there will be many negative factors in your investigation, and if you become depressed or discouraged because these minus factors show up, you don't belong in business. Nothing is perfect . . . and if you are looking for something that is, it's in the next world. The point is, evaluate in the light of total potential, not on individual minus or plus factors.

114. *The intangible assets* . . . is there a real desire on the part of customers for the product or service . . . or are they simply transitory, using it because of convenience?

115. How do the customers react to the owner? If the relationship is highly personal, it may be dangerous to buy, particularly in a small town where strangers are viewed with suspicion.

116. Is there a way to improve this business at once with an infusion of capital, machines, or better working force?

117. If there are trademarks, patents, licenses, copyrights involved, they should be checked for legality.

118. If the land and building are included, is title clear?

119. Is the title clear on all equipment? If anything is encumbered, will it be cleared as part of the sale?

If you assume any mortgages, what are the terms (watch for balloon payments)?

120. Are all necessary licenses available to you . . . and what do they cost?

121. Are there any back taxes, liens or unsettled government claims against the business?

122. Are there any long term contracts for goods and services that have been all or partially prepaid, or are they at non-profitable prices? These must be cleaned up.

123. If there are dealer franchises for lines of merchandise, or other business materials, will you also get these on the same terms?

124. Are all insurance policies in order and transferable?

125. Point—Never buy the receivables. Let the former owner have them . . . this prevents you from losing on the bad ones, and allows you a fresh start with everyone. Make sure all suppliers are notified of the sale, and all payables are the responsibility of the previous owner. Make sure all suppliers you intend to use are paid in full out of escrow so you won't start off on the wrong foot with them.

126. Employees . . . It may sound cruel, but as soon as you can, hire new employees, particularly in key positions. The employees of the former owner invariably resent a new owner, and since you are going to be making changes, there will be resistance from them either overt or covert—get your own people in who will do things your way.

127. Tax angles . . . Often a sharp accountant can get the business for you for a lower price by working out the seller's tax problems.

128. He can help you create a much faster cash flow by using techniques to turn cash assets into liabilities during the first few years of operation.

129. For example, he can reduce the selling price by increasing the interest on the unpaid balance . . . interest is a business expense and as such is tax deductible.

130. He can reduce the selling price, particularly where the seller will be in a high tax bracket by retaining the seller as an employee as a consultant, and these payments to him come out of business income and are tax deductions.

131. If there is an agreement the seller will not re-enter that business over a period of time, he can set a yearly stipend to be paid to keep the agreement in force, which is also a deductible business expense.

132. If you want tax protection, your first year should have value on inventory set as high as possible, which will reduce taxable profits without affecting available cash. For example, if the seller is using FIFO (first in, first out) inventory value systems, the buyer can change to LIFO (last in, first out) and cut taxable inventory profits dramatically the first year.

If there is land and buildings involved in the sale, you should have your accountant look into a sale leaseback arrangement to recover a substantial portion of your investment at the start and have deductible expense for leasing the property. This gives you a working capital cushion and puts a solid tax deduction in that would otherwise be unavailable.

The key to deciding whether to buy or lease equipment is the longevity of it. If the equipment has a long life, you should own it . . . if it needs to be replaced every few years, leasing is your best bet.

Caution . . . a lease that gives you title at the end of the leasing period is considered a purchase by the IRS and is not deductible as a business expense, although you can take depreciation. The leased item must revert to the leasing company at the end of the lease period in order to qualify as a genuine lease.

Check with your accountant about the investment tax credit. It comes and goes with political whims, but if it is available, you can take the credit personally and then if you wish, shift the value to a new corporation.

If you lease more than one property (as in branch stores, plants, etc.), set up the leases in different corporations. So, if one goes bad, the only assets liable are those of that corporation; the total assets of the entire corporation are not behind it.

You should avoid taking over anyone else's corporation. It's a far better idea to form a new one of your own, and let the seller keep his. If you want to keep the trade name, arrange for the seller to transfer the name only to your new corporation.

133. Putting high values on machinery and equipment that will have to be replaced in a few years will give maximum tax saving depreciation.

134. The buildings and machinery with long life should be given low values . . . and anything that can be recovered only in a resale should have a low value assessment.

135. You need a tax expert at your side when you get ready to close the deal. It can save you thousands of dollars, give you a head start on profitability, and perhaps make the difference between success and failure.

136. Finally, in making your decision to buy a business, keep this in mind. It is the only way left to amass capital with a limited amount to start with, and a 20% to 30% annual growth rate of invested capital is not at all unusual . . . Paul Getty, one of the richest men in the world, said it best . . . "To make a fortune, you must start in a venture of your own, no matter how small."

CHECK LIST FOR STARTING OR BUYING A BUSINESS

Are You The Type?

Have you rated your personal qualifications using a scale similar to that presented in this book?

Have you had some acquaintances rate you on such scales?

Have you carefully considered those qualities you are weak in, and taken steps to improve them or to get an associate whose strong points will compensate for them?

What Business Should You Choose?

In what business have you had previous experience?

In what business do you know the characteristics by the goods or services you will sell?

Do you have special technical skills, such as those needed by a pharmacist, plumber, electrician, or radio repair man, which may be used in a business?

Have you studied current trends to be certain the new business you are planning is needed?

Have you considered working for someone else to get more experience?

What Are Your Chances for Success?

Are general business conditions good or bad?

Are business conditions in the city and neighborhood where you are planning to locate good or bad?

Are current conditions in the line of business you are planning good or bad?

What Will Be Your Return On Investment?

How much will you have to invest in your business?

What will be your probable net profit?

Will the net profit divided by the investment result in a rate of return which compares favorably with the rate you can obtain from other investment opportunities?

How Much Capital Will You Need?

What income from sales or services can you reasonably expect in the first six months? The first year? The second year?

What is the gross profit you can expect on these volumes of business?

What expenses can you forecast as being necessary?

Is your salary included in these expenses?

Are the net profit and salary adequate?

Have you compared this income with what you could make as an employee?

Are you willing to risk uncertain or irregular income for the next year? Two years?

Have you made an estimate of the capital you will need to open and operate this business until income equals expenses, in accordance with the suggestions outlined in this book?

Where Can You Get The Money?

How much have you saved which you can put into the business immediately?

How much do you have in the form of other assets which you could, if necessary, sell, or on which you could borrow to get additional funds?

Have you some place where you could borrow money to put into the business?

Have you talked to a banker? What does he think about your plan?

Does he think enough of the venture to lend you money?

Do you have a financial reserve available for unexpected needs?

How does the total capital, available from all sources, compare with the estimated capital requirements?

Should You Share The Ownership Of Your Business With Others?

Do you lack technical or management skills which can be most satisfactorily supplied by one or more partners?

Do you need the financial assistance of one or more associates? If you do (or do not) share the ownership with associates, have you checked the features of each form of organization (individual proprietorship, partnership, corporation) to determine which will best fit your operation?

Where Should You Locate?

To help you choose a location, have you answered all of the questions about location?

If you are planning to operate a factory, have you answered these questions in addition to the appropriate ones concerning the location?

a. Should you locate nearer to your source of material supply, your labor, or your market, measured by relative freight, labor, distribution, power, and other costs?

b. Which is more desirable, a city, suburban, or country location, measured by cost and availability of labor, transportation, power, etc.?

c. Where will you find an adequate supply of labor of the types you require?

d. What transportation, power, water supply, fuel, do you need, and where will you find them adequately?

e. Are climatic conditions important to your product or process?

f. How do tax rates compare, allowing for differences in municipal services?

What type of building will you need?

How much space do you need?

What provision are you making for future expansion?

What special features do you require, such as particular types of lighting, heating, ventilating, air conditioning, or dust collecting facilities?

What equipment do you need?

If proper equipment is not in the building site you have selected, where can it be obtained?

If you are planning a manufacturing plant, what structural strengths are required in the building you select to support the machinery and other equipment? Have you complied with the building code in this regard?

After selecting a location on the basis of the above factors, are you and members of your family satisfied that the community will be a desirable place to live and rear your children?

If the proposed location does not meet nearly all your requirements, is there a sound reason why you should not wait and continue seeking a more ideal location?

Should You Buy A Going Business?

Have you considered the advantages and disadvantages of buying a going business, as presented in this report?

Have you compared what it would take to equip and stock a new business with the price asked for the business you are considering buying?

How Much Should You Pay For It?

Have you checked the owner's claims about the business with his copies of his income tax returns?

Are the sales increased by conditions which are not likely to continue?

Is the stock a good buy? How much would have to be disposed of at a loss? How much is out of date, unsalable, or not usable?

Are the fixtures and equipment and/or the machinery modern? Or would they be unsuitable? Overvalued? In poor condition?

Are you going to buy the accounts receivables? Are you sure they are worth the asking price?

Does the present company have good will to offer? Have you been careful in your appraisal of its worth?

Would you assume the liabilities? Are the creditors willing to have you assume the debts?

Have you consulted a lawyer to be sure that the title is good?

Has your lawyer checked to see if there is any lien on record against the assets you are buying?

Are there any accumulated back taxes to pay?

Is this a bulk sale? Has the bulk sales law been complied with?

Why does the owner wish to sell?

What do the suppliers think of the proposition?

Are You Familiar With The Problems of Buying?

In estimating your total stock, have you considered:

a. In what quantities and how often does the user buy your product?

b. What share of the market do you think you can get?

c. Have you broken this total estimate down into the major lines to be carried?

d. What characteristics, specifications, or properties will you require in your materials or parts?

e. Has your stock selection been guided by an analysis of customer preference?

f. Have you set up a model stock assortment to follow in your buying?

g. Will it be cheaper to buy large quantities infrequently or small quantities frequently, weighing price differentials for large orders against capital and space tied up?

h. Have you decided what merchandise to buy from manufacturers? From wholesalers?

i. Have you planned to make your account more valuable by concentrating your buying?

j. Have you considered affiliating with a voluntary or cooperative group?

k. Have you worked out any stock control plants to avoid overstocks, under-stocks, out-of-stocks?

How Will You Price Your Products and Services?

Have you decided on your price ranges?

What prices will you have to charge to cover your costs and obtain a profit?

How do these prices compare with prices of competitors?

Have you investigated possible legal restrictions on your establishment of prices?

What Are The Best Methods of Selling In Your Proposed Business?

Have you studied both the direct and indirect sales promotional methods used by competitors?

Have you outlined your promotional policy? Why do you expect customers to buy your product or service—price, quantity, distinctive styling, other?

Are you going to do outside selling?

Are you going to advertise in the newspapers? Magazines?

Are you going to do direct mail advertising?

Are you going to use handbills?

Are you going to use radio advertising?

Are you going to use television?

Are you going to use display?

How Will You Select And Train Personnel?

Will employees supply skills you lack?

What skills are necessary?

Have you written job descriptions for prospective employees?

Are satisfactory employees available locally?

What is the prevailing wage scale?

What do you plan to pay?

Would it be advantageous or disadvantageous to hire someone now employed by a competitor?

What labor legislation will affect you?

Have you planned your training and follow-up procedures?

What Other Management Problems Will You Face?

Are you going to sell for credit?

Do you have the additional capital necessary to carry accounts receivable?

What will be your returned goods policy?

Have you considered other policies which must be established in your particular business?

Have you planned how you will organize the work?

Have you made a tentative plan to guide the distribution to meet your own time and effort?

What Records Should You Be Prepared to Keep?

Have you planned a bookkeeping system?

Have you planned a merchandise control system?

Have you obtained any standard operating ratios for your type of business which you plan to use as guides?

What additional records are necessary?

What system are you going to use to keep a check on costs?

Do you need any special forms or records? Can they be bought from stock? Must they be printed?

Are you going to keep the records yourself? Hire a bookkeeper? Have an outsider come in periodically?

What Laws and Regulations Will Affect You?

Have you checked the police and health regulations as they apply to your business?

Are your operations subject to interstate commerce regulations?

Have you received advice from your lawyer regarding your responsibilities under Federal or State statutes or local ordinances pertaining to such matters as advertising, pricing, purity of product, royalties, labeling, trade practices, patents, trademarks, copyrights, brand names?

What Tax and Insurance Problems Will You Have?

Have you worked out a system for paying the withholding tax for your employees?

Have you worked out a system for handling sales taxes? Excise taxes?

Has fire insurance been purchased? Windstorm? Use and occupancy?

Has insurance protecting against damage suits and public liability claims been purchased?

Has workmen's compensation insurance been provided?

Has burglary and hold-up insurance been considered?

What other hazards should be insured against?

Will You Keep Up To Date?

How do you plan to keep up with improvements in your trade or industry?

HOW TO PRICE A BUSINESS

The following is a suggested formula for arriving at a price for a business. It is approached from the point of view of the buyer, but should also be of help to the seller. Since all businesses are different, this cannot cover all types. It can only be a rough guideline to point up some of the key considerations.

Step 1. Determine the adjusted tangible net worth of the business. (The total value of all current and long-term assets less liabilities.)

Step 2. Estimate how much the buyer could earn with an amount equal to the value of the tangible net worth if he invested it elsewhere. This is just an arbitrary figure, used for illustration. A reasonable figure depends on the stability and relative risks of the business and the investment picture generally. The rate should be similar to that which could be earned elsewhere with the same approximate risk.

Step 3. Add to this a salary normal for an owner-operator of the business. This combined figure provides a reasonable estimate of the income the buyer can earn elsewhere with the investment and effort involved in working in the business.

Step 4. Determine the average annual net earnings of the business (net profit before subtracting owner's salary) over the past few years. This is before income taxes, to make it comparable with earnings from other sources or by individuals in different tax brackets. (The tax implications of alternate investments should be carefully considered.) The trend of earnings is a key factor. Have they been rising steadily, falling steadily, remaining constant, or fluctuating widely? The earnings figure should be adjusted to reflect these trends.

Step 5. Subtract the total of earning power and reasonable salary from this average net earnings figure. This gives the extra earning power of the business.

Step 6. Use this extra, or excess earning figure to estimate the value of the intangibles. This is done by multiplying the extra earnings by what is termed the "years of profit" multiplier pivots on these points. How unique are the intangibles offered by the firm? How long would it take to set up a similar business and bring it to this stage of development? What expenses and risks would be involved? What is the price of goodwill in similar firms? Will the seller be signing a noncompetitive agreement? If the business is well established, a factor of five or more might be used, especially if the firm has a valuable name, patent or location. A multiplier of three might be reasonable for a moderately seasoned firm. A younger, but profitable firm might merely have a one-year profit figure.

Step 7. Final price = Adjusted Tangible Net Worth + Value of Intangibles. (Extra earnings x "years of profit.") Here is how the formula described might work in evaluating two businesses for sale:

1. Adjusted value of tangible net worth (assets-liabilities).
2. Earning power—at 10%—of an amount equal to the adjusted tangible net worth if invested in a comparable risk business, security, etc.
3. Reasonable salary for owner-operator in the business.
4. Net earnings of the business over recent years—this means net profit before subtracting owner's salary.
5. Extra earning power of the business (line 4—lines 2 & 3).
6. Value of intangibles—using three year profit figure for moderately well established firm (3 times line 5).
7. Final Price—(lines 1 & 6).

Business A	Business B
$50,000	$50,000
5,000	5,000
8,000	8,000
15,500	11,500
2,500	–1,500
7,500	None
$57,000	$50,000 (or less)

In example A, the seller gets a substantial value for intangibles (goodwill) because his business is moderately well established and is earning more than the buyer could earn elsewhere with similar risks and effort. Within three years the buyer should have recovered the amount paid for goodwill in this example.

In example B, the seller gets no value for goodwill because his business, even though it may have existed for a considerable time, is not earning as much as the buyer could through outside investment and effort. In fact, the buyer may feel that even an investment of $50,000—the current appraised value of net assets—is too much because he cannot earn sufficient return.

There are ways that a dedicated business seeker can use to take over a business venture with little or no capital of his own to invest. It should be understood that these will be businesses that are in dire straits, and the owners have few if any options left other than to simply fold up and quit. There are very few successful businesses that can be acquired (except by fraud) using these systems.

The business seeker who wants to take over a failing venture should have more going for him than just the desire to own a business. What he is looking for is a "turnaround" situation where he can take control of a failing business and by using some ideas and techniques he's sure will work, turn it into a profitable venture in a relatively short time.

These opportunities do exist, and by careful looking and evaluating, you can very well find one.

HOW TO BUY A BUSINESS

THE SANDWICH LEASE

This is a method of taking over a business, that you don't intend to manage, but carries a sufficient cash flow to pay off whatever is owed, and pay for somebody to operate it.

You lease the business, with the proviso you have a right to sub-lease. Then you sub-lease the business to an operator, who pays you enough to cover the cost of your lease, plus a profit, plus the fact that they are buying the business for you with no investment of your own.

INSTITUTION OWNED BUSINESSES

If you find a business that is behind in its payments to a bank, insurance company, loan company, etc., that is on the verge of being foreclosed, you can go to the institution and make them a proposition that can allow you to take over the business and have a substantial chunk of money in your pocket as well.

Under this plan you use a piece of property to take over a business. You find a business owing money to banks, finance companies, etc., and you go to the bank or finance company and offer to trade your property for the note on the business. You make this provision, that they will loan you back 80% of the money owed by the business, on your property. You then take over the business, have a mortgage on the property, and have 50% of the original cost of the business in your pocket.

GETTING A BUSINESS AT HALF PRICE

Under this plan, you go out and buy trust deeds at 50% of their value, and trade them at 100% of the value of the business. You point out to the seller that the trust deeds give him an income, and he no longer has to worry about the business. If the cash flow is sufficient, you've taken over a business at half price, and have extra cash to put in your pockets.

The final point is, in any of these deals, always have a slip-out clause, that is, a statement in the contract that it is subject to somebody's approval other than your own. Thus, if things get down to the point where you have to fish and cut bait, and it looks like a sour deal, you can fall back on your slip-out and walk away without being stuck.

HOW TO TAKE OVER GOING BUSINESSES

THE DEBT CONSOLIDATION METHOD

If you find a business whose problem is overwhelming current debt, but with a little breathing space and some better management can be made profitable, then you might try this program.

Your first problem when you discover this situation will be to have a "Dutch Uncle" talk with the present owner. You honestly point out that he's headed down the tubes because of his debt situation. That under these circumstances no one will buy his business with all that debt to clean up. However, if he will agree to some reasonable terms, you can see that he will get something for his business, rather than losing everything. If he agrees that this makes sense, and will let you see what you can work out, you then contact the creditors.

Get a list of everything he owes, with an aging (how old) report on the debts. Now you sit down and figure out the total income the business can produce. As an example, let's say that the business can produce $10,000 a year toward retirement of a debt load that is $25,000. This is after operating expenses and a reasonable salary for you.

Now, working through a banker you contact all the creditors and tell them you will arrange for a bank escrow of $833 a month, and that each creditor will receive 40 cents on the dollar for their account, to be paid proportionally each month out of the escrow fund. That you will continue to do business with them on a COD basis. If you get an agreement, then you can go back to the present owner and arrange to pay him something for the business out of second year (after the debt load has been retired) and take him off the hook on the debts. The amount and terms will depend on his degree of desperation, and the actual value of the business.

This plan, in effect, puts you in control of a business on a basis where you buy it from the income it generates, and if you can increase that income, obviously you will have a valuable piece of property.

Now obviously, the problem here is with the creditors. Why will they agree to take a 60% loss on their accounts? It's a simple reason that goes likes this: *Something is better than nothing.* They are aware that unless something is done, they will get little or nothing as the present owner will go into bankruptcy. With your offer they have a chance to collect something on the bad debts, and keep an account on which they can make future profits without any future credit risk. You have to convince them that you can do the job, of course.

THE EQUIPMENT GAMBIT

If you find a business with a lot of equipment (printing shop, machine shop, small manufacturing plant, etc.) that is free and clear, but there is little or no income and not too much debt, you can try this method.

If you can see a way to pump up the income, get the business going again, then you have an opportunity to take over using the equipment as your capital.

To be successful with this policy, you have to determine how much the owner could get for his operation selling it out piecemeal at auction, or by selling the equipment (if land and building are included, so much the better) to individuals. With an estimate of what the owner can get for the equipment (which is probably his only option), you can arrive at a figure that will do better than if he gives you some reasonable terms. Now, the sticky part of the negotiations will be over your getting title to the equipment. He may want to retain title until he is paid. You point out that without the equipment, you have nothing to buy, and unless you can obtain more financing, there is no way to make the business grow and prosper.

When he agrees to your terms, you take a list of your equipment to the bank, and see what kind of capital you can raise on it. Assuming that you can get enough for a small down payment to the owner along with an operating capital cushion, you can take over. If you cannot get all you need from a bank, run an ad in a local paper looking for someone with some capital who would like to get into a sale leaseback deal. You sell them the equipment, and they lease it back to you. There are firms and individuals who engage in this type of business, and you can find many of them by subscribing to the *Business Opportunity Digest* ($24 a year, 312 FRANKLIN ST. ✆ CLARKSVILLE, TN 37040). As a subscriber, you can run a free ad asking for a sale leaseback deal, or you'll find many of them listed in the publication.

If real estate is involved, and there is a mortgage, you take over the first, refinance it with a second to get your capital.

THE CAPTURED ACCOUNT METHOD

If you have a large captive account or two that will buy from you no matter what, then you can use them to acquire an interest in a business. This is common practice in the advertising agencies, and printing and professional practices and fields.

The idea here is to find a business that is small, solid but struggling. You can offer them a large chunk of the business in exchange for a partnership or controlling interest.

The main problem here is to find the firm. It will not be for sale as a rule, but very interested in getting more business. An ad in the trade magazines will usually bring results. If you must stay in a specific geographical area, then contact suppliers in your field and talk to some of the salesmen or sales managers about likely prospects.

The obvious problem here is negotiating the terms by which you will throw your business in the pot. The best vehicle for an arrangement like this is probably a corporation. If you key share holding to volume produced, you may be able to control.

THE DOUBLE LOAN SYSTEM

This is a system where you buy the owner out for cash, take over the business as it sits, assets and liabilities. This is strictly for small deals that can be picked up for very little cash.

It works like this. Let's say you have a little business that the owner is just not doing a good job with. It's in no particular trouble, but the owner wants out because he doesn't like the business and will take a quick cash buyout.

This method requires you have some borrowing capacity at a bank or other source. You arrange to borrow enough to take the owner out of the picture and take over. Now it is possible that repayments on the loan, plus normal business expenses will be more than the business can stand at the start, so you use the double loan technique.

This requires the help of a friend or relative. Let's say you borrowed $5,000 to take over the business, and payments are $225 a month, too much at the start. So, you go to a friend or relative and have them borrow $2,700 (enough for one year of payments on the first loan). They take the $2,700 and make the required monthly payments on the first loan each month. You take over the payments on the second loan, roughly $115 a month, which the business can produce. At the end of the first year you can refinance both loans into one package and be on your way.

With this system you are buying a business, and buying time for the business to get turned around and produce the needed income.

CASH BIND TAKEOVER

If you find a business doing a pretty good volume on credit but haven't enough working capital to sustain credit growth because of slow collections, etc., you have an excellent takeover prospect.

Most businesses don't understand the use or potential of private factors. A factor is someone who will put up immediate cash for accounts receivable, less a discount, and wait the normal 30 to 60 days to collect. Commercial factors won't handle small business volume as a rule, and if they do they charge too much in the way to hold back for bad debts, service charges and the like. But, there are lots of people with idle cash that aren't even staying even with inflation that would love to earn 10% on their money with little risk.

By running ads in the papers, you can find these people, and working through their banker, set up a factoring system that will provide them an excellent return, and you with a business.

With this system, you buy the business by simply factoring accounts receivable, using the money as a down payment, and then factoring the new business as fast as it comes in to obtain working capital.

The key to this situation is the collectibility of the accounts, and the potential of quickly increasing the business. There is another potential you can often find in businesses in this kind of trouble, a lot of fat in the overhead. They have expanded on paper profits and have built in too high a fixed overhead. You may be able to cut outgo in relation to income as much as 50% in situations of this kind.

THE CORPORATION SYSTEM

This method is very simple. If you have the capability of forming a corporation with, say, ten others, you use the stock in the corporation to take over the business. The reason for having ten stockholders is that there is the opportunity for the owner of the business you take over to have more than one place to sell his stock; it's kind of a mini-public corporation.

This system is only for a business on its death bed, and you know that can be revived quickly. For example, you know where to get an instant dose of more business that will put life back into the body. The owner takes the stock because it's all he can get. You obviously pay no cash for the business; he has the sales potential of ten customers for his stock when the business gets going.

The corporation has the added advantage of protection of your personal assets. If you gamble and fail, the only liability will be the assets of the corporation, which is the business.

THE NEW BUSINESS AT THE SAME OLD STAND

On occasion you will run across a deal where the business is in hock to a lot of creditors, but the operational guts of the business (building lease, fixtures, equipment, etc.) are held by one person. The business is broke, and there is no chance to revive it, no way to pay off the other creditors. In this case you go to the owner of the building, etc., and offer to take over the lease. Since the present owner is probably way behind, and there is no possibility of collecting, the owner will surely agree. You simply move in then, change the name of the business, contact all the customers of the former owner, and get to work ... When the creditors of the former business come around to collect, you have no obligation to pay off, and you have grabbed a business for peanuts.

This situation obviously does not occur everyday, but is often common in very small retail service businesses. Usually there have been a parade of failing owners who have left various pieces of equipment or fixtures behind them as they left, until the location owner has in effect gone into renting a business rather than just a building. The former operators were always under capitalized, and probably poor managers. If you can quickly build the business volume while keeping the overhead at a minimum, you could make it go.

THE CHAPTER 10 ROUTE

This is a variation of method one, the debt consolidation deal. It can be used when one or more of the creditors refuses to go along with your pre-payment idea. You take over the business with a corporation, and immediately declare Chapter 10 bankruptcy, which allows the business to keep operating while the court works out a repayment schedule that the business can live with. The advantage here is the creditors cannot harass the business, and the court will direct a settlement whether the creditors like it or not.

By using a corporation, the take over vehicle, you limit your personal liabilities to those of the corporation should the business fail anyway.

THE BUST OUT SYSTEM

This is a system you can use where there is a large inventory involved. You scrape up the money to buy the business from the owner with a series of short loans. Then you take over the business, you have an emergency cash sale and sell out the inventory at big cuts, say 50% off . . . then repay the notes you let out to take the business over. Then go to the bank, and arrange for inventory financing to replace your stock.

This is valid where there is a situation that shows the business is way over stocked on inventory as the result of a lot of bad buying . . . If you are a good negotiator, you mark down the total inventory value at least 75% for the sale, and still make a profit when you hold your bust out sale. This situation often occurs where the owner has had no previous experience in the business and has been victimized by supplier salesmen. He winds up with all his capital in inventory, and no credit left to do what you can do. In this case you pay the owner a small down, give a note for inventory, and reasonable monthly payments.

There are variations on all these situations, but the thing to remember at all times is that you are taking over a bad situation without anything much behind you except your wits and steady nerves. The thing to be sure of is that you know what you are doing after you take over the business, or your career in that particular venture is going to be very short indeed.

SOURCES OF FURTHER INFORMATION

U.S. Government Publications
Practical Business Use of Government Statistics, by Thomas T. Semon (Small Business Management Series No. 22). 1959. Small Business Administration. 20 cents. *Equity Capital and Small Business,* edited by Edward L. Anthony (Small Business Management Series, No. 24). Small Business Administration, 1960. 35 cents.

Guides for Profit Planning, by B. LaSalle Woelfel (Small Business Management Series No. 25). 1960. Small Business Administration. 25 cents.

Insurance and Risk Management for Small Business, by Mark R. Greene (Small Business Management Series No. 30). 1963. Small Business Administration. 30 cents.

Cash Planning in Small Manufacturing Companies, by Joseph C. Schabacker (Small Business Research Series No. 1). 1960. Small Business Administration. $1.25.

The First Two Years: Problems of Small Firm Growth and Survival, by Kurt B. Mayer and Sidney Goldstein (Small Business Research Series No. 2) 1961. Small Business Administration. $1.

Suggested Management Guides, by H. Earl Sangston. 1962. Small Business Administration. $1.75.

Guides for Business Analysis and Profit Evaluation. 1959. Business and Defense Services Administration, U.S. Deparment of Commerce. 30 cents.

Management Aids for Small Business: Annual No. 2 (contains 21 articles, including the following: Loan Sources in the Federal Government; Figuring and Using Break-even Points; Sales Forecasting for Small Business: How to Choose Your Banker Wisely; Borrowing Money from your Bank) Rev. ed. 1958. Small Business Administration. 55 cents.

The following publications are available free at SBA field offices or on request to the Small Business Administration, Washington, D.C. 20416. Specify individual numbers in your request.

Management Aids for Small Manufacturers, New Depreciation Guidelines (No. 147); What Kind of Money Do You Need? (No. 150); Financial Planning in Closely Held Businesses (No. 156); Bank Loan Limitations; Living Within Them (No. 158).

Small Marketers Aids, Depreciation Costs—Don't Overlook Them (No. 68); Can You Afford Installment Selling? (No. 76); Keeping Score With Effective Records (No. 94).

Small Business Bibliographies, Operating Costs and Ratios—Retail (No. 8); Operating Costs and Ratios—Wholesale (No. 11).

Management Research Summaries, Facts About Small Business Financing (MRS-10); Forecasting in Small Business Planning (MRS-23); Investment Decision Making in Small Businesses (MRS-54); A Study of Industry Financial and Operating Ratios MRS-61); Accounting in Small Business Decisions (MRS-66); Equity Financing of Small Manufacturing Firms (MRS-67); Sources of Equity and Long-term Financing for Small Manufacturing Firms (MRS-68); Insurance Management in Small Retail Firms (MRS-153); Accounting and Financial Data for Small Retailers (MRS-211).

CHAPTER 10
HOW TO BAIL OUT FOR A SOFT LANDING

How To Bail Out For A Soft Landing

We discovered in our interviews, that the smart S.O.B. looks on bankruptcy as simply another form of doing business. He is no more concerned about the threat of going bankrupt than he is concerned about the price of yaks in Afghanistan.

It is simply a business procedure that the smart S.O.B. uses when necessary. It can either buy him time to get a business reorganized and back on its feet, or gives him the opportunity to simply walk away and start over again without any handicaps

Since all business is a game, and all business is risk, bankruptcy should simply be looked on as part of the game. You should never be tremendously upset if somebody that owes you money goes bankrupt (it is all part of the game), nor should they be that upset if you have to.

So remove any doubts about bankruptcy being any great stigma, we've known successful S.O.B.'s who have gone bankrupt 25 or 30 times (you have to use corporations to do this, you can only go bankrupt personally once every seven years), and are still in business, still have good credit, and are making a lot of money.

They looked on bankruptcy simply as a time at bat when they struck out, but never considered the possibility that they wouldn't get up to bat again.

In this chapter, we are going to give you the details on how to use the bankruptcy laws to save your ass and your assets.

Don't hesitate to use them, because there is always another opportunity and another chance, and it is better to get out from under a loser than let a dead horse crush you to death.

CHAPTERS X & XI

The problem of bankruptcy is not as complex as the average businessman might think. For the small businessman operating as a proprietorship, or even a small partnership, the process of bankruptcy may be little different than personal bankruptcy. In this section we are going to cover the three major areas of bankruptcy.

CHAPTER X

Under a Chapter X, either you or three creditors with claims in excess of $5,000, may petition the court for bankruptcy. If the court sees fit to grant the petition, it will appoint a trustee who will take title of all assets to prevent their dispertion and then will instigate a plan for reorganization. In order for this plan to be accepted, there has to be at least 2^3 of the creditors who are in agreement, as well as 2^3 of the stock holders if it happens to be a publicly held corporation. If this agreement between both creditors and the stock holders fails, the company is liquidated and the creditors are paid off according to the priority. And don't forget who is always at the top of that list—good old Uncle.

The major problem that you encounter with a Chapter X is that even if you are able to get agreement between the creditors and the stock holders or just the creditors if it's a privately held corporation, it becomes very costly because you are put in the position of having to come up with a reorganization plan that could ultimately be rejected by the stockholders after all the work has been done. It becomes very costly and the only winner usually ends up being the attorneys who are handling the case.

CHAPTER XI

A whole book could be written just about the advantages of a Chapter XI proceeding. Chapter XI involves fewer steps and fewer people and alot less cost. In some cases it can be totally handled by the debtor himself. Generally what you are asking for is for the court to give you protection from your creditors while you are getting a chance to get back on your feet. This is especially useful if you are in a position where you have a large asset that you feel could be sold, but will take some time to do so. By filing a Chapter XI, it will give you the breathing space needed to try to dispose of the property which would also satisfy all your other debts. It's pretty hard for the court to turn down this type of plan as it is equitable for all concerned, except the person holding a mortgage or mortgages on the piece of property that is in question, as no further payments will be made until the property is disposed of.

Under a Chapter XI you also, like in Chapter X, have to submit some sort of plan. This has to be a plan for paying back the creditors while your business is still in operation. Generally you can get by with paying interest only on several of the larger debts and just reduce the smaller debts by paying a percentage of them each month.

The ratification of this type of plan only requires the majority of the number of dollars claimed and doesn't require any concurrence from the stockholders or secured creditors. Then, upon ratification, the court can make it binding upon all creditors. But while the creditors are considering the plan, they are barred from harrassing the debtor who is free to continue running the business. When the plan is approved it is the total responsibility of the debtor to make sure that the plan is put into action.

Since secured creditors and stockholders have no vote, it is far easier to get a Chapter XI plan approved than a Chapter X. The most important factor of a Chapter XI is the fact that you can stay in control of the company and if you are able to pull the plan off, you can then be declared out of bankruptcy. Another interesting aspect of this plan is that you can even borrow additional funds, thereby allowing the lenders preference over the old unsecured creditors as far as paying them back is concerned.

HOW DO YOU SET UP A PLAN OF REORGANIZATION?

To set up a plan of reorganization for a Chapter XI would be the same as if you were trying to put together a budget to convince your wife that you could afford a new sports car. It must be done in such a way as to convince some very skeptical people that you have the ability and the company has the potential to come up with a profitable solution if you are given a chance. Of course there is going to be some guestimates involved in this, as you are not going to be able to get exact market data, exact financial projections and exact product information. Being that it is your business, you are in a better position than anybody else to give estimates of what you think you can do and what you think the capabilities are. Probably the most important part of your plan is how you are going to take care of the people who are going to have to wait, or better known as your creditors.

The national averages show that when a business goes into a Chapter XI, its chances of pulling out and not going into a total bankruptcy are generally pretty slim. Therefore you could start off by offering 10 cents on the dollar as a majority of the creditors will feel that this will be better than nothing at all, even if they were to have to take on a payment plan over a period of time that you are trying to bring the company out of its problem.

DON'T PANIC

The most important thing to remember when you get yourself in a position where your back is against the wall, and yet you have a business that has all the prospects of succeeding, rather than doing like the majority and throwing in the towel or giving up and just sitting there and letting business die a slow death by having it drained by the creditors that you presently have, take a firm stand and get your shit together. First, get yourself a hold of a good attorney. You can refer back to Chapter 5. Then, if in his judgement the only logical route to take is to file a Chapter XI, do it fast before the creditors can get together and organize themselves and force you into a Chapter X position where you don't have any control and where you won't be able to maintain any control over any appointed referee. Then after you have your petition filed, you will have a little time to sit down and work out a plan and take a breather and not have everybody hounding you. After you work out your plan, make a sincere effort to convince the creditors that are holding out, that this is the only way they will get any money at all, otherwise you will have to go into a total bankruptcy and nobody will win.

Now once you have your petition filed and you are in Chapter XI, get your ass in gear and put your plan to work. If you believe in your plan, you should be able to pull out of it. If you don't believe in your plan, and you are using it only as a stalling method, then it is just a matter of time before you will go into a total bankruptcy. But give your Chapter XI a good try. Find out how you can function on less cash than you have ever done before. Learn how to cut your staff and your overhead to the bone. Cut out all of your development and other costs that aren't necessary. Be very careful about working on your advertising, as of course this is the backbone of most businesses.

WHO CARES

Don't forget that your primary interest is still the customer, because he's the guy that brings the cash in the door. So what you have to do is to get over the negative reaction that is going to prevail after he understands that you have taken bankruptcy. The best thing to do is some good public relations—call them up, write them, let them know that it's only a temporary problem and that their source of supply is secure and you are going to have business back just like it was, in a very short time. In fact tell him that things will even be better now because alot of the pressures have been taken off and you will be able to deliver quicker and be able to carry a better inventory because you won't be hampered by the past hounding of creditors.

Do more advertising than you used to. Let everybody know that you are still around. Don't let any of the other competitors that you have run you down because they have heard this has happened. Stand right up and let them know that this is strictly a technical manuever in order for you to save a good business.

CREDITORS

Don't let the fact slip by that the whole reason that you've gone into this is because of the creditors. Donate a certain amount of your time to letting them know where you are and what progress you are making. The worst thing that you can do is to avoid them. What you want to do is to win their confidence and let them know that you are confident in the plan that you are putting together, and that you are going to pull out of it and consequently they are going to be able to come out of it financially better than if they were to put extreme pressure on you and force you into total bankruptcy.

STOCKHOLDERS

If your company is owned by other stockholders, don't let them hang out to dry either. Let them know what you are doing. Let them in on your plan. You'd be surprised how much help they could be if they really think that you are trying to pull it together. You might find some new capital in these stockholders that wasn't available before. Set yourself up a monthly letter to all your stockholders letting them know the progress you have made and how your plans are progressing.

EMPLOYEES

As soon as the decision is made that you are going to file a Chapter XI, you should have a meeting with your employees and explain to them the ramifications. Show them how this is a good business manuever for you and that it is going to mean a longer, more permanent situation for them. Rather than being gloomy and down on everything that is going on, take a positive attitude and by keeping in contact with them and letting them know, you will be a source of inspiration to them and you won't have to worry about them chickening out on you

IN SUMMATION

As you can see, Chapter XI is indeed a management tool. What it really does is to give you a license to raise working capital by a very simple method (stealing it from your unsecured creditors). Now you can go on with business as usual, except now you are working with a little higher program than you did in the beginning. This is probably the last chance you will have to make it, because if you repeat the same mistakes that got you into the problem to begin with, you will, for sure, become part of that large majority that never makes it out of Chapter XI. Don't forget, a good S.O.B. isn't going to punch anybody else's clock.

APPENDIX

NOTE: ALL LEGAL FORMS ARE FROM
CALIFORNIA—CHECK YOUR LOCAL
STATE CLERK'S OFFICE BEFORE
USING.

JONES APPLIANCE STORE

DATE _____

JONES APPLIANCE STORE HEREBY ACKNOWLEDGES RECEIPT OF THE SUM

OF _____ FROM JOHN J. JONES FOR WHICH IT AGREES TO

ASSIGN ATTACHED ACCOUNTS RECEIVABLE IN THE AMOUNT OF _____.

SETTLEMENT WILL BE MADE BY JONES APPLIANCE STORE & JOHN JONES

WITHIN 30 DAYS OF THE ABOVE DATE. ACCOUNTS WILL EITHER BE PAID

FOR IN CASH IN SUCH' SETTLEMENT OR BY REPLACEMENT WITH ANOTHER

ACCOUNT OR ACCOUNTS IN LIKE AMOUNT. ALL ACCOUNTS, NOT PAID

WITHIN 30 DAYS - WILL EARN AN ADDITIONAL 2% INTEREST FOR THE

NEXT 30 DAYS OR A PERCENTAGE THEREOF.

                                    JONES APPLIANCE STORE

                        BY_____ _

JONES APPLIANCE STORE

A S S I G N M E N T

ON THE 1ST DAY OF DECEMBER, 1977, FOR VALUE RECEIVED, JONES APPLIANCE STORE, ASSIGNOR, HEREBY SELLS, ASSIGNS, AND TRANSFERS TO JOHN J. JONES, ASSIGNEE, ALL OF ITS RIGHTS, TITLE, AND INTEREST IN THE FOLLOWING ACCOUNTS RECEIVABLE:

NAME	NET AMOUNT
L. L. TYLER	$ 284.44
MARISON MOTEL	916.00
COUNTY SCHOOL DIST.	1,214.40
B. B. DECKER	100.00
FRED'S MARKET	132.00
TOTAL	$2,646.84

RECAP: CHECK RECEIVED

WITHIN 30 DAYS OF THE ABOVE DATE, THE ASSIGNOR WILL SETTLE WITH THE ASSIGNEE ON THE ABOVE ACCOUNTS. ON ACCOUNTS WHICH THE ASSIGNOR HAS COLLECTED, THE ASSIGNEE SHALL BE PAID THE NET AMOUNT SHOWN ABOVE PLUS A PREMIUM OF 2% ON THE SAID NET AMOUNT. ON ACCOUNTS NOT YET COLLECTED, THE ASSIGNOR AT SIXTY (60) DAYS FROM THE ABOVE DATE SHALL MAKE SETTLEMENT BY CASH PAYMENT IN THE NET AMOUNT AS SHOWN ABOVE, OR BY SUBSTITUTION OF ANOTHER ACCOUNT IN LIKE AMOUNT.

ASSIGNOR { JONES APPLIANCE STORE

{ BY _____

Appendix

DEC. 5	L. L. TYLER	284.44	284.44
DEC. 5	COUNTY SCHOOL DISTRICT	1,214.40	1,498.84

TO JONES APPLIANCE COMPANY, THESE ASSIGNED ACCOUNTS HAVE BEEN
PAID AND MAY BE CREDITED ON YOUR BOOKS.

_____

Appendix

```
 1   XYZ Attorneys
     000 Anywhere St.
 2   Anywhere, USA
     Tel:  (000) 000-0000
 3

 4   Plaintiff

 5

 6

 7

 8              MUNICIPAL COURT OF THE STATE OF ANYWHERE
 9
                         COUNTY OF ANYWHERE
10

11
     J. Able,
12                     Plaintiff,        NO. 37751312

13   VS.                                 PLAINTIFF'S FIRST SET
                                         OF INTERROGATORIES TO
14                                       DEFENDANT

15   J. Doe
                       Defendant.
16

17   TO:   DEFENDANT JOHN DOE, IN PRO PER:

18        Pursuant to the provisions of Section 2030 of the Code of
19   Civil Procedure, Plaintiff above named requires that the Defendant
20   above named answer in writing and under oath the following
21   INTERROGATORIES, and that such answers by filed herein and a
22   true copy thereof served upon Plaintiff's attorneys within thirty
23   (30) days of the date of service hereof upon you.  If any of
24   the following interrogatories cannot be answered in full, please
25   answer to the extent possible, specifying the reason for your
```

inability to answer the remainder and stating whatever information or knowledge you have concerning the unanswered portion. These interrogatories are intended to elicit information not only within your personal knowledge, but obtainable by you, including information in the possession of anyone acting on your behalf.

1. What is the full name of the person answering these interrogatories, whether on behalf of himself or some other person, firm, or company?

2. What is the address of the place of business of the person identified in the answer to Interrogatory Number 1?

3. What is the residence address of the person identified in the answer to Interrogatory Number 1?

4. In the last four years, was the Defendant engaged in business?

5. If your answer to the preceding interrogatory is "yes" please answer the following (separately for each such business, if more than one);

    A.   What was the name of the business?

    B.   What was the address of its principal place of business?

    C.   Did the business conduct business at other addresses, and if so, what were those addresses?

    D.   What was the legal composition of the business (i.e., corporation, business trust, partnership, limited partnership, or any other form)?

E. If your answer to D. indicates it was a corporation, state the names and addresses of the original incorporators, the original officers (and their offices) and any subsequent officers (and their offices), and the state in which the corporation was incorporated.

F. If your answer to D. indicates it was a partnership or limited partnership, state the names and addresses of all persons who are or have been partners.

G. If your answer to D. indicates it was a proprietorship, state the name and address of the proprietor.

H. Did the business ever do business under a fictitious name and if so, what?

I. What was the nature of the business, i.e., what products or services did it deal in, was it a manufacturer, processor, distributor, retailer, dealer, service organization, etc?

6. Within the last four years have you, any employee, agent officer or director of the Defendant ever ordered or agreed to sell any merchandise, and/or services to the Defendant?

7. If your answer to the preceding interrogatory is "yes" please answer the following:

A. The date or dates on which each sale was made or agreement to sell was made.

B. The manner (i.e., by phone, letter, person-to-person conversation, wire, etc.) that each order (or agreement to purchase was placed or agreement to purchase was received.

1   C. The name and last known address of each person
2 receiving each order or making each agreement to sell.

3   D. Describe in detail the merchandise, and/or
4 services that were sold or agreed to be sold on each such
5 occasion.

6   E. If any quantities were involved, state the quantity
7 sold on each such occasion, or agreed to be sold.

8   8. If your answer to preceding interrogatories 6 and 7
9 indicate that Plaintiff did receive orders or make agreements to
10 sell, state, as to each such sale or agreement, whether the
11 same was oral or written, and if written, answer the following:

12   A. As to each such sale or agreement, the date of
13 the writing, the addressee, general subject matter and signatory.

14   B. As to each of such writings, the name and address
15 of the present custodian of the writing, or any copy thereof.

16   C. As to each of such writings, whether the same
17 will be produced at the offices of Plaintiff's attorneys for
18 inspection and copying without the necessity of making a motion
19 to produce the same, upon written request of the Defendant.

20   D. Whether you claim any such writings are privileged,
21 and if so, the nature of the claim of privilege.

22   9. If your answer to preceding interrogatories 6 and 7
23 indicate that Plaintiff did receive orders or make agreements
24 to sell, state, as to each order or agreement, whether the same
25 was oral or written, and if oral, answer the following:

Appendix

1   A.   Between what persons did the conversation take

2   place?

3   B.   Relate, in narrative style, as to each transaction

4   or conversation, what was said between the parties, and by whom.

5   C.   State the names and addresses of any persons present

6   other than those identified in 9A above.

7   D.   Were any notes or memoranda made of the conversation?

8   E.   If your answer to preceding interrogatory 9A is

9   "yes" state the name and address of the custodian of such notes

10   and or memoranda, and identify the same as to date, writer and

11   general content.

12   F.   As to each such note or memorandum, state whether

13   the same will be produced at the offices of Plaintiff's attorneys

14   for inspection and copying without the necessity of making a

15   motion to produce the same, upon written request of Defendant.

16   G.   Were any letters written or other documents produced

17   confirming any part of all of any of such conversations?

18   H.   If your answer to preceding interrogatory 9G is

19   "yes", state the name and address of the custodian of such writings

20   or documents, and identify the same as to date, writer and general

21   content.

22   I.   As to each such writing or document, state whether

23   the same will be produced at the offices of Plaintiff's attorneys

24   for inspection and copying without the necessity of making a

25   motion to produce the same, upon written request of Defendant.

10. As to each such sale or agreement to sell heretofore identified, state the agreed price for each item, and the total price for each order or agreement to sell.

11. As to each such order or agreement to sell heretofore identified, state whether there were any conditions relating to such sale or agreement, such as (but not limited to) time of delivery, manner of delivery, style, color, number, size, quantity, design, tolerances, performance, sales ability, consignment, returns, allowances, etc.

12. If your answer to Interrogatory Number 11 indicates there were conditions, state with particularity what the conditions were, as to each sale or sale agreement

13. Respecting your answer to Interrogatory Number 12, if the same indicates such conditions, please answer the following:

A. Are such conditions customary in your trade?

B. Were such conditions specified in writing or orally?

C. If the conditions were specified orally, state all the surrounding circumstances, including persons present agreeing to the conditions, when and where this occurred, who was present, what the parties actually said, the dates in question and how the conversation occurred.

D. If the conditions were specified in writing, identify the writing by date, writer, general content and signatory, give the name and address of the custodian of the writing, and indicate whether the same will be produced for

1 inspections and copying without the necessity of making a motion

2 to produce the same upon written request of Defendant.

3   14.   If any part of the Plaintiff's case is based upon a

4 failure of condition indicated in your answer to Interrogatories

5 11-13, answer the following:

6   A.   As to each item of merchandise or service or

7 business entity sold, the specific condition not satisfied.

8   B.   As to each item of merchandise or service sold,

9 the exact facts which indicate or tend to indicate that the

10 condition was not satisfied.

11   C.   As to each item of merchandise or service sold,

12 whether Plaintiff obtained or attempted to obtain any independent

13 evaluation of the product or service, and if so, the name and

14 address of the person or company consulted, and the results of

15 such evaluation, if any.

16   D.   Was notice of such alleged failure of condition

17 given to Defendant?

18   E.   If your answer to Interrogatory 14D is "yes", state

19 when notice was give, by whom and to whom, the manner of giving

20 notice and the exact contents of the notice.

21   F.   Do you have in your possession or under your control

22 any documents, writings, notes, or memoranda concerning the

23 alleged failure of condition; if so, identify the same by date,

24 writer, general content, and give the name and address of the

25 custodian of the same and indicate whether the same will be

1 produced for inspection and copying without the necessity of

2 making a motion to produce the same, upon written request of

3 Defendant.

4   G.   If any such failure of condition relates to

5 identifiable merchandise, products or other tangible things,

6 state whether the same are available for inspection, and whether

7 the same can be inspected without the necessity for motion

8 therefor, and where they may be inspected, and the name and

9 address of the person or persons having custody and control

10 thereof.

11   H.   If any such failure of condition relates to

12 identifiable merchandise, products or other tangible things, and

13 they are not available for inspection, state why they cannot

14 be inspected.

15   15. Withing four years last past, have you sold any

16 merchandise or goods to Defendant (including constructive

17 receipt)?

18   16. If your answer to the preceding interrogatory is "yes"

19 please answer the following:

20   A.   What item or items were sold in each instance,

21 and in what quantities?

22   B.   What was the date of sale of each instance?

23   C.   What was the manner of delivery of each shipment

24 (i.e., truck, rail, parcel post, UPS, etc.) and what was the

25 name of the delivering carrier of each shipment?

11

Appendix

1   D.   What records or memoranda of receipt of each ship-

2 ment do you have (identifying the same by date, content and party

3 making the record)?

4   E.   What is the name and address of the custodian of

5 the records identifed in 16D above, and can the same be inspected

6 without the necessity of a motion therefor, upon written request

7 therefor by Defendant.

8   F.   Was anything incorrect or irregular with respect

9 to each such delivery, and, if so, what?

10   G.   If your answer to 16F above indicates such an

11 irregularity, state whether you have made any claim against

12 any carrier, insurer or other person relating to such irregularity,

13 and if so, all particulars of the claim (i.e., against whom it

14 was made, when, what was claimed, what disposition was made of

15 the claim, etc.)

16   H.   If your answer to 16F above indicates such an

17 irregularity, state whether notice thereof was given to Defendant

18 and if so, all particulars of the manner of giving notice (i.e.,

19 when given, to whom, the manner of giving, what response was

20 received, etc.).

21   I.   If your answer to 16F above indicates such an

22 irregularity, state whether you claim any damage or loss as a

23 result of such irregularity.

24   J.   If your answer to 16I above is "yes", state how

25 the damage or loss is related to the irregularity, the exact

Appendix

12

amount of damage or loss claimed, and how that amount was computed.

17. As to each such sale or agreement to sell heretofore identified, state whether there were any representation or express warranties relating to such order or agreements.

18. If your answer to Interrogatory Number 17 indicates there were representations or express warranties, state with particularity what the representations or express warranties were, as to each sale or sales agreement.

19. Respecting your answer to Interrogatory Number 18, if the same indicates either representations or express warranties were made, please answer the following:

A. Are such representations or express warranties customary in your trade?

B. Were such representations or express warranties specified orally or in writing?

C. If the representations or express warranties were specified orally, state all the surrounding circumstances, including persons present making or hearing the representations or express warranties, when and where this occurred, what the parties actually said, the dates in question and how the conversation occurred.

D. If the representations or express warranties were specified in writing, identify the writing by date, writer, general content and signatory, give the name and address of the custodian of the writing, and indicate whether the same will be

Appendix

produced for inspection and copying without the necessity of

making a motion to produce the same upon written request of

defendant.

    20. If any part of the plaintif's case is based upon

a breach or failure of such representations or express

warranties indicated in your answer to Interrogations 17-19,

please answer the following:

    A. As to each item of merchandise or services sold,

the specific representation or express warranty breached.

    B. As to each item of merchandise or service sold,

the exact facts which indicate or tend to indicate that the

representation or warranty was breached.

    C. Was notice of such breach given to defendant?

    D. If your answer to Interrogatory 20C is "yes",

state when notice was given, by whom, and to whom, the manner

of giving notice and the exact contents of the notice.

    E. Do you have in your possession or under your

control any documents, writings, notes or memoranda concerning

the alleged breach of representation or express warranty; if

so, identify the same by date, writer and general content, and

give the name and address of the custodian of the same and

indicate whether the same will be produced for inspection and copying without the necessity of making a motion to produce the same, upon written request of defendant.

F. If any such breach of representation or express warranty relates to identifiable merchandise, products, or other tangible things, state whether the same are available for inspection, and whether the same can be inspected without the necessity for motion therefore, and where they may be inspected, and the name and address of the person or persons having custody and control thereof.

G. If any such breach of representation or express warranty relates to identifiable merchandise, products, or other tangible things, and they are not available for inspection, state why they cannot be inspected.

21. Is any part of plaintiff's case to this action related to a claim of breach of implied warranty of fitness for the purpose intended by the parties as to any such merchandise or service or business entity supplied plaintiff by defendant?

22. If your answer to Interrogatory Number 21 is "yes", please answer the following:

A. as to each such item of merchandise or service, or

Appendix

business entity, what was the intended purpose?

B. If the intended use or purpose was communicated by Defendant to Plaintiff's assignor, state when the communication was made, by whom it was made, to whom it was made, whether it was oral or written, and the exact content of the communication.

C. Do you have in your possession or under your control any documents, writings, notes, or memoranda concerning the communication identified in your answer to Interrogatory 22B above; if so, identify the same by date, writer and general content, and give the name and address of the custodian of the same and indicate whether the same will be produced for inspection and copying without the necessity of making a motion to produce the same, upon written request of defendant.

D. State specifically in what manner or characteristic the merchandise or service did not conform to the use or purpose intended.

E. Was notice of the non-conformity of the merchandise or services or business entity to the use or purpose intended given to defendant?

F. If your answer to Interrogatory 22E is "yes", state when notice was given, by whom and to whom, the manner of giving notice and the exact contents of the notice.

23. Do you claim to have made any payment or payments for the merchandise or services heretofore identified in your answers to these interrogatories?

24. If your answer to the preceding interrogatory is "yes", state the date and the amount of each payment, and the manner of payment (i.e., cash, check, money order, etc.)

25. Do you have in your possession or under your control any document or writing evidencing such payments?

26. If your answer to Interrogatory Number 25 is "yes", identify each document as to date, nature and content of the document, and give the name and address of the custodian thereof, and indicate whether the same will be produced for inspection and copying without the necessity of making a motion to produce the same, upon written request of defendant.

27. Do you claim any other set-offs or allowances against the defendant in this action?

28. If your answer to the preceding interrogatory is "yes", state with particularity the legal nature of the set-off or claim, the facts giving rise to the set-off or claim, the sum or amount of set-off or claim and whether such sum or amount has

Appendix

1 been entered upon your books and records of account.

2   29. If your answer to interrogatory 27 is "yes", state

3 whether you have any documents, writings, notes or memoranda

4 relating to such set-off or claim in your possession or under

5 your control, and if so, identify each document or writing as

6 to date, nature and content of the document, and give the name

7 and addresses of the custodian thereof, and indicate whether

8 the same will be produced for inspection and copying without

9 the necessity of a motion to produce the same, upon written

10 request of respondent.

11

12   30. Do you have in your possession or under your control

13 any documents, writings, memoranda or notes, not otherwise

14 described in your answer to the preceding interrogatories, which

15 establish or which you believe would tend to establish a cause

16 of action in this action.

17

18   31. If your answer to the preceding interrogatory is "yes",

19 identify each document or writing as to date, nature and content

20 of the document, and give the name and address of the custodian

21 thereof, and indicate whether the same will be produced for

22 inspection and copying without the necessity of a motion to

23 produce the same, upon written request of defendant.

32. Does the plaintiff keep or maintain books, and/or records of account which indicate the persons to whom plaintiff is obligated or a creditor of, and the amounts of the obligations or account receivable (accounts payable and receivable, ledgers, journals, cards, and the like)?

33. If your answer to Interrogatory Number 32 is "yes", please answer the following:

A. What is the name and address of the person (or persons) responsible for keeping and maintaining such books and/or records?

B. Do such books and/or records contain an account for the defendant and if so, what balance, if any, was shown in such account on the date this action was commenced?

C. As to each such book and/or records, state whether the same will be produced at the offices of plaintiff's counsel for inspection and copying without the necessity of making a motion to produce same upon written request of respondent.

Dated: Any Date

XYZ Attorneys

BY: _____
J. ABLE

19

<u>PROOF OF SERVICE BY MAIL</u>
1013a, 2015.5 C.C.P.

ANY STATE   )
) ss.
ANY COUNTY   )

   I am a citizen of the United States and employed in

the aforesaid county;

   I am over the age of eighteen years and not a party

to the within entitled action; my business address is 123 ANY

STREET, ANY TOWN, ANY STATE ZIP; on ANY DATE I served the

within <u>REQUEST FOR ADMISSIONS AND PLAINTIFF'S FIRST SET OF</u>

<u>INTERROGATORIES TO DEFENDANT</u> on the <u>DEFENDANT</u> in said action

by placing a true copy thereof enclosed in a sealed envelope

with postage thereon fully prepaid, in the United States mail

at ANY TOWN, ANY STATE, addressed as follows:

    J. Doe
    Any Street
    Any Town, Any State, Zip

   ·I, J. Able, certify (or declare), under penalty of

perjury, that the foregoing is true and correct.

   Executed on ANY DATE at ANY TOWN, ANY STATE.

           _____

1   Your name _____

2   Address _____

             _____

3   Phone _____

  Defendant, in pro per

4

5

6

7

8   MUNICIPAL COURT OF THE STATE OF CALIFORNIA

9   _____

10

11   _____,   No._____

          Plaintiff(s)

12   vs.

                            ANSWER

13   _____,

         Defendant(s)

14

15   Defendants(s) answer the complaint as follows:

16   I

17   Admit the allegations contained in paragraph(s)____, ____,

18   and ____ (of the 1st Cause of Action, and paragraphs(s)_____,

  ____ and ____ of the 2d Cause of Action).

19   II

20   With the exception of the admissions set forth above,

21   defendeant(s) deny each and every, all and singular, generally

  and specifically the allegations contained in paragraphs(s)____,

22   ____ and ____ (of the 1st Cause of Action, and paragraphs _____,

  ____ and ____ of the 2d Cause of Action).

23

24   WHEREFORE Defendant(s) pray that Plaintiff(s) take nothing

  by this action; that defendant(s) recover costs of suit including

25   reasonable attorneys fees; and for such other relief as may be

  deemed just.

26   21   **Appendix**

27

```
 1                                    _____
 2                                    Defendant
 3                                    _____
 4                                    Defendant
 5                    VERIFICATION
 6         I am (a) defendant in the above action; I have read the
    foregoing Answer, and know the contents thereof; and I certify
 7  that the same is true of my own knowledge.
 8         I certify, under penalty of perjury, that the foregoing is
    true and correct.
 9         Executed on _____(date)_____, 197__, at _____(place)_____,
    California.
10
11                                    _____
12
                   PROOF OF SERVICE BY MAIL
13
         I am a citizen of the United States and a resident of the
14  county of _____, I am over the age of 18 years and
    not a party to the above action; my residence address is:
15  _____, California.  On _____,
16  197__, I served the within Answer on the Plaintiffs in said action
    by placing a true copy thereof enclosed in a sealed evelope with
17  postage thereon fully prepaid, in the United States post office
    mail box at _____(city)_____, California, addressed as follows:
18  _____
19  I, _____, certify under penalty of perjury
    that the foregoing is true and correct.  Executed on ___(date)___,
20  197__, at _____, California.
21
22
23                                    _____
24                                            (signature)
25
26  Appendix                    22
27
```

INSTRUCTIONS FOR FILLING OUT COMPLAINT

Type in the title of the court, exactly as it appears on the Complaint.

Type in the names of the parties, exactly as it appears on the Complaint.

Don"t forget to type in the number of the case. Get it from the Complaint.

Read the Complaint very carefully and type in here the number of each paragraph which you can agree with completely. Do not list here any paragraph which has anything in it with which you do not agree. If there is more than one Cause of Action in the Complaint, continue as shown by the words within the parentheses.

Type in the number of each paragraph of the Complaint which has anything in it with which you do not agree. Use the words in the parentheses if there is more than one cause of action.

The Answer must be signed by each person who has been named by the Complaint, because any person not signing has not answered and may lose by default.

Any one of the defendants can sign the verification. Type in the date and place where signed.

Enter here the name of the creditor of his attorney, as it appears in the upper left of the first page of the Complaint.

Signature of person mailing Answer to plaintiffs.

SMALL TAX CASE PETITION FORM

....
                    (Petitioner(s)
                    vs.
COMMISSIONER OF INTERNAL REVENUE,   Docket No.
                    Respondent,

PETITION

1. Petitioner(s) request(s) the Court to redetermine the
tax deficiency(ies) for the year(s)............. as set forth
in the notice of deficiency dated................, a copy of
which is attached. The notice was issued at the Office of the
Internal Revenue Service at ....(City and State)
....
2. Petitioner(s) taxpayer identification (e.g., social
security numbers(s) is (are) ....
3. Petitioner(s) make(s) the following claims as to his
tax liability:

Year	Amount of Deficiency Disputed	Amount of Addition to Tax, if any Disputed	Amount of Over-Payment Claimed
....	....	....	....
....	....	....	....

4. Set forth those adjustments, i.e., changes, in the notice
of deficiency with which you disagree and why you disagree.
....
....

Petitioner(s) request(s) that the proceedings in this case
be conducted as a "small tax case" under section 7463 of the
Internal Revenue Code of 1954, as amended, and Rule 1/2 of the
Rules of Practice of the United States Tax Court. A decision
in a "small tax case" is final and cannot be appealed by either
party.

....
  Signature of Petitioner   Present Address
  (Husband)

....
  Signature of Petitioner   Present Address
  (Wife)

....
Signature and address of counsel, if retained by petitioner(s)

REQUEST FOR PLACE OF TRIAL FORM

UNITED STATES TAX COURT

....
       Petitioner(s)
          vs.
COMMISSIONER OF INTERNAL REVENUE,   Docket No.
             Respondent

REQUEST FOR PLACE OF TRIAL

Petitioner(s) hereby request(s) that trial of this case be
held at............(city)...............(state)

Dated..................., 19....

                ....
                Signature of petitioner or counsel

Here is a longer, more detailed form:

FORM OF ARTICLES OF INCORPORATION

We, the undersigned, do hereby associate ourselves in order to form a corporation for the purpose hereinafter stated and do hereby certify as follows:

1. The name of this corporation shall be ---------------

---.

2. The general nature of the business is to be transacted by this corporation together with, and in addition to, those powers conferred by the law of this state and the principles of common law upon corporations is the following:

(The Kind of Business You're In)

3. In furtherance, and not in limitation, of the general powers conferred by laws and the objects and purposes herein set forth, this corporation shall also have the following powers:

a. To take, own, hold, deal in, mortgage or otherwise give liens against, and to lease, sell, exchange, transfer, or in any manner whatsoever buy or dispose of real property wherever situated.

b. To manufacture, purchase or acquire, and to hold, own, and in any manner dispose of and deal with goods, wares, merchandise and personal property wherever situated.

c. To enter into and perform contracts of every kind; to
acquire and deal with its own stock or stock in other
corporations; to guarantee another's debts in furtherance of
the lawful purposes of the corporation; to become a partner
in any lawful business or venture.

d. To establish profit-seeking, pension, and other
employee plans.

e. To acquire the assets and good will of any person,
firm or corporation, and to pay for such assets and good
will in cash, stock of this corporation, or otherwise, or
by undertaking any of the liabilities of the transferer; to
hold or in any manner dispose of the property so acquired,
to conduct in any lawful manner the whole or any part of
any business so acquired, and to exercise all the powers
necessary to convenient in and about the conduct and
management of such business.

f. To apply for, purchase, register, or in any manner
to acquire and dispose of patents, licenses, copyrights,
trademarks, tradenames, inventions, or other rights; to
work, operate, or develop the same and to carry on any
business which may directly or indirectly effectuate these
objects.

g. Without limits as to amount, to draw, make, accept, endorse, discount, and issue notes, drafts, bills of exchange, bonds, debentures, and other negotiable instruments and evidences of indebtedness, to the maximum extent permitted by law.

h. To have one or more offices; to conduct its business and promote its objects within and without the state.

i. To carry on any other business in connection with the foregoing and with all the powers conferred upon corporations by the laws and statutes of the state.

4. The aforesaid enumerated powers are to be construed both as purposes and powers and shall not be limited or restricted by reference to or inference from the terms of any provision herein; nor shall the expression of one thing be deemed to exclude another, although it be of like nature.

5. The amount of the total authorized capital stock which may be issued by the corporation is -------------------- shares of common stock of (check applicable line and preferred stock, if any).

--------------- a. No par value.

--------------- b. Par value of $ ---------- per share.

--------------- c. Preferred stock, as follows: ------------

--.

All or any part of said capital stock may be payable
either in cash, property, labor, or services at a just
valuation to be fixed by the Board of Directors, and the
judgment of such Directors as to the value shall, in the
absence of fraud, be conclusive upon the stockholders and
parties dealing with the corporation. The capital stock
may be issued and paid for at such time or terms and
conditions as the Directors may determine and the amount
of the capital stock increased or decreased in the manner
provided by law; provided, however, that the stock of the
corporation shall be non-assessable.

6.   The amount of capital with which this corporation
shall begin business is $ --------------------.

7.   The existence of this corporation shall be perpetual.

8.   The principal office of this corporation in the state
is to be located at --------------------------- in the city of
-------------------------, and the agent in charge thereof
shall be -------------------------.

9.   The number of directors of this corporation shall be
not less than (check applicable line):

---------------- a.   Three.

---------------- b.   Four.

---------------- c.   Five.

-------------- d. Other: ---------------.

10. The names and mailing addresses of the Board of
Directors and Officers who subject to the provisions of these
Articles and the By-Laws to be adopted, shall hold office
until their successors are elected and qualified are:

NAME   POSITION   ADDRESS

11. The names and mailing addresses of each subscriber
to these articles of Incorporation and the number of shares
of stock of this corporation which each agrees to take and to
pay for are as follows:

NAME   POSITION   ADDRESS

the proceeds of which shall amount to at least the sum stated
in paragraph 6 of these Articles.

IN WITNESS WHEREOF we being all of the original subscribers
to the capital stock of this corporation for the purpose of
forming a corporation, do make and file these Articles, and
accordingly set out hands and seals this the ---------- day of
--------------- 19 ------.

--(SEAL)

--(SEAL)

--(SEAL)

STATE OF --------------------.
COUNTY OF -------------------.

Before me, the undersigned authority, personally appeared
------------------------, each to me known and known to me
to be the persons described in and by this document.

The stockholders and directors shall have power to hold
their meetings and keep the books, documents, and papers of
the corporation outside the state of -------------------------,
at such places as may be from time to time designated by the
By-Laws or by resolution of the stockholders or directors,
except as otherwise required by laws of ----------------------.

It is the intention that the objects, purposes, and powers
specified in the third paragraph hereof shall, except where
otherwise specified in said paragraph, be nowise limited or
restricted by reference to or inference from the terms of any
other clause or paragraph in this Certificate of Incorporation,
but that the objects, purposes, and powers specified in the
third paragraph and in each of the clauses or paragraphs of
this charter shall be regarded as independent objects,
purposes, and powers.

WE THE UNDERSIGNED, for the purpose of forming a
Corporation under the laws of --------------------------------,
do make, file, and record this Certificate and do certify that
the facts herein stated are true; and we have accordingly
hereunto set our respective hands and seals.

31

Dated at ----------------------------------(SEAL)

---------------------- 19 -------------(SEAL)

---(SEAL)

STATE OF ---------------------.

COUNTY OF -------------------.

BE IT REMEMBERED, that on this --------------- DAY OF

------------------- A.D. personally appeared before me,

-------------------------------- a Notary Public, ----------

--.

PARTIES TO THE FOREGOING Certificate of Incorporation, known

to me personally to be such, and I having first made known to

them and each of them the contents of said certificate, they

did each severally acknowledge that they signed, sealed, and

delivered the same as their voluntary act and deed, and each

deposed that the facts therein stated were truly set forth.

GIVEN under my hand and seal of office the day and year

aforesaid.

(NOTARY SEAL) ---.

Notary Public

ARTICLE I.   NAME AND LOCATION. The name of this
corporation shall be --.
Its principal office shall be located at --------------------
---------------------- IN THE City of ----------------------,
State of ------------------------. Other offices for the
transaction of business shall be located at such other places
as the Board of Directors may from time to time determine.

ARTICLE II. CAPITAL STOCK. The total authorized capital
stock of this corporation shall be --------------------------.
SHARES OF COMMON STOCK OF (check applicable line and preferred
stock, if any):

--------------- a. No par.

--------------- b. Par value of $ ---------------.

--------------- c. Preferred stock, as follows: ------------.

All certificates of stock shall be signed by the President
and the Secretary and shall be sealed with the corporate seal.

Treasury stock shall be held by the corporation subject
to the disposal of the Board of Directors and shall neither
vote nor participate in dividends.

The corporation shall have a first lien on all the shares
of its capital stock and upon all dividends declared upon the

same for any indebtedness of the respective holders thereof to the corporation.

Transfers of stock shall be made only on the books of the corporation; and the old certificate, properly endorsed, shall be surrendered and cancelled before a new certificate is issued.

In case of loss or destruction of a certificate of stock, no new certificate shall be issued in lieu thereof except upon satisfactory proof to the Board of Directors of such loss or destruction; and upon the giving of satisfactory security against loss to the corporation; any such certificate shall be plainly marked "Duplicate" upon its face.

ARTICLE III. STOCKHOLDERS' MEETINGS. An annual meeting of the stockholders shall be held at ------------ o'clock ----- M. on the --------- day -------------- each year, commencing on the --------- day of --------- 19 -----------, or if said date shall be a holiday, on the following day, at the principal office of the corporation. At such meeting, the stockholders shall elect directors to serve until their successors are elected and qualified.

A special meeting of the stockholders, to be held at the

same place as the annual meeting, may be called at any time whenever requested by stockholders holding a majority of the outstanding stock.

Unless prohibited by law, the stockholders holding a majority of the outstanding shares entitled to vote may, at any time, terminate the term of office of all or any of the directors, with or without cause, by a vote at any annual or special meeting, or by written statement, signed by the holders of a majority of such stock, and filed with the secretary or, in his absence, with any other officer. Such removal shall be effective immediately even if successors are not elected simultaneously, and the vacancies on the Board of Directors shall be filed only by the stockholders.

Notice of the time and place of all annual and special meetings shall be given 10 days before the date thereof, except that notice may be waived on consent of stockholders owning the following proportion of the outstanding stock (check applicable line).

--------------- a. A majority.

--------------- b. Two-thirds majority.

--------------- c. Three-fourths majority.

--------------- d. Other: ---------------.

The President, or in his absence, the Vice-President, shall preside at all meetings of the stockholders.

At every such meeting, each stockholder of common stock shall be entitled to case one vote for each share of stock held in his name, which vote may be cast by him either in person or by proxy. All proxies shall be in writing and shall be filed with the Secretary and by him entered of records in the minutes of the meeting.

ARTICLE IV. DIRECTORS. The business and property of the corporation shall be managed by a board of not less than three or by an executive committee appointed by said board.

The regular meeting of the directors shall be held immediately after the adjournment of each annual stockholders' meeting. Special meetings of the Board of Directors may be called by the president.

Notice of all regular and special meetings shall be mailed to each director, by the Secretary, at least 10 days before each meeting, unless such notice is waived.

A quorum for the transaction of business at any meeting of the directors shall consist of a majority of the members of the board.

The directors shall elect the officers of the corporation

and fix their salaries. Such election shall be held at the directors' meeting following each annual stockholders' meeting. Any officer may be removed, with or without cause, by vote of the directors at any regular or special meeting, unless such removal is prohibited by law.

Vacancies in the Board of Directors may be filled by the remaining directors, at any regular or special meeting of the directors, except when such vacancy shall occur through removal by stockholders holding a majority of the outstanding shares, as hereinabove provided.

At each annual stockholders' meeting, the directors shall submit a statement of the business done during the preceding year, together with a report of the general financial condition of the corporation and of the condition of its property.

ARTICLE V.   OFFICERS. The officers of the corporation shall be President, a Vice-President, a Secretary, and a Treasurer (and, in the discretion of the directors, an assistant secretary), who shall be elected for a term of one year and shall hold office until their successors are elected and qualified.

The President shall preside at all directors' and

stockholders' meetings; shall sign all stock certificates and written contracts and undertakings of the corporation; and shall perform all such other duties as are incident to his office. In case of disability, or absence from the city, of the President, his duties shall be performed by the Vice-President, who shall have equal and concurrent powers.

The Secretary shall issue notice of all directors' and stockholders' meetings; shall attend and keep the minutes of such meetings; and shall perform all such other duties as are incident to his office. In case of disability or absence, his duties shall be performed by the assistant secretary, if any.

The Treasurer shall have custody of all money and securities of the corporation. He shall keep regular books of account and shall submit them, together with all his vouchers, receipts, records and other papers, to the directors for their examination and approval as often as they may require; and shall perform all such other duties as are incident to his office.

ARTICLE VI. DIVIDENDS AND FINANCE. Dividends, to be paid out of the surplus earnings of the corporation, may be declared from time to time by resolution of the Board of Directors by vote of a majority thereof.

The funds of the corporation shall be deposited in such bank or banks as the directors shall designate and shall be withdrawn only upon the check of the corporation, signed as the directors shall from time to time resolve.

ARTICLE VII. AMENDMENTS. Amendments to these By-Laws may be made by a vote of the stockholders holding a majority of the outstanding stock at any annual or special meeting, the notice of such special meeting to contain the nature of the proposed amendment.

We hereby adopt and ratify the foregoing By-Laws.

Here is a standard form for the minutes of the first meeting of incorporators and subscribers. It can be prepared in advance and noted on and added to at the meeting.

MINUTES OF INITIAL MEETING OF
INCORPORATORS AND SUBSCRIBERS

The initial meeting of the incorporators and subscribers to the capital stock of ------------------------------------ WAS HELD AT --------------------------------- in the city of

------------------------------- at ---------------------------.

The following were present, being all of the incorporators and
subscribers:

On motion duly made and carried, --------------------- was

elected temporary chairman, and -------------------------------

was elected temporary chairman, and --------------------------

was elected temporary secretary.

It was reported that the corporate charter heretofore

filed with the Secretary of State had been approved. On motion

duly made and carried, those certain By-Laws preceding these

minutes were adopted and approved.

Thereupon, the incorporators and subscribers took the

following action (check applicable part):

--------------- 1. Announced that they had transferred and

assigned their subscriptive rights to stock to ------------

--.

--------------- 2. Proposed that the following shares be

issued:

    Name   Cert. N.   N. of Shares   Consideration

Thereupon, on motion duly made and carried, the following

were ratified and elected as directors of this corporation for the following year, and until their successors are chosen:

Thereupon, on motion duly made and carried, the following resolution was passed:

RESOLVED: That the Board of Directors is hereby authorized to manage the affairs of the corporation and to exercise all powers vested in said board by the foregoing by-laws, the corporate charter, and the laws of the state.

Other business:

Whereupon, the meeting was adjourned.

The undersigned hereby waives notice of the foregoing meeting.

For the first meeting of your directors, you can prepare this form in advance and verify it at the meeting.

MINUTES OF DIRECTORS' ANNUAL MEETING

The annual meeting of directors of ----------------------- was held at its office in the city of ----------------------- at --------------------------------- o'clock -------------M. on the ----------------- day of ---------------- 19 -------.

41

The following were present:

constituting ----------------------- all ---------------- a

majority (check applicable provision) of the directors.

The minutes of the annual meeting of the stockholders were

read and approved.

On motion duly made and carried, the following were

nominated and elected as officers of the corporation for the

following year and until their successors are chosen:

Other Business:

Whereupon, the meeting was adjourned.

                                              Secretary

If you desire to waive the directors' meeting, this form can

be used:

WAIVER OF NOTICE OF DIRECTORS' MEETING

The undersigned, being the following proportion of the

directors of the corporation:

--------------- 1. All.

--------------- 2. Three-fourths majority.

--------------- 3.   Two-thirds majority.

--------------- 4.   Majority.

--------------- 5.   Other: ---------------.

do hereby waive notice of the foregoing meeting and consent

to any and all action taken there at, as evidenced by the

foregoing minutes.

For the annual stockholders' meeting, you can use this form

properly filled in and have it attested to.

MINUTES OF STOCKHOLDERS' ANNUAL MEETING

     The annual meeting of the stockholders of ---------------

--- was held at its

office in the city of ------------------------------------ at

--------------- o'clock ---------- M. on the ----------- day

of ----------------------- 19 ----------. The following were

present:

constituting --------------- all --------------- a majority

(check applicable provision) of the stockholders.

     The meeting was called to order by the President. The

directors' statement of the business done during the

preceding year, and a report of the general financial

43

condition of the corporation was submitted to the stockholders
and approved.

On motion duly made and carried, the following were
nominated and elected as directors of the corporation for the
following year and until their successors are chosen:

Other Business:

Whereupon, the meeting was adjourned.

                                                           Secretary

If you desire to waive the stockholders' meeting, use this
form:

WAIVER OF NOTICE OF

STOCKHOLDERS' MEETING

The undersigned, being the following proportion of the
stockholders of the corporation:

--------------- 1. All.

--------------- 2. Three-fourths majority.

--------------- 3. Two-thirds majority.

--------------- 4. Majority.

--------------- 5. Other: ---------------.

do hereby waive notice of the foregoing meeting and consent to any and all action taken there at, as evidenced by the foregoing minutes.

One of the first functions you will perform after the corporation is formed will be to open a bank account...you can use this form to authorize the opening and use of the account by the proper officers of the corporation.

RESOLUTION OF DIRECTORS AUTHORIZING

DEPOSIT AND WITHDRAWAL OF FUNDS IN

--(Name of Bank)

I certify that the following is a true copy of a certain resolution of the Board of Directors of ---------------------- -------------------------------------- (Name of Corp. in full), a Corporation duly organized and existing under the laws of ------------------------- (Name of state where organized), having its principal place of business in -------------------- --------------------- (Name of City or Town and State) duly adopted in accordance with the By-Laws, and recorded in the minutes of, a meeting of said Board held on ----------------- (Date of meeting), 19 ----------, and now in full force and effect:

RESOLVED

1. An account or accounts be opened for and in the name of this Corporation with ----------------------------------- (hereinafter referred to as the Bank), that the persons whose titles are listed below are authorized to sign and agree to those provisions of said Bank's customary corporation signature card, and that said Bank is hereby authorized to pay or otherwise honor any checks, drafts, or other orders issued from time to time, for debit to said account when signed by --------------------------------- (Please insert above titles, not names, of officers; for example, President, Treasurer, etc. Also, if more than one is inserted, indicate whether they are to sign singly, any two, jointly or otherwise) including any such payable to or for the benefit of any signer thereof, or other officers, or employee, individually, without inquiry as to the circumstances of the issue or the disposition of the proceeds thereof.

2. That the Bank is hereby authorized to accept for deposit for account of this Corporation, for credit, or for collection, or otherwise, any and all checks, drafts, and other instruments of any kind endorsed by any person, or by

hand stamp impression, in the name of this Corporation, or without endorsement.

3. The aforesaid officers of this Corporation, be and they hereby are authorized to act for this Corporation in all matters and transactions relating to any of its business with the Bank, including the withdrawal of property at any time held by the Bank for account of this Corporation.

4. That the Secretary is directed to furnish the said Bank a certified copy of these resolutions, the names of all officers and other persons herein authorized to deal with said Bank, together with a specimen of the signature of each, under the Seal of the Corporation, and that, until receipt by the Bank of notice to the contrary, in the form of a certificate signed by the Secretary, under the Corporate Seal, the Bank is authorized to reply upon all statements made or furnished in accordance herewith.

I FURTHER CERTIFY that the following are the officers of said Corporation, duly qualified and now acting as such:

NAME   TITLE OF OFFICE HELD

----

47   **Appendix**

IN WITNESS WHEREOF, I have hereunto subscribed my name
and affixed the seal of the said Corporation this ------- day
of ---------------, 19 -----.

(Corporate Seal)

_____

Secretary

INFORMATION REQUIRED IN CERTIFICATE OF INCORPORATION

Many states have standardized certificate of incorporation forms which may be used by small businesses. Copies of this form may be obtained from the State official who grants charters and, in some States, from local stationers as well. The following information is required.

1. The corporate name of the company—Legal requirements generally are: (a) That the name must not be so similar to that of any other corporation authorized to do business in the State that the names might be confused; and (b) that the name chosen must not be deceptive so as to mislead the public. In order to be sure that the name which you selected is suitable, it would be well to submit it to your State officer handling incorporation.

2. Purposes for which corporation is formed—Great care should be taken in writing this section because in some states the activities of the corporation will be limited to the powers set forth here. If so, you must petition your State incorporation officer for an amendment to the charter before deviating from these approved activities. In some states, the corporation laws are very rigid, protecting the right of a corporation to expand its activities, and at the same time limiting such expansion to activities related to those specified in its certificate of incorporation. When this is the case, the object for which the corporation is being formed may be stated precisely and simply, since the corporation's rights are protected and its activities limited by the corporation laws.

In states where the corporation laws are less rigid however, the purposes of the corporation may be presented in broad legal terms which will protect the right of the corporation to expand its future activities, including entry into other lines of business. For example, a corporation may have several specific statements to set forth its objectives, with one of these statements sufficiently inclusive to allow for future contingencies, typical of such phrasing is the statement, "The foregoing acts will be interpreted as examples and not as limitations."

3. The length of time for which the corporation is being formed—this may be a period of years or may be perpetual.

4. The names and addresses of the incorporators—in certain states one or more of the incorporators is required to be a resident of the state within which the corporation is being organized.

5. Location of the principle office of the corporation in the state of incorporation—although most small corporations find it advisable to obtain their charter from the state in which the greater part of their business is conducted, you should consider the benefits which may be gained from incorporating in another state. Such factors as cost of organization fees, state taxes, restrictions on corporate powers and lines of business in which a company may engage, capital requirements, restrictions upon "foreign" corporations in your state, and so forth, should be taken into consideration in the selection of the state of incorporation.

If you decide to obtain your charter from another state, you will be required to have it in an office. However, rather than establish an office there, you may appoint an agent to act for you. The agent will be required only to represent your corporation, maintain a duplicate list of stockholders, and to receive or reply to suits brought against the corporation in the state of incorporation.

6. The maximum amount and type of capital stock which the corporation wishes authorization to issue—allowance should be made for a greater amount of capital stock than is really needed at the time of incorporation.

7. Capital required at time of incorporation—some states require that a specified percent of the par values of the capital stock be paid in cash and banked to the credit of the corporation before the certificate of incorporation is submitted to the proper state official.

8. The names of the subscribers and the number of shares to which each subscribes.

9. Names and addresses of persons who will serve as directors until the first meeting of stockholders or until their successors are elected and qualify.

BOOKS, MINUTES, STOCK CERTIFICATES

When you have your charter you will need books, minutes, stock certificates and a corporate seal. These are usually available from stationery stores in your area, but you can save a little money buying from a specialist: Excelsior Legal Stationery Company, Inc., 62 White St., New York, NY (Phone 212-966-5868); Corporation Supply Co., 38 S. Dearborn,

Chicago, IL (Phone 312-726-3375); Allen Pacific Corp., 5022 Melrose Ave., Los Angeles, CA Phone 213-464-3944).

SECTION 1244 STOCK PLAN

WHEREAS, the Board of Directors of this corporation deems it advisable to undertake to raise additional capital up to the amount of $100,000 through the offer, sale and issue of shares of the common stock authorized by the Certificate of Incorporation , and

WHEREAS, it is further deemed advisable that the offer, sale and issue of such shares be effectuated in such manner that qualified holders of such shares may receive the benefits of Section 1244 of the Internal Revenue Code, and

WHEREAS, no portion of a prior offering of any stock of this corporation is now outstanding or remains unissued, and

WHEREAS, this corporation qualifies as a small business corporation as defined in Section 1244, and the aggregate amounts received from prior plans offering Section 1244 stock and for stock as contributions to capital, does not exceed $500,000.

NOW, THEREFORE, BE IT RESOLVED, that the Board of Directors is hereby authorized and directed to offer for sale, sell and issue shares of the common stock of this corporation, to the extent authorized by the certificate of corporation, in such amounts and for such consideration in cash or in property, other than stock or securities, as from time to time shall be determined by the Board of Directors, in its discretion, and as may be permitted by law, subject to the following terms, conditions, limitations or restrictions:

(1) The offer, sale and issue of such shares shall be effected in such manner as shall qualify such stock as "Section 1244 stock," as such term is used and defined in the Internal Revenue Code and the Regulations issued thereunder.

(2) The offer, sale and issue of such stock shall take place only during the period commencing with the date when, under the application rules or regulations of any governmental agency of competent jurisdiction, the stock may lawfully be offered, sold or issued, and ending on (date within two years of adoption of resolution and plan) or on the date when the corporation shall make a subsequent offering of any stock, whichever shall be sooner.

(3) The maximum amount to be received by the corporation for the stock to be issued and sold pursuant to this Resolution and Plan shall be $100,000 in cash, or property, other than stock or securities.

AGREEMENT FOR SUBCHAPTER S ELECTION

(1) The parties hereto acknowledge their intention that the Corporation shall elect to be taxed as a "small business corporation" under Subchapter S of the Internal Revenue Code, or such other provisions of law now or hereafter applicable to such election. The parties, accordingly, agree to consent to such election and to execute and cause the Corporation to execute the forms necessary to effect such election and cause all of said forms and other necessary documents to be timely filed with the appropriate district director of the Internal Revenue Service. The parties further agree to take such further action as may be deemed necessary or advisable by counsel to the Corporation to exercise and perfect such election.

(2) The parties further acknowledge their intention to continue such election unless they unanimously agree otherwise. Accordingly, the parties hereto, severally and separately, agree that from and after the time the said election is made and perfected they will do nothing, either directly or indirectly, which causes or which might have the effect of causing the termination of such election. More specifically, without limiting the generality of the foregoing, none of the parties shall make any transfer or other disposition of his shares, or any of them, by will, deed or other instrument, and whether by sale, gift, bequest, assignment, mortgage, pledge, security interest, hypothecation, lien or encumbrance, trust (voting or otherwise), or any other means whatsoever, the effect of which is or may be to terminate such election. Further, the parties, severally and separately, agree to take such action as may be required to continue such election from year to year or from time to time, and to prevent its termination.

(3) The parties further agree that each party shall execute a will or codicil directing his executor to consent to such election within the time required to prevent its termination and to take whatever other action is necessary and execute and file whatever forms are necessary, or may be considered necessary by counsel of the Corporation, to prevent the termination of such election. The parties further agree that each party shall cause such direction to his executor to be included in all subsequent wills and codicils executed by him, including his Last Will.

(4) The provisions of this agreement shall be binding upon each and all of the parties hereto, their heirs, beneficiaries, legal representatives, and successors.

On the death of any party to this agreement, unless termination of such election is prevented by action of the executor or personal representative of the deceased, the price to be paid by the Corporation under this agreement for each of the shares of such deceased shareholder shall be $50, and the estate and all beneficiaries of the deceased shall transfer all of said shares to the Corporation at said price per share.

(5) The provisions of this agreement shall be binding on any person who acquires any shares of this Corporation under any judicial process, attachment, bankruptcy, receivership, execution or judicial sale, and such person shall take whatever action is necessary to prevent a termination of said election, failing which, whether or not due to the fault of such person, said person shall transfer all of said shares to the Corporation at a price per share of $50 whenever requested by the Corporation to do so.

(6) The fact that the appropriate tax authorities revoke the termination, or allow a reelection,.shall not effect the obligation of the Corporation to pay no more than the amount provided for in the two preceding paragraphs of this agreement for said shares, nor validate any transfer or other disposition of shares prohibited by this agreement.

THE ANATOMY OF A POLITICAL CAMPAIGN

THE GENERAL STAFF

CANDIDATE

>Campaign manager...Total control of campaign activities.
>
>Big wheel...fund raising, endorsements, party leverage.
>
>Legal counsel...keeps campaign out of legal difficulties.
>
>Fund raiser...gets the money.
>
>Precinct organizes precinct work.
>
>Public relations...media contact, speeches, appearances, publicity.

THE ARMY

Under campaign manager

Headquarter's manager...opens headquarters, decorates, keeps it staffed, gets out mailings, keeps master chart of campaign in headquarters, stores signs, literature, campaign materials, sees that votermaster lists are maintained, has telephone facilities for workers, arranges meeting and rallies during campaign.

Precinct chairman...organizes precinct captains...gets maps, voter cards literature,etc. to captains who get to workers... captains organize candidate coffees, secure canvassers, transportation, baby sitters, poll watchers, envelope stuffers etc.

Fund raiser...will have volunteers among business and professional men (with help of big wheel) to solicit their peers...Have volunteers to get out mailings for funds.

Public relations chairman...have special events chairman, assigns chairman, speakers bureau chairman, advertising chairman.

Supplemental chairmen work under campaign manager.

"Independent committees" chairman...ie. Lawyers for, Labor for, Democrats for, etc.

Youth chairman...organize youth activities for candidate.

Ethnic chairman...work with ethnic groups for campaign.

PRE-ELECTION PLAN

1. Get involved with party, see which positions they are seeking candidates for, which positions are sewed up. The party is often looking for candidates, particularly to run against incumbents of opposition

party.

2. Pick your spot and make a list of "pressing point" contacts relating to the office you'll be seeking.

3. Appoint your campaign manager, and begin coffee's in the precincts to find volunteer workers and possible contributors.

4. Contact your big wheel and have small get togethers with some movers and shakers in the community or area. Don't ask for money, ask for advice...the money comes later.

5. Lock up billboard space for primary with deposits.

6. Hire your legal eagle and have him check election laws, submit instructions on what you need to qualify and dates of importance.

7. Check election officials about boundry changes in precincts, get results of last election.

8. Begin research into last campaign to see who did what and why.

9. Get a fund raising program developed, appoint your fund raising chairman.

10. Get public exposure...speak before groups... attend party functions.

THE CAMPAIGN PLAN

Gather key staff. Manager, fund raiser, big wheel, precinct chairman, public relations chairman...plan private cocktail party for influentials.
Week 2

Hold luncheons with potential large contributors, party wheels, influentials to build power base...Set up research program............use college student volunteers.
Week 3

Hold cocktail party for influentials...Build card file of potential contributors, set campaign theme...Plan literature, layout signs, letterheads, other graphics.

Set pre-announcement talks before local groups........Begin precinct work...Setting up captains, planning coffees... Making maps, getting voter lists, secure sign locations...Book T.V. time, radio time for final days...Order signs, bumper stickers, order ad specialties.
Week 4

Develop basic speeches, prepare news conference plans for announcements...Use research material to build position papers...Fill in literature copy...Begin appearances at coffees, speak before local groups...Recruit volunteers and build potential contributor file...Plan rally for announcement eve for workers...Locate a suitable headquarters...Arrange for phones...Plan mailings for funds for furniture, phones and staffing of headquarters...Plan announcement night rally at headquarters for workers.

Week 5

Prepare ad budget...Have campaign pictures taken, get literature layout and copy to printer...Send out news conference invitations for formal campaign announcement...Rent suitable location for conference...Arrange catering for food and drinks for press...Hold it at lunch hour to assure maximum press attendance...Arrange candidate appointments with editors and news directors of broadcast media. Hire a good photographer to cover functions.

Week 6

Make preparation for fund raising banquet...in 13th week... Secure "name speakers"...Have ticket books printed for sale by volunteers...Get direct mail material ready...Secure mailing lists...Form youth groups...Volunteer committees... special event committees.

Week 7

Hold announcement news conference...Open headquarters, hold rally at headquarters for all workers...Open house next day for public.Be sure plenty of volunteers are scheduled to man headquarters...Schedule twice as many as needed...Start crews placing signs about 50% of those available...Getting bumper stickers on...Get first fund raising mailing out on time.

Week 8

Start speeches...Keep a steady flow of news releases going out to media...Get registration drive going in precincts to register all favorable voters...Get researchers busy on all other announced candidates...Pay particular attention to incumbents of big names...Get youth groups busy on getting "I'm for" petitions out to prepare for large endorsement ads. Set up telephone operation and take a snap poll on which names voters recognize.

Week 9

Make T.V. and radio tapes...Layout newspaper and specialty publication ads...Get set into tape...Place ads in monthly or bi-monthly specialty publication...Break publicity and fund raising dinner...Start shopping center, industrial plant, street corner appearances.

Week 10

Arrange for personal interviews by editors of school papers (they are taken home)...Start telephone calls to beef up fund raising dinner attendance...Renew efforts in precincts... Weed out the do nothings, get canvassing on firm footing with a special precinct rally...Hold out some tickets to the big dinner to give to good precinct captains.

Week 11

File officially for office...Finish up research work and build it into speeches get ads "Lawyers for," "Labor for," etc. worked up through volunteer committees.

Week 12

Final week before dinner, push tickets harder, break stories on "Head Table Attendees." Remember on these dinners 50% come in the last few days.

Week 13

The dinner...get press coverage, plenty of pictures from your own photographer...Have blank checks and pens on every table...Hit them with your "Give 'em hell" speech, get the money!

Week 14

Constant precinct work, volunteer affairs, coffees, speeches.

Last Week

Put out balance of signs...Start newspaper ads...T.V. spots, radio spots, sound trucks ' car caravans... Get out in public again...Make it a point to see all precinct captains personally or at a rally...Get out the vote theme... Get a bandwagon philosophy rolling among your workers...If you're ahead according to polls be sure to raise enthusiasm and don't be complacent...If you're behind, remind them of Harry Truman.

E Day

Make sure your people deliver every known voter who favors you to the polls. Poll watchers keep track, at four hours before polls close, non-show voters are contacted, offered rides, babysitters etc.

Have an election watch party arranged, all workers and supporters invited. Win or lose thank them all! There's always next time.

PRIMARY STRATEGY

Against an incumbent!

1. Hit him where he lives right at the start.

2. Get an issue and beat him over the head with it.

3. Build a strong precinct organization and get the name of every party member on a card.

4. Use direct mail and the telephone, pound away at them on the issue.

5. If he refuses to debate you, and he will, send every eligible primary voter a "shame on him" letter...People like a fighter, don't respect a coward.

6. Get petition crews out to get signatures for "We're for you" ads to be run the last couple of days before election... This builds a bandwagon psychology.

7. Be controversial...Make hard nosed statements...This gets press attention...You want to be characterized as the "wave of the future", "the new breed".

8. On the final days use your "We're for you" ads and get out a final summation mailing with a poll showing you ahead...Hit radio and T.V.

9. With all you can afford, you want the bandwagon effect, to start a stampede, and you can.

10. Be sure your poll watchers get every known favorable voter to the polls. . Primaries are lightly voted, it may seem like life and death to you, but it's nothing much to the voters.

11. Stage a telephone blitz, have plenty of cars available to get your people to the voting booth...You've got 14 hours to work, so burn up the wires.

RUNNING against a non-incumbent in a pack or for non-partisan office.

1. File first...Get a good slogan, get signs, billboards, bumper stickers, mug shot and name ads started in local specialty, club, religious publications that have only one or two issues prior to election.

2. Get precinct captains organized, start canvas of precincts at once, registor all favorable...Have coffees, meetings, appearances of all kinds scheduled...Get lawn signs up on every street possible.

3. Get literature crews out on street corners and in shopping centers every Wednesday and Friday to hand out a simple position paper.

4. Have a major publicity stunt scheduled that will attract press coverage...A nothing over $1.00 flea market sale pointing up the need to fight inflation, reduce taxes... What ever the stunt, relate it to a campaign issue.

5. Create a short, succinct speech attacking the opposition party vigorously, ignoring your primary opponents entirely...Keep your party loyalty intact.

6. Avoid candidate nights that give you three minutes to speak. This is a meat show, it does no good...Plead prior commitment and offer to appear at a later time by yourself...Have your campaign manager be the S.O.B. in these cases.

7. Get petition crews out to sign "We're for you" ads to be run in the last few days before election.

8. Your precinct workers should canvas every home of uncommitted party members asking what problems bother them... Get names of household members, work these into a personalized computer letter to give your stand on the specific problem mentioned...Delay this program until it is too late for any opponent to copy it...This will give the voter a personal letter from you to every uncommitted voter, and it will firmly implant your identity in his or her mind.

9. If your name is stuck in the middle of the pack on the ballot, develop literature that tells the voter to count down five (or whatever number of names are above yours) for better government. Show that section of the ballot, circle your name and the number in bright red...Get that "Count down" into every voter's hands.

10. Use radio to bolster your final days. Quote a poll showing you ahead...Use the "Count down" theme...When you break you're "We're for you" ads, use count down theme too.

11. On "E" Day have poll watchers on hand with cards to count off your sure votes as they appear, and at 3 o'clock, turn non-voters cards over to

phone crew to follow-up. Get all the sure votes in.

Win or lose, be sure to personally thank every worker on your campaign. There is always next time.

THE CANDIDATES ARE A PRODUCT!

They have to be packaged and sold to the voters.

A successful product is not:

MODEST
TIMID
COMMONPLACE
UNKNOWN

and neither is a successful political candidate.

When you decide to sell a product you've got to find out what its' selling points are going to be. Why it offers the buyer a better deal than the competitive products. What it will do for those who buy it, and where it can be purchased.

Your job right now is to answer these questions in terms of your candidate of his opposition.

What are the major selling points?

What will he do for those who vote for him.

Why he offers more than opponents to the electorate?

Where they can vote for him, and when.

How logical are you? Can you appraise people honestly? Do you know what their strengths and weaknesses are?

PERSONAL EVALUATION.

We have prepared a list of twenty factors for candidate evaluation. You will rate them from 1 to 10 on each point. Example, point number one, "good looks". If they are Rock Hudson or Raquel Welch, rate them 10. If they are something, be honest. The average person should not go over 5.

When you finish the list, if you have 200, you are lying to yourself. If you rate between 60 and 100, you are being fair with yourself, and have a good chance of picking a winner.

Once you have done this rating job for yourself, you should run the same check on your opposition. This will give you a relative strength report when the race starts, and you will know how much ground you as a candidate, or the opponent, has to make up during the race. You will find a rating sheet at the end of this section, you can Xerox it, and start putting the numbers in place. It would not be amiss to get some practical help from people who know you (if you can let your wife tell the truth without getting mad she'll be of great help.)

HERE THEY ARE TAKEN ONE AT A TIME

PERSONAL LOOKS

How a candidate looks to a voter is important, don't kid yourself about that. Handsome men and beautiful women have advantages. In recent races you could rate Ronald Reagan as 8, Gerald Ford as 2, John Kennedy was 8, (Jackie's was 10), and Richard Nixon 2. Don't forget all we are talking about here is physical appearance with the mouth closed.

ABILITY TO LEAD AND CONVINCE

Can he lead people? Do they ask him for advice? Can he convince people to buy things, to accept his suggestions on personal matters? Is he usually a chief or an indian in a group? Example in national elections, Dwight Eisenhower would rate 10, Stevenson 2 or 4 at best. Roosevelt was 10, Landon 1, Nixon 4, Humphrey 4.

IS HE WELL ORGANIZED?

Is he a highly organized person? Does he keep meticulous records? Can you say he has his time planned to the minute. Does he always know exactly how much is in his checking account? Can he remember issues, positions and past statements clearly? Example, Nixon 8, Humphrey 2, Johnson 6, Goldwater 1. (Note: even if he can't, he can hire people who can).

COMMAND LOYAL FOLLOWING

Has he the nucleus of a campaign organization right now? Does he know 200 people who will rally to his banner with cash and labor the minute he files. Does he know 10 people who will? If he knows 10, give him 2, if he knows 200, give him 10.

ACCOMPLISHED PUBLICITY GETTER

If he can pick up the phone and call a news conference and all the media will attend and report what he says, give him 10. If he does not quite know who to call to get a story in the paper, give him 0. If he knows some media people, can plant a story on occasion, give him 4.

RELIGIOUS AFFILIATION

Is he a member of the predominate religious group in your area? If he a church leader? Does he command respect in church circles? If he is a leader of the biggest church in the area, has rapport with all the ministers, priests and rabbis and can count on support, go 10. If he doesn't know which church has the most members, go 0.

STRONG SPEAKER

If you have an Orson Wells, rate him 10. If his knees get weak when he rises to speak, rate him 0. Example, Roosevelt 10, Regan 10, Nixon 4.

VETERAN

If he has an honorable discharge, give him 2. If he served overseas , go 4. If he saw combat go 6. If he is a known war hero with big medals, or a leader of the American Legion, go 10.

RACIAL ADVANTAGE

If he is of racial extraction of predominate group, go 2. If he is of a minority race, in a predominately minority area of his extraction, go 4. If he is a leader of the minority group go 6 or 8 depending on his identity among the electorate. If your area is 100% ethnic and he is ''the leader'', go 10.

INFLUENTIAL GROUP CONNECTIONS

If he is a chief among influential groups, labor, farm, business or industry, youth, conservationists, etc. rate him 1 to 6 depending on his positions and identification with the group or groups. If he can command the vote of more than one group, rate accordingly. The key is his ability to swing the group vote regardless of party affiliation.

SURE MEDIA SUPPORT

If he will get the endorsement of all major media during the campaign, rate him 10. If he doesn't understand how to get the endorsements, rate him 0. If he will get the biggest paper, go 4.

STRONG FUND RAISING POTENTIAL

In this important catagory, rate him one to ten. If he can tap all the fat cats for everything you will need for the campaign, go 10. If he doesn't know how to raise money, and had no sure contributors except his relatives, go 0. If you rate him 5, for example, he has sure sources for at least half the campaign expenses he will need.

VERY WELL KNOWN

If he is a Johnny Carson in your area, go 10. But, if like most of us, he is not on late night TV, or has daily exposure in the mass media, he'll rate from 1 to 2 at best. Very, very few people are really well known by the general public.

PARTY BACKING

In the primary he will get little if any help from the party. If he is after an incumbent, he will get hostility and pressure to get out. But, on a rare occasion where you will be running against a "turncoat" candidate, he may get party help. Mostly this one will be 0.

CAMPAIGN EXPERIENCE

If he is an old war horse who has come up through the precincts to state level in the party, and has lots of campaigns under his belt, go 10. If this is his first time in the lists, go 0.

ON THE SIDE OF THE ANGLES

If his positions are those of the majority of the voters, and your opponents are directly opposed, go 10. But, if everyone is on the side of the angles (as will be the case 99% of the time) go 1 or 2. If he is against the angles, go 0.

LOYAL FAMILY SUPPORT

If his family is large and all become dedicated workers, are 100% enthusiastic about the prospective campaign, go 10. If they are tolerant, and rather passive, go one to 5, if they are hostile, go 0.

HIGHLY COMPETITIVE

There's an old saying, "it isn't the size of the dog in the fight that counts, it's the size of the fight in the dog." If he likes a fight and tries always to win, can take it as well as dish it out, and is a person who can come up off the floor swinging, go 10. Harry Truman gets 10.

SKELETONS IN YOUR CLOSET

If he is clean as a hound's tooth, go 10, but if he's got trouble in his past that will embarrass him if discovered, better be realistic here. Bad trouble, can wipe him out. Serious trouble can hurt him badly and common trouble merely embarrass and harass him. Bad trouble is jail, serious difficulties with the law. Accusations never cleared up of dishonesty etc. Serious trouble can be over women, booze, gambling, other moral laxness, and embarrassments can be almost anything that he has done from being a dead beat in credit matters, to being too often found at local bars at closing time. If he starts to look like a winner, you can be sure that all the opposition can dig up will be used in one form or another, so be ready.

There is your breakdown, and if you could honestly come out with 180, all he has to do is file, and he will win.

Calculator—

CALCULATORS

The small pocket calculator is new to our lives. Unknown five years ago, they are becoming as popular as television or hi-fi sets. The potential use for the pocket calculators are many and varied, but at present all we are going to be interested in is how to use them in performing simple calculations that will help you with your business.

We will use several different words in this text to describe the operations of the calculator and ways to use it. The following diagram will show you some of these and where they are located in relation to the small calculator.

DIGITS AND NUMBERS

DIGITS are like letters. NUMBERS are like words. Words are made of letters and numbers are made of digits. For example, the number 841 is made up of digits eight and four and one. Or, it can be said that 841 is a three-digit number.

FUNCTIONS AND OPERATIONS

These are: add, subtract, multyply and divide. An operation on your calculator is what you do with one number to another number. We will refer to these functions that you do with these numbers as adding, subtracting, multiplying and dividing. When using the combination of the numbers on the number keys and then the functions on the function keys, you get a read-out.

You also will be concerned about the clear button and the clear entry button. The clear button removes all the information that has been previously put into the calculator and starts from zero. The clear entry button removes only the last information that was put into the calculator. The last and probably most important function key would be the equals. When you've completed a particular calculation, you punch the equals button for the result.

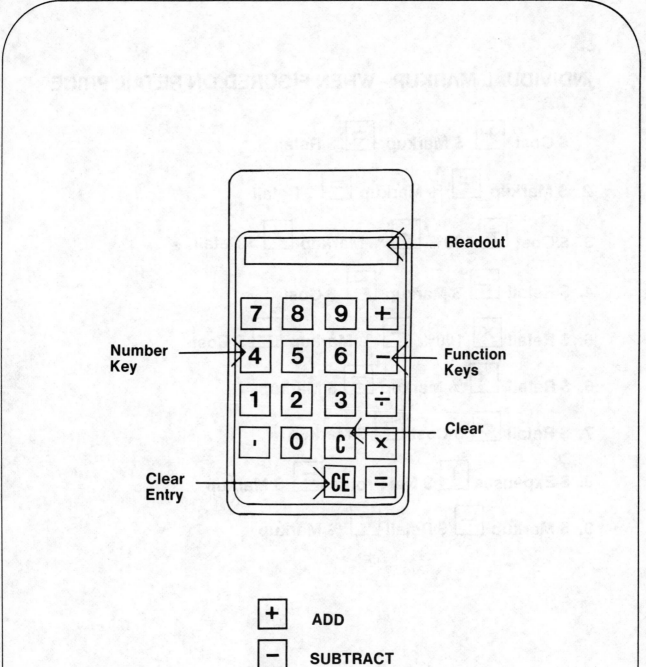

Label	
	Readout
Number Key	
	Function Keys
	Clear
Clear Entry	

$+$ ADD

$-$ SUBTRACT

$\times$ MULTIPLY

$\div$ DIVIDE

67

INDIVIDUAL MARKUP—WHEN FIGURED ON RETAIL PRICE

1. $ Cost $+$ $ Markup $=$ $ Retail

2. $ Markup $\div$ % Markup $=$ $ Retail

3. $ Cost $\div$ 100% $-$ % Markup $=$ $ Retail

4. $ Retail $-$ $ Markup $=$ $ Cost

5. $ Retail $\times$ 100% $-$ % Markup $=$ $ Cost

6. $ Retail $\times$ % Markup $=$ $ Markup

7. $ Retail $-$ $ Cost $=$ $ Markup

8. $ Expenses $+$ $ Net Profits $=$ $ Markup

9. $ Markup $\div$ $ Retail $=$ % Markup

INDIVIDUAL MARKUP—WHEN FIGURED ON COST PRICE

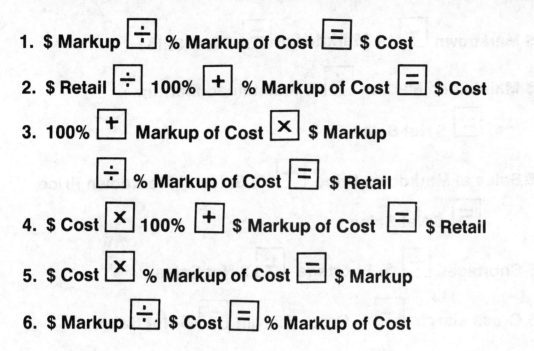

1. $ Markup ÷ % Markup of Cost = $ Cost

2. $ Retail ÷ 100% + % Markup of Cost = $ Cost

3. 100% + Markup of Cost × $ Markup

   ÷ % Markup of Cost = $ Retail

4. $ Cost × 100% + $ Markup of Cost = $ Retail

5. $ Cost × % Markup of Cost = $ Markup

6. $ Markup ÷ $ Cost = % Markup of Cost

SALES—

1. $ Markdown $\div$ % Markdown $=$ $ Net Sales

2. $ Maintained Markup $\div$ % Maintained Markup $=$ $ Net Sales

3. $ Sales at Markdown Price $\div$ % Sales at Markdown Price $=$ $ Net Sales

4. $ Shortages $\div$ % Shortage $=$ $ Net Sales

5. $ Gross Margin $\div$ % Gross Margin $=$ $ Net Sales

6. Capital Turnover $\times$ $ Average Inventory at Cost $=$ $ Net Sales

7. Stock Turnover $\times$ $ Average Inventory at Retail $=$ $ Net Sales

8. $ Net Profit $\div$ % Net Profit $=$ $ Net Sales

9. $ Average Sale $\times$ Number of Transactions $=$ $ Net Sales

10. Stock Turnover at Cost $\times$ $ Average Inventory at Cost $=$ Cost of Goods Sold

SHORTAGES—SHRINKAGE

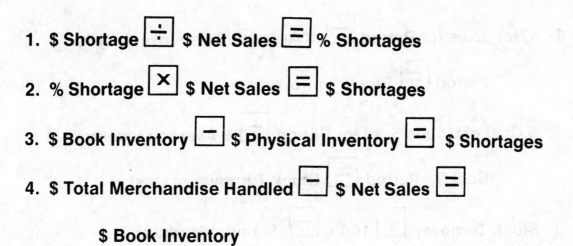

1. $ Shortage ÷ $ Net Sales = % Shortages

2. % Shortage × $ Net Sales = $ Shortages

3. $ Book Inventory − $ Physical Inventory = $ Shortages

4. $ Total Merchandise Handled − $ Net Sales =

       $ Book Inventory

TURNOVER—

1. $ Net Sales for Period $\div$ $ Average Retail Inventory for Period $=$ Stock Turnover

2. $ Cost of Goods Sold for Period $\div$ $ Average Inventory at Cost for Period $=$ Stock Turnover at Cost

3. Stock Turnover $\div$ 100% $-$ % Initial Markup $=$ Capital Turnover

4. $ Net Sales for Period $\div$ $Average Cost Inventory for Period $=$ Capital Turnover

PROFIT—

1. $ Net Profit $\div$ $ Net Sales $=$ % Net Profit

2. % Net Profit $\times$ $ Net Sales $=$ $ Net Profit

3. $ Gross Margin $-$ $ Expenses $=$ $ Net Profit

4. $ Markup $-$ $ Expenses $=$ $ Net Profit

5. $ Gross Margin $-$ $ Operating Expense $=$ Operating Profit

6. $ Operating Profit $\div$ $ Net Sales $=$ % Operating Profit

AGREEMENT AND CONTRACT

FOR INDEPENDENT OR SUB-CONTRACTOR

KNOW ALL MEN BY THESE PRESENTS:

That this Contract made by and between_____
Party of the first part, and_____, address
_____Party of the second part,
for the purpose of establishing an independent contract relationship and contractual agreement between the parties hereto
absolutely excluding any employee-employer style relationship.

That the Contract entered into by the parties hereto
expressly recognizes as its basis the Constitution of the United
States and the Constitution of the State of_____ and
the Common Law; and further that each of the parties hereto
demand their independent sovereign rights as secured by the
Declaration of Independence and rely upon their natural God
given rights to freely enter into an independent contract
relationship with each other unconditioned by any unconstitutional or illegal governmental interference.

That the party of the first part and the party of the second
part do covenant and agree as follows:

1. That the party of the second part will provide the
   following kinds of services:_____
   _____.

2. That the party of the second part will be compensated
   as follows:_____per_____or_____payable
   in cash or check, at the option of the first part.

3. All equipment, tools or supplies will be provided by
   the second party except as follows:_____
   _____.

4. The party of the second part states and affirms that
   he is acting as a free agent and independent contractor,
   holding himself out to the General Public as an independent contractor for other work or contracts as he
   sees fit; that he runs ads in the newspapers offering
   services to the General Public, maintains his office
   and principle place of business at his address above

stated and carries business cards; that this contract is not exclusive. First party possesses no right hereunder to discourage or inhibit the second party's rights to enter any other contracts as he sees fit.

5. This contract shall run from day to day or until the project second party is hired for is completed, thereby making it impossible for the first party to fire second party; both parties are equally bound to this contract; second parties pay may be received at any time upon reasonable demand for work or performance of the contract up to the time of the demand; all of the amounts shall be paid in full with no deductions of any kind.

6. Second party may start work or cease work at will as long as the contract is performed and accomplished satisfactorily and promptly; no supervision of second party will be made by first party in the details of the work to be performed after the initial period of introduction to the object of the contract described herein.

7. Second party agrees to accept full responsibility for any and all taxes that may be lawfully due to any governmental unit and to hold party of the first part harmless from any liability from the non-payment of taxes due from second party to any governmental unit.

8. Both parties recognize the validity of the belief in the First and Fifth Amendments to the Constitution of the United States and agree to mutually and individually exercise those rights for the protection of each party.

9. The parties hereto recognize that any kind of State or personal coercion which forces either party, against his own free will, to surrender any of the rights secured to him by the Constitution of the United States is unlawful, ungodly and immoral.

10. Second party waives any and all claim from first party to any form of Workmen's Compensation Insurance coverage or compensation provided under Federal, State or Local compulsion or compulsory legislation which affects Employees and Employers, and agrees to carry

and provide his own insurance for injury or sickness or retirement, whether in the form of social security or otherwise as and for a consideration for entering into this agreement.

The both parties claim the protection of the U.S. Constitution as spelled out in Article I, Section 10 as follows: "No State ...shall pass any bill ... or law impairing the obligation of contracts...".

That both parties invoke the following legal protection of the U.S. Constitution to guarantee the sanctity of this lawful contract between two freely consenting adult citizens.

Art. I, Sec. 1 provides that only Congress has the power to make laws; consequently any rules, regulations and procedures which are not passed into law by Congress are void, and do not affect a free citizen.

Art. I, Sec. 8 provides that only Congress has the power to coin money and regulate the value thereof, and any abdication of this power to other agents is unconstitutional and void. Further, that Congress shall make all laws necessary and proper for carrying into execution the foregoing powers... but this provision does not grant any extra Constitutional power to Congress whatsoever.

Amendment IV provides that no warrants shall issue but on probable cause...which protects us in all our contractual affairs from being forced to reveal any information or produce any records unless a valid search warrant executed by the Judicial Branch of Government is presented to us.

Amendment V provides that no person ... shall be compelled in any criminal case to be a witness against himself, nor be deprived of life, liberty or property without due process of law. This provision guarantees us protection in this contract against all encroachments such as the Internal Revenue Code or State Revenue Codes which are null and void in any place where they violate the constitution.

In Witness Whereof, the parties hereto set their hands
this date_____.

_____   _____
Witness   First Party

_____   _____
Witness   Second Party

Appendix